Diverse Futures

NEW SUNS:

RACE, GENDER, AND SEXUALITY IN THE

SPECULATIVE

Susana M. Morris and Kinitra D. Brooks, Series Editors

Diverse Futures
Science Fiction and Authors of Color

Joy Sanchez-Taylor

THE OHIO STATE UNIVERSITY PRESS
COLUMBUS

Copyright © 2021 by The Ohio State University.
All rights reserved.

Library of Congress Cataloging-in-Publication Data
Names: Sanchez-Taylor, Joy, author.
Title: Diverse futures : science fiction and authors of color / Joy Sanchez-Taylor.
Other titles: New suns: race, gender, and sexuality in the speculative.
Description: Columbus : The Ohio State University Press, [2021] | Series: New suns: race, gender, and sexuality in the speculative | Includes bibliographical references and index. | Summary: "An examination of science fiction tropes in Octavia E. Butler, Ted Chiang, Sabrina Vourvoulias, and many others, demonstrates how authors of various races and ethnicities write SF that pays homage to the genre while also creating a more diverse and inclusive portrait of the future"—Provided by publisher.
Identifiers: LCCN 2021000211 | ISBN 9780814214732 (cloth) | ISBN 0814214738 (cloth) | ISBN 9780814281338 (ebook) | ISBN 0814281338 (ebook)
Subjects: LCSH: Science fiction, American—Minority authors—History and criticism. | Science fiction—Minority authors—History and criticism.
Classification: LCC PS648.S3 S25 2021 | DDC 813/.0876208—dc23
LC record available at https://lccn.loc.gov/2021000211

Cover design by Black Kirby
Text design by Juliet Williams
Type set in Adobe Palatino

To my husband, Sam Taylor, who always helps me remember that I have something important to say and who never makes me feel guilty for taking the time to say it.

And to my daughter, Alessia Luna Taylor, who centers my universe.

CONTENTS

Acknowledgments		ix
Introduction	"An Image of Tomorrow"	1
Chapter 1	Space Travel and First Contact Narratives	25
Chapter 2	Race, Genetics, and Science Fiction	55
Chapter 3	The Apocalypse Has Already Come: Post-Apocalyptic Landscapes	84
Chapter 4	"Our Knowledge Is Not Primitive": Indigenous and Eurowestern Science	118
Conclusion	"How Long 'Til Black Future Month?"	147
Bibliography		165
Index		177

ACKNOWLEDGMENTS

This book is a long time in the making. I have to thank Dr. Diane Price-Herndl, Dr. Tova Cooper, Dr. Ylce Irizarry, and Dr. Quynh Nhu Le from the University of South Florida for their initial guidance and support on this project. I would also like to thank Dr. Jessica Cook and Dr. Katherine McGee for never letting me give up on my dream to study science fiction by authors of color.

I am fortunate to work at one of the premiere community colleges in the US, LaGuardia Community College, CUNY, a school that values both teaching and research. One of the most important factors in academic publishing success is time for writing and research. LaGuardia gave me release time, which allowed me to complete *Diverse Futures*. Working at CUNY offered me the opportunity to connect with other scholars through the Faculty Fellowship Publication Program (FFPP), and I would like to thank Bridgett M. Davis and my fellow FFPP members who stayed reading my chapters long after the program ended, Dr. Rebecca D. Mazumdar and Dr. Jill F. Strauss. I would also like to thank CUNY's Futures Initiative and Dr. Jonathan Gray for giving me the amazing opportunity to coteach a class on Afrofuturism at the CUNY Graduate Center in 2019. And to my students in this course and at LaGuardia, thank you for inspiring me with your enthusiasm, perseverance, and amazing intelligence.

I would also like to thank all of my friends in the ever-growing field of science fiction studies who gave me feedback on initial ideas for this project. Specifically, I would like to thank Grace L. Dillon and Isiah Lavender III for their generosity in mentoring me and giving me feedback on my ideas and writing. They are both truly wonderful scholars and amazing human beings!

I am grateful for the opportunity that the New Suns series at Ohio State is giving me in publishing this work, and so I want to thank the series editors, Susana M. Morris and Kinitra D. Brooks, as well as the editorial team of Kristen A. Elias Rowley and Ana Jimenez-Moreno.

Finally, I would like to thank my husband, Sam Taylor; my parents, Raymond and Theresa Sanchez; and my sister, Amanda Sanchez-Phillips, for their love and support throughout this process. I would also like to thank our family friend, Becky Asai, for taking the time to read my published works.

Not everyone understands the work of academia, so to all of the graduate students and new professors out there—keep writing; there is always someone who will read and be inspired by your work.

INTRODUCTION

"An Image of Tomorrow"

I grew up reading science fiction and fantasy novels. I started by reading my father's entire collection of Piers Anthony fantasy novels and quickly worked my way into the major authors of the science fiction and fantasy canons: J. R. R. Tolkien, Frank Herbert, Issac Asimov, and the like. It never occurred to me to question the lack of diversity in these texts; as a Latina "nerd," I viewed myself as an anomaly. I was the girl of color who happened to be a fan of a "white" genre. Then, in 2008, I read Junot Díaz's *The Brief Wondrous Life of Oscar Wao*, a novel whose main character, Oscar, is a Dominican nerd who wants to become a science fiction and fantasy author. Suddenly, I realized that there was at least one other Latinx nerd in the world! I identified with Díaz's story in a way that I had never identified with any of the other novels I had read. Although I have to teach *Oscar Wao* these days with some heavy but necessary conversations about the racial and gender bias that protected Díaz, accused of misconduct and abuse toward several women of color, from facing major ramifications for his behavior,[1] reading his references to science fiction writers of color in *Oscar Wao* piqued my curiosity and eventually led to my decision to study science fiction by authors

---

1. For more information, see Alison Flood's "Junot Díaz welcomed back by Pulitzer prize after review into sexual misconduct claims" (2018).

of color. Samuel R. Delany, one of the most well-known Black science fiction authors, a prolific critic of the genre, and an award-winning African American science fiction author, argues in *Starboard Wine: More Notes on the Language of Science Fiction* (1978), "We [Black peoples] need images of tomorrow; and our people need them more than most" (14). Like Delany, I wanted to not only experience a tomorrow where I felt included, but also to explore how authors of color are revising the tomorrows science fiction readers will encounter.

I am sure that my story is reflected in the experiences of many peoples of color who are fans of science fiction. The stereotype that science fiction is a "white" genre leads people of color either to refuse to engage with the genre or, like me, to see themselves as oddities or outsiders. Science fiction stereotypes also lead to science fiction authors of color facing difficulties getting their works published or promoted. Delany faced decades of racism from publishers and the science fiction community, an experience he relates in his 1998 critical essay "Racism and Science Fiction." Although there are currently more science fiction works written by authors of color on the market than when Delany began writing in the 1960s, the notion of diversity in futuristic works often becomes a political statement about what groups of peoples have the right to exist in the future. On March 3, 2018, a public art project billboard in Pittsburgh, PA, designed by artist Alisha B. Wormsley and featuring the statement "There are Black People in the Future" was forcibly removed at the request of the landlord.[2] The fact that a statement affirming the existence of Black peoples in the future is still viewed as offensive in 2018 demonstrates a disconnect between the rhetoric of equality espoused by many Eurowestern countries and the lived reality of people of color in these countries. One of the goals of this project is to raise awareness about how authors of color are combatting the idea of science fiction as a "white" genre by writing their racial and cultural experiences into these genres.

Diverse Futures examines the contributions of late twentieth- and twenty-first-century US and Canadian science fiction authors of color to the genre. By examining intersections between science fiction authors of multiple races and ethnicities, this text seeks to explain how science fiction authors of color are juxtaposing tropes of science fiction with specific cultural references to comment on issues of inclusiveness in Eurowestern cultures. Fortunately, there are too many science fiction or science fiction–related texts written

---

2. For more information, see the article "'There Are Black People in the Future'—Tale of a Billboard."

by authors of color to include them all; therefore, this project will focus on science fiction texts that go beyond including characters of color in the narrative and, instead, make people of color and their cultural experiences an integral part of their narratives, a distinction that Isiah Lavender III defines as an "ethnoscape," or racialized science fiction environment that both highlights and reconceives depictions of race to unpack the assumptions about race and ethnicity often made in science fiction writing ("Ethnoscapes" 189). While some of the authors or texts included in this work may not be currently classified as science fiction, all the texts can be considered ethnoscapes, and each text includes an element or trope that is associated with the science fiction genre.

The definition of science fiction is constantly in flux as authors and critics shape and reshape its boundaries. I am less interested in arguing for a strict definition of science fiction than I am in showing how the authors I examine are working to challenge the genre's Eurocentricity. Many of the authors in this study juxtapose descriptions of technology and myth, blurring genre distinctions in favor of creating texts that avoid the binary of primitive versus advanced cultures. Kinitra D. Brooks notes that women of color who blur genre distinctions between science fiction, fantasy, and horror often have their works overlooked or oversimplified by literary critics (56). While categorization of a text such as Octavia E. Butler's genetically-manipulated-vampire novel, *Fledgling*, makes for an interesting conversation about genre conventions, it is not the focus of this work. I understand that some of the texts in this collection could also be classified as fantasy or horror; however, I choose to employ a broad definition of science fiction that allows for the scientific views of non-Eurowestern cultures. Sherryl Vint argues for a more expansive reading of science fiction when discussing Butler's *Kindred* (1979):

> Instead of trying to sort out whether *Kindred* is really sf [science fiction] (how are we to understand its refusal to provide a scientific rational for time travel?), we should instead consider how it enables us to think of sf in new ways. Just as realist representations must be understood not as the neutral reflection of "the way things are" but as ideological constructs, so traditional claims about what "counts" as sf should be understood as tending to exclude the perspective and experiences of peoples of color. ("Only by Experience" 241–42)

Current definitions of science fiction do not account for the history of cultures of color being stereotyped as "primitive" while simultaneously being denied access to technology.[3] In an effort to highlight the resiliency and innovativeness of cultures of color, which often recycle and re-purpose "old" technologies[4] or blur distinctions between science and spirit,[5] I will employ an expansive definition of science fiction.

I also choose to include texts that utilize what Grace L. Dillon (Anishinaabe) names "Indigenous scientific literacies," or Indigenous practices not typically recognized by the Eurowestern scientific method as science, as science fiction ("Imagining" 7). This choice evokes Arthur C. Clarke's famous science fiction law which notes that "any sufficiently advanced technology is indistinguishable from magic" (21). In her discussion of the works of Andrea Hairston, Nalo Hopkinson, and Nnedi Okorafor, Dillon explains the shift in science fiction criticism to include works which highlight Indigenous knowledge, which include conjuring practices:

> These dynamic shifts in the SF field, recognizing the science of more than Euro-Western ways of thinking, along with numerous other examples such as indigenous science fiction stories, express better the stance of Hairston's forms of conjuration as science and embedded experiences of life itself. . . . As a native science, conjuring may have multiple layers, including not merely its symbiogenesis and coevolution, in quantum mechanics and organic physic terms (spelled out explicitly in Hairston's SF novel, *Mindscape*), but also forms of conjuration such as reading, writing, and literacy in general. ("Haint" 103, 107)

Rather than always looking to aliens for the "advanced" technology, I challenge readers to look at Indigenous scientific literacies as markers of advanced civilizations that have been passed down through generations. Since many of the cultures being discussed in this text contain scientific literacies that acknowledge the connection of all life on Earth, including the spiritual realm, I do not consider myself as creating a new definition of science fiction; rather, I am expanding the boundaries of what constitutes science fiction by challenging the Eurowestern privileging of the Western scientific method and rational thought over non-Eurowestern forms of science and logic. Social Darwinism is based on the ideal that man's rational thought differentiates Eurowestern "evolved" man from animals and peo-

---

3. See Adriano Elia's "The Languages of Afrofuturism."
4. See the introduction to Nelson, Tu, and Hines, *Technicolor: Race, Technology, and Everyday Life*.
5. See Nisi Shawl's "Ifa: Reverence, Science and Social Technology."

ples of color (Dennis 244). However, many of the texts in this collection create an alternate view of modernity where mankind acknowledges the need to coexist with its environment. Acknowledging Indigenous scientific literacies is one of many ways critics of science fiction can make room for science fiction authors of color.

I am also specifically choosing the phrase "science fiction" over the broader descriptor "speculative fiction" because while speculative fiction is quickly gaining traction in scholarly texts, the majority of publishers and science fiction fans do not use this term. P. L. Thomas notes that many authors who resisted the label of "science fiction" in favor of "speculative fiction," such as Kurt Vonnegut and Margaret Atwood, mainly did so because of the scholarly association of science fiction as not literary and, therefore, not worthy of serious study (1–2). Brooks also notes, "In its contemporary iteration, speculative fiction has developed into a lackadaisical umbrella term for any fiction remotely related to genre literature" (65). I argue that this extremely broad genre term creates confusion among publishers and fans, which leads to many science fiction authors of color not being recognized and supported by the science fiction community. In *Diverse Futures*, I am taking my study back to the original term "science fiction" to acknowledge the place of authors of color in this genre and the presence of people of color in alternate and future worlds. Many of the authors discussed in this collection are also recipients of some of science fiction's most prestigious awards such as the Hugo and Nebula awards. It is my hope that discussing the authors in these works as science fiction authors, rather than speculative authors, will help readers interested in science fiction discover texts and authors that do not always make it to the science fiction sections of bookstores and book-reviewing websites. I am not speculating that there will be people of color in the future; I am stating an important fact.

For the purposes of this project, I address science fiction as a diverse group of texts which all employ at least one trope of science fiction. This definition follows the example of John Rieder in *Colonialism and the Emergence of Science Fiction* (2008) when he refuses to define science fiction and instead argues that there is not one established defining trait that links all science fiction.[6] Rieder chooses to define science fiction both through its common tropes and through its production and reception:

---

6. Rieder acknowledges Paul Kincaid's essay "On the Origins of Genre" (2003) as the basis of his argument. Kincaid notes that science fiction critics are unable to "extract a unique, common thread" that binds together all science fiction texts, or a "unique, common origin" for the genre (415).

> Science fiction is "a web of resemblances" that can be traced backward from Gernsback's baptism of the genre along a variety of paths, and that can be extended in an unpredictable number of new and different ways. Its fluid boundaries have been defended and contested in many ways for many reasons, but the existence of the category as a condition of literary and cultural production and reception is incontrovertible. (17)

This looser, more inclusive definition of science fiction recognizes the most powerful influences on the genre: the tropes that shape the expectations of science fiction fans, who are increasingly gaining influence through their ability to recognize and fund new science fiction projects through online mediums. Rieder also notes that science fiction has from its earliest imaginings (whether that is the mythic monsters or fantastical voyages of Mary Shelley and Jules Verne in the nineteenth century, or the alien and robot stories of the twentieth) been linked to the social consequences of colonialism "including the fantastic appropriation and rationalization of unevenly distributed colonial wealth in the homeland and in the colonies, the racist ideologies that enabled colonialist exploitation, and the cognitive impact of radical cultural differences on the home culture" (20–21). Each chapter of *Diverse Futures* addresses a specific trope of science fiction to demonstrate how the authors featured in this collection utilize these tropes to challenge the racial/cultural binaries and hierarchies that underlie much of the Eurowestern narrative of cultural progress.

The authors featured in *Diverse Futures* often choose to write science fiction because the genre's world-building capabilities create space for critiquing Eurowestern race relations without the pressures of becoming a token representative for a racial or ethnic group. Carl Freedman notes that though science fiction and historical fiction have certain commonalities (both use other time periods—the past and future, respectively—as a way of commenting on the present), the main difference between the genres is the freedom of form and content: "As knowledge . . . of the past becomes ideologically more and more difficult to attain, the historical novel, necessarily tied as it is to such knowledge, is bound to become increasingly susceptible to reification. But science fiction is comparatively free of the burden of the past . . ." (57–58). Grace L. Dillon gives a concrete example of this perspective in her introduction to *Walking the Clouds: An Anthology of Indigenous Science Fiction* (2012) when she describes an Indigenous play titled *alterNatives*. In this play, an Indigenous character states that he prefers to write science fiction as opposed to "the great Canadian aboriginal novel" he is expected to produce. Dillon references *alterNatives* to demonstrate how science fiction offers

Indigenous authors "an equally valid way to renew, recover, and extend First Nation peoples' voices and traditions" (9–10). Science fiction, therefore, offers authors of color the ability to write stories that address issues of colonization without the burden of needing to address past historical representations of their race or culture.

Additionally, I argue that by using recognizable science fiction tropes, the authors in this collection create a "double estrangement" for science fiction readers, a term I use to juxtapose Darko Suvin's definition of cognitive estrangement with W. E. B. DuBois's concept of double consciousness.[7] Suvin argues that science fiction is defined by *"the presence and interaction of estrangement and cognition"* (7, emphasis in original). His argument centers on the idea that science fiction estranges readers by presenting the unfamiliar in familiar terms while also applying cognition to achieve "a dynamic transformation . . . of the author's environment" (10). Suvin ultimately argues that science fiction authors utilize the genre's ability to create cognitive estrangement to critique the society of their time. Science fiction authors of color present the unfamiliar as familiar to estrange their readers, but I argue that they also frequently include critiques of science fiction by altering established science fiction tropes to highlight the racial estrangement that DuBois describes in *The Souls of Black Folk* as double consciousness, or the knowledge that peoples of color are always forced to view themselves through a lens of whiteness. Science fiction authors of color understand that historically, they have been the "other" or "alien" depicted in science fiction. Greg Tate notes that "Black people live the estrangement that science fiction writers imagine" (qtd. in Dery 212). For peoples who are more likely to identify with the alien "other" in traditional science fiction than a white human narrator, science fiction becomes a space where authors of color (who are typically fans of the genre themselves) can employ recognizable aspects of science fiction—tropes like the alien, time travel, and immortality—yet also rework these tropes to make room for non-Eurowestern cultures. The fact that the term "alien" is also used to refer to foreigners or immigrants in the US demonstrates the ways that peoples of color are further alienated by Eurocentric depictions of "American" culture. Gloria Anzaldúa describes this feeling in terms of the mestiza figure as an "'alien' consciousness" which is painfully aware of how the dominant, Eurowestern culture

---

7. The term "double estrangement," while not established, has been used before in Lindsey Garrat's article on race and education titled "Doubly Estranged: Racism, the Body and Reflection" (2016) and in a book review of Benjamin Kwakye's *The Other Crucifix* authored by Peter Wuteh Vakunta (2010). For DuBois's description of double consciousness, see *The Souls of Black Folk* (1903).

of the US views Mexican/Chicanx peoples and how both groups alienate Indigenous peoples (99–100). This awareness of racial and cultural alienation creates an additional metaphoric layer in the science fiction works discussed in this collection. The authors featured ask readers to consider not only the ways that people of color are alienated in Eurowestern cultures but also how science fiction depictions of othered beings or aliens have contributed to this alienation by privileging a Eurocentric perspective.[8]

My choice to use the term "people of color" to discuss the authors in this work is intentional, yet in no way intended to homogenize all races and ethnicities. I am not implying that the authors discussed have the same experiences and that all their works are engaging science fiction in the same way. I am arguing, however, that there are thematic connections between science fiction authors of multiple races and ethnicities, a fact that is already demonstrated in academic anthologies of science fiction such as Nalo Hopkinson and Uppinder Mehan's postcolonial science fiction anthology *So Long Been Dreaming* (2004) and Isiah Lavender III's multiethnic critical anthologies *Black and Brown Planets* (2014) and *Dis-Orienting Planets* (2017). Despite the diverse representation in these and other science fiction anthologies, science fiction critics continue to separate science fiction texts written by authors of color into specific racial and ethnic categories (Afrofuturism, Indigenous futurism, Chicanafuturism, etc.) which, I argue, leaves little room for examining connections between science fiction authors whose racial and cultural experiences share commonalities. Displacement, diaspora, and marginalization are experiences that are not limited to one race or ethnicity, which is why bringing science fiction authors of color into conversation with one another serves to highlight the diversity of texts working to shift the focus

---

8. I am not implying that white science fiction authors cannot write science fiction that takes a non-Eurocentric perspective to highlight racial alienation. One example is Neil Gaiman. His novel *American Gods* features references to African and Native American mythology and features a diverse cast of characters. *Anansi Boys* features a character descended from Anansi, a West African trickster god. The character Shadow in *American Gods* is described ambiguously as mixed race, and the main characters' races in *Anansi Boys* are never explicitly discussed; both choices have been discussed by Gaiman in interviews as a deliberate challenging of the default-white-character assumption in European and Eurowestern literature (https://www.npr.org/templates/transcript/transcript.php?storyId=91303720, https://mic.com/articles/175489/american-gods-reinvents-itself-through-its-black-protagonist#.ekt29bfDo). Gaiman was also sure to insist that the racial diversity of the *American Gods* TV series (based on his novel of the same name) be retained: http://blacknerdproblems.com/the-mythology-of-the-black-man-in-american-gods/. It is clear that Gaiman's use of race in these novels is a deliberate choice to draw attention to a history of racism in European and Eurowestern countries and also highlights the racial assumptions readers in these cultures often make.

of science fiction away from a Eurocentric perspective. Such an argument aligns with Chela Sandoval and Angela Y. Davis's discussion of the overcategorization of racial and gender theories in *Methodology of the Oppressed* (2000), which, she argues, results in such theories being "submerged and underutilized" (70). This project hopes to draw attention to science fiction authors of color who are often overlooked by critics and publishers when categorized into strict ethnic literary subgenres rather than being included in the broader genre of science fiction.

Because this project is designed to be a comparative examination of the contributions of contemporary science fiction authors of color, each chapter is arranged thematically around a major science fiction trope rather than chronologically. Many of the works discussed could be included in multiple chapters because, as Brooks notes, a defining principle of speculative writing by authors of color is a purposeful obfuscation of the limits of genre; for example, a novel like Octavia E. Butler's *Fledgling* is a vampire novel that also utilizes genetic manipulation technologies. In such cases, I have elected to discuss these texts as science fiction and to limit my discussion of each work to one of the discussed tropes to avoid repetition. The choice of texts is also designed to reflect authors who employ the specific science fiction trope discussed in each chapter in a way that challenges science fiction's history of Eurocentric representation through a depiction of communities of color in fantastic or futuristic settings, specifically by showcasing these communities' cultural beliefs and practices as an integral part of the narrative. I limit my study to the US and Canada because these countries—through colonization, immigration, and forced migration—have science fiction authors of color representing a variety of races and ethnicities who are responding to issues of marginalization and diaspora within Eurowestern cultures. This book is not meant to be a comprehensive history of science fiction writing by authors of color; rather, it explores how a representative sample of such authors create possible futures where peoples of color not only exist but also contribute to the well-being of humanity. I hope this project is the start of a larger conversation about how the science fiction genre can work to be more inclusive of authors of color and the non-Eurocentric futures these authors imagine.

Because the chapters in this collection are arranged by tropes rather than chronologically, each can each be read independently; read together, they provide a broader context of the current state of science fiction writing by authors of color in US and Canadian cultures. Chapter 1 discusses Octavia E. Butler's *Dawn* (1987), Celu Amberstone's "Refugees" (2004), Rosaura Sánchez and Beatrice Pita's *Lunar Braceros 2125–2148* (2009), Ted Chiang's "Story of Your Life" (2010), and Gina Ruiz' "Chanclas and Aliens" (2012) to demonstrate how authors of color are utilizing the science fiction tropes of space travel and first contact to disrupt narratives of colonization. The authors discussed in this chapter take a dual approach to first contact narratives: They employ the stereotypical, othered view of aliens and peoples of color when necessary to draw attention to issues of colonization, yet these texts also add plot points where alien and human communities are forced to adapt to and learn from one another to survive. Ultimately, each author in this chapter draws attention to power structures to show the effects of colonization from the view of the colonized. The authors in this chapter also look ahead to new possibilities by demonstrating how acceptance of non-Eurowestern cultural views can lead to the salvation of the human race.

Chapter 2 discusses Larissa Lai's *Salt Fish Girl* (2002), Octavia E. Butler's *Fledgling* (2005), Nnedi Okorafor's *The Book of Phoenix* (2015), and N. K. Jemisin's Broken Earth Trilogy (2015–2017) to examine how science fiction authors of color are reworking the tropes of genetic engineering, genetic mutation, and genetic manipulation to critique the history of scientifically justified violence against peoples of color. In this chapter, I argue that genetically engineered characters, as markers of difference, have the potential to demonstrate how humanity can resist racist and xenophobic views by complicating essentialized, often Eurowestern-privileged views of race and ethnicity. None of the authors in this chapter are arguing that genetics will create a "race-blind" future; in fact, all the genetically altered characters in this chapter have their lives threatened because of their differences. But the depiction of genetic engineering in these texts does open interesting conversations for how genetics may allow specific groups to challenge long-held views about race and ethnicity. One fact that all the texts in this chapter highlight becomes clear: An adjustment to views of racial essentialism is necessary to avoid continuing the cycle of oppression that is currently affecting many peoples of color in Eurowestern cultures.

Chapter 3 discusses Sabrina Vourvoulias's *Ink* (2012), Gabby Rivera's "0.1" (2019), Colson Whitehead's *Zone One* (2011), and Ling Ma's *Severance* (2018) to discuss how these authors employ the trope of a postapocalyptic setting to disrupt the idea of a "race blind" future. Each of the authors discussed is utilizing the postapocalyptic setting to challenge the view of cultural intermixture as negative and to imagine alternative worlds where characters of color are not few and exceptional, but instead are unexceptional norms. The postapocalyptic space is a space of physical hardship, and the characters in these texts face dangers linked to their status as immigrants or peoples of color; however, the post-apocalyptic space also highlights how cultures who have already experienced the hardships of colonization, forced migration, and slavery are best equipped to survive. I argue that the authors in this chapter utilize postapocalyptic and dystopic tropes to demonstrate how cultures who refuse to address essentialist cultural views about racial or ethnic purity are doomed to failure.

Chapter 4 discusses Nalo Hopkinson's *Brown Girl in the Ring* (1998), Tananarive Due's African Immortals series (1997–2011), Carlos Hernandez's "The Assimilated Cuban's Guide to Quantum Santeria" (2016), and Rivers Solomon's *An Unkindness of Ghosts* (2017) as examples of science fiction texts that combine elements of Eurowestern and Indigenous sciences and technologies. I argue that the incorporation of Indigenous practices such as environmental sustainability, the promotion of balance between living beings, objects, and spirits, and "conjure science"[9] expand the definition of "technology" in science fiction. Such an expansion is a direct challenge to Eurowestern notions of Indigenous cultures as "primitive"; it also highlights how Indigenous scientific literacies, which have been passed down in Indigenous cultures for centuries, are only now truly being studied and understood by Eurowestern scientists. The characters in each of these texts combine Eurowestern and Indigenous sciences and technologies to survive, whether that means cheating death in the near future or living forever. Their refusal to die exposes the biopolitics currently informing Eurowestern cultures that views peoples of color as disposable bodies.

Science Fiction and Theories of Race

Diverse Futures aligns with recent science fiction criticism that seeks to examine non-Eurocentric contributions to the science fiction genres. There is no denying that science fiction has a history of representing cultures of color through a Eurocentric, colonial gaze.[10] For science fiction authors of color, this history of negative representation can create a problematic self-consciousness. In the introduction to *So Long Been Dreaming: Postcolonial Science Fiction and Fantasy* (2004), Nalo Hopkinson refers to "the unholy marriage of race consciousness and science fiction sensibility" (7) when describing the struggle for science fiction writers of color to write science fiction without being accused of participating in a genre viewed as reinforc-

---

9. See Dillon's "Haint Stories Rooted in Conjure Science: Indigenous Scientific Literacies in Andrea Hairston's *Redwood and Wildfire*."

10. For an in-depth explanation of the history of colonialism and science fiction, see John Rieder's *Colonialism and the Emergence of Science Fiction* (2008).

ing stereotypes of colonization. She notes later, "To be a person of color writing science fiction is to be under suspicion of having internalized one's colonization" (7). Hopkinson's words capture the hesitation many authors of color express at the idea of writing science fiction: How can science fiction authors write stories that respect both the conventions of the science fiction genres and their cultural experiences? Or, as Hopkinson describes: "that take the meme of colonizing the natives and, from the experience of the colonizee, critique it, pervert it, fuck with it, with irony, with anger, with humor, and also, with love and respect for the genre of science fiction that makes it possible to think about new ways of doing things" (9). Science fiction authors often begin as fans of the genre, but for science fiction authors of color, this fandom is tainted by science fiction texts that reinforce ideals of racial essentialism and white supremacy.[11] Science fiction authors and fans of color also find themselves subject to racist attacks such as the decades of racism faced by Samuel R. Delany and the Sad Puppy/Rabid Puppy attacks against authors of color such as N. K. Jemisin.[12] Although science fiction is becoming more diverse every year, its history of reinforcing colonial, racist views still has strong effects for authors of color who engage with this genre.

One reason why science fiction authors of color are willing to risk racism and accusations of internalized colonization to write science fiction is that this genre allows authors to create entirely new worlds where people of color are not only present but crucial to the narrative. Rieder notes that while many early science fiction texts reinforced the colonial ideologies of the societies they were created in, "the invention of other worlds very often originates in a satirical impulse to turn things upside down or inside out" (4). Rieder also points to H. G. Wells's *The War of the Worlds* (1898) as an early science fiction text that goes beyond satire to reverse the colonial gaze and create an experience of estrangement for its intended European audience (10). Science fiction has a vexed history of reinforcing a Eurocentric perspective, yet from its inception, authors like Wells have recognized science fiction's potential for subverting a colonial, white-dominant perspective.

---

11. For analysis of racism in American science fiction texts, see Isiah Lavender III's *Race in American Science Fiction* (2011) and André M. Carrington's *Speculative Blackness: The Future of Race in Science Fiction* (2016).

12. For commentary on the science fiction community's racism toward science fiction authors of color, see Samuel R. Delany's "Racism and Science Fiction" (1998) and N. K. Jemisin's 2018 Hugo Award acceptance speech. For information on racism in science fiction fan communities, see the Sad Puppies/Rabid Puppies Hugo Awards controversy discussed in Amanda Marcotte's "The alt-right attacks sci-fi: How the Hugo Awards got hijacked by Trumpian-style culture warriors" (2016).

Considering science fiction's history of both reinforcing and challenging colonial paradigms, it is no surprise that authors are beginning to look to science fiction themes to revise the Eurocentric rhetoric that dominates colonial history and literature. Agnieszka Podruczna explains how the defining features of the science fiction genre lend themselves to postcolonial critique:

> The pattern of subversive denial of the old norms and establishing a new order, so characteristic of this genre, is precisely why the postcolonial literary tradition has been one of the first to recognize the possibilities of science fiction and seize it for itself, in order to use its endless world-building capabilities to construct narratives that would challenge the colonial, binary status quo and attempt to dismantle the discourse from within, using the discourse of the coloniser to infuse it with the ethnic identity of those who had been denied their voice by the colonial paradigm. (Podruczna 264)

The science fiction genre is defined by its ability to create new worlds. By applying this notion of reinvention, science fiction authors challenge the genre's Eurocentricity through the creation of non-Eurocentric worlds and narratives. The "new order" of science fiction that is "infused" with the identities of colonized peoples that Podruczna describes are the types of texts this project seeks to examine.

Although people of color have engaged in speculative writing arguably for centuries,[13] it is only in the last few decades that critics have begun to examine the connections between science fiction and themes of racial identity. The term "Afrofuturism" was defined by critic Mark Dery in his 1993 essay "Black to the Future" as speculative fiction that addresses African American themes.[14] Afrofuturism has since become a powerful movement of science fiction authors, artists, and critics who have expanded the original definition to include multiple forms of media. Authors and artists of African, Afro-Latinx, and Caribbean backgrounds are often included in definitions of Afrofuturism, but it is important to note that one criticism of the Afrofuturist

---

13. In 2016, science fiction author Nisi Shawl shared an annotated list of Black science fiction that began with Martin R. Delany's *Blake: Or the Huts of America* (1859). See a link for this list in Leah Schnelbach's *Tor.com* article "This Crash Course in the History of Black Science Fiction Will Change Your Reading Life!" Ytasha Womack also notes in *Afrofuturism: The World of Black Sci-Fi and Fantasy Culture* (2013) that Afrofuturist critics have discovered "a tradition of sci-fi or futuristic works created by people of African descent that stretched back to precolonial Africa" (19).

14. De Witt Douglass Kilgore notes that while Dery was not the first critic to use the term "Afrofuturism," his usage was the first to gain critical attention and ultimately sparked other artists and critics to adopt the term ("Afrofuturism" 2).

movement is that it is not always inclusive of non-African/African American authors. There is also currently a debate in Afrofuturist criticism as to whether African artists and writers should be defined as part of the Afrofuturist movement or should be labeled "Africanfuturist."[15] Several African authors and critics, including Nnedi Okorafor, Mohale Mashigo, and Sofia Samitar, have argued that Afrofuturism was originally intended to describe African American artistic production and that many works of Afrofuturism depict an African American projection of an African future.[16] Like science fiction, the definitions of Afrofuturism are constantly in flux as creators find new ways to connect their specific experience of Blackness to science fiction themes.

Author and critic Ytasha Womack explains in *Afrofuturism: The World of Black Sci-Fi and Fantasy Culture* (2013) that the many unseen and underrepresented science fiction fans of color were engaging in Afrofuturism well before the movement was defined:

> I was an Afrofuturist before the term existed. And any sci-fi fan, comic book geek, fantasy reader, Trekker, or science fair winner who ever wondered why black people are minimized in pop culture depictions of the future, conspicuously absent from the history of science, or marginalized in the roster of past inventors and then actually set out to do something about it could arguably qualify as Afrofuturist as well. (6)

Womack explains that Afrofuturism is not simply a term created by critics to discuss theoretical concepts of literature or history; it is a lived movement made relevant by the artists and authors who create Afrofuturist worlds that highlight the erasure of peoples of color in futuristic settings. This recognition led to an excavation of the works of Black artists, filmmakers, musicians, and writers, such as W. E. B. DuBois ("The Comet," 1920), Sun Ra (*Space Is the Place*, 1973), and John Sayles (*Brother from Another Planet*, 1983) as critics began to argue that although the term Afrofuturism was rela-

---

15. Nnedi Okorafor created the term "Africanfuturism" to differentiate her work from works of Afrofuturism. Okorafor explains on her blog that the current definitions of Afrofuturism do not fit her creative works. For more information, see "Africanfuturism Defined" at http://nnedi.blogspot.com/.

16. See Mashigo's "Afrofuturism is not for Africans living in Africa'—an essay by Mohale Mashigo," excerpted from her new collection of short stories, *Intruders*," https://johannesburgreviewofbooks.com/2018/10/01/afrofuturism-is-not-for-africans-living-in-africa-an-essay-by-mohale-mashigo-excerpted-from-her-new-collection-of-short-stories-intruders/.

tively new, the concept of using science fiction themes to combat a dystopic, Eurowestern-controlled vision of Black futures has a rich history.[17]

This idea of combatting a Eurocentric vision of the future is a defining feature of Afrofuturism. De Witt Douglass Kilgore explains in the entry "Afrofuturism" for *The Oxford Handbook of Science Fiction* (2014) that science fiction's imagining of the future is directly linked to racial hierarchy: "In Euro-American Futurism, the ability to imagine things to come is the property of a dominant class distinguished from the rest of the human species by race" (2). In Eurowestern cultures, historical narratives and science fiction are each dominated by texts that privilege whiteness. People of color living in these cultures find themselves simultaneously written out of both the past and future. Afrofuturism, as the first highly visible science fiction movement to address issues of Eurocentrism and racism in these genres, is bringing conversations about racial representation in alternate and futuristic settings into critical and public consciousness. Through its interweaving of Black cultural references and science fiction themes, Afrofuturist artists create texts that "[subvert] the genre which speaks so much about the experience of being alienated, but contains so little written by alienated people themselves" (Hopkinson qtd. in Leonard 253). Afrofuturism demonstrates how science fiction authors can combat Eurocentrism by employing a historically white-dominated genre to highlight racial inequity in Eurowestern cultures.

The depiction of possible futures in Eurowestern science fiction has been influenced for centuries by the modern versus primitive binary, which leaves little room for the inclusion of marginalized or diasporic cultures. Adriano Elia explains that "Afrofuturism is therefore a transnational and transdisciplinary cultural movement based upon the unusual connection between the marginality of allegedly 'primitive' people of the African diaspora and 'modern' technology and science fiction" (84). Afrofuturism thus becomes a space where authors and artists can imagine "modern" worlds that also incorporate Black cultural practices and beliefs. Toni Morrison argues that African slaves were the first peoples to experience the existential crisis of alienation that critics like Nietzsche define as inherent to modern civilization, and therefore the first modern peoples (Noudelmann 288). As a result, critics like Kodwo Eshun note that a principal feature of Afrofuturism is recognizing the modernity of Africa, which is the antithesis of Eurowestern depictions of Africa as a "metaphor for dystopia and catastrophe" (Elia 84). Projections of a technologically advanced Africa are currently making their

---

17. For a literary analysis of Afrofuturist texts that predate the term, see Isiah Lavender III's *Afrofuturism Rising: The Literary Prehistory of a Movement* (2019).

way into the public consciousness through films like *Black Panther* (2018) and the works of authors such as Nnedi Okorafor.[18] The popularity and high box-office earnings of *Black Panther* in particular may lead to a greater number of diverse representations of science fiction reaching a mass market than ever before. Afrofuturism will become increasingly visible as Black artists and critics continue to examine how the creation of Black futures draws attention to the presence and contributions of Black cultures worldwide.

The idea of utilizing the science fiction genres to question issues of racial futurity, particularly the modern versus primitive binary which dominates Eurowestern narratives of colonization, is also a defining theme within the Latinx,[19] Indigenous, and Asian futurisms movements. Catherine Ramírez's "Deus ex Machina: Tradition, Technology, and the Chicanafuturist Art of Marion C. Martinez" and "Afrofuturism/Chicanafuturism: Fictive Kin," published in *Aztlan* in 2004 and 2008, respectively, draw direct parallels between the concepts of Afrofuturism and her definition of "Chicanafuturism." Ramírez expressly states in "Deus ex Machina" that she draws from Alondra Nelson's work in defining Afrofuturism to create her definition, which she later updates in "Afrofuturism/Chicanafuturism" to include specific elements of Chicanx culture:

> Chicanafuturism explores the ways that new and everyday technologies, including their detritus, transform Mexican American life and culture. It questions the promises of science, technology, and humanism for Chicanas, Chicanos, and other people of color. And like Afrofuturism, which reflects diasporic experience, Chicanafuturism articulates colonial and postcolonial histories of indigenismo, mestizaje, hegemony, and survival. (187)

---

18. Although Okorafor's work is widely known to Afrofuturist scholars, her writing is set to come into public view through the planned HBO series based on her novel *Who Fears Death* as well as the new *Shuri* comic series.

19. For the purposes of this text, I have decided to use the terms "Latinx," "Latinx futurisms," and "Latinx science fiction" as descriptors for peoples living in the US who originate from Spanish-speaking cultures and the science fiction texts written by these groups. I recognize that any catch-all descriptor comes with issues, so I am choosing the term that is, to date, the most contemporary and inclusive term available. When discussing a specific author's culture or a culture referred to in a text, I will use more specific cultural terms. My choice follows trends in Latinx popular culture and science fiction criticism, such as Frederick Luis Aldama and Christopher González's *Reel Latinxs* (2019) and Matthew David Goodwin's science fiction anthology *Latinx Rising* (reprinted 2020 edition), which both represent the term as inclusive of people of Latin American, Central American, Chicanx, and Latino-Caribbean origins.

Ramírez's work highlights the ways that Chicanx peoples, as well as many other peoples of color, have been stereotyped as "primitive" peoples who do not engage with technology while simultaneously being forced to use technology in exploitative labor practices, such as factory work. Ramírez also uses her definition of Chicanafuturism to educate non-Chicanx peoples on Chicanx use of technology, whether that be using the internet to speak to relatives in another country or recycling circuit boards to make art.

Cathryn Josefina Merla-Watson notes that Ramírez's definition of Chicanafuturism has since expanded into a movement titled "Latin@ futurism":

> Latin@futurism references a spectrum of speculative aesthetics produced by US Latin@s, including Chican@s, Puerto Ricans, Dominican Americans, Cuban Americans, and other Latin American immigrant populations. It also includes innovative cultural productions stemming from the hybrid and fluid borderlands spaces, including the US-Mexico border.

Latin@futurism or Latinxfuturism takes the concept of the hybrid, yet alienated Latinx figure at the center of Latinx borderland studies and examines how Latinx authors are utilizing the science fiction genre to challenge Eurowestern-dominant narratives of Latinx culture. Such authors are literally creating the "alien" consciousness described by Gloria Anzaldúa in 1987 to define the *mestiza* experience in *Borderlands/La Frontera*. The hybridity and alienation that Anzaldúa describes as integral to anyone who lives in a border area comes to life in the works of Latinx science fiction authors, who utilize tropes like ghosts and aliens to represent the liminal existence of Latinx peoples in Eurowestern cultures.

Although Indigenous futures have been discussed for decades by critics such as Gerald Vizenor in his theory of Native survivance, or by critics who engage with Indigenous constructions of time,[20] the term "Indigenous futurisms" came into critical view through the publication of Grace L. Dillon's seminal anthology *Walking the Clouds* (2012). Dillon's critical explanation of the intersections of Indigenous cultural values and themes of science fiction in the titled sections of her critical introduction—"Native Slipstream," "Contact," "Indigenous Science and Sustainability," "Native Apocalypse," and "Biskaabiiyang, 'Returning to Ourselves'"—makes a clear case that Indigenous science fiction authors have been overlooked in the genre. Dillon also

---

20. See works by Marijo Moore, Trace A. Demeyer, Conrad Scott, Stina Attebery, David M. Higgins, Lois Red Elk, Suzanne Zahrt Murphy, and Amy Krout-Horn.

notes that an emerging movement of Indigenous authors, many of whom use more easily recognizable tropes of science fiction, are challenging science fiction's exclusion of Indigenous cultural values. She explains that one of main goals of *Walking the Clouds* is to "[open] up science fiction to reveal Native presence" (2). Dillon's seminal anthology and her work in supporting new Indigenous science fiction authors through the annual Imagining Indigenous Futurisms Science Fiction Writing Contest has led to the publication of more Indigenous science fiction anthologies, such as *Love Beyond Body, Space, and Time* (2016), and the emergence of Indigenous science fiction authors like Rebecca Roanhorse and Daniel H. Wilson. Dillon's explanations of Indigenous cultural values and practices have also influenced many science fiction critics. One example is Amandine Faucheux and Isiah Lavender III's cowritten article "Tricknology: Theorizing the Trickster in Afrofuturism," which examines how the Indigenous trickster figure influences themes of Afrofuturism.

Discussions of Asian futurism in the US and Canada emerged from Asian and Asian American studies critics' examinations of Orientalist depictions in science fiction texts, defined as "techno-Orientalism" or "the phenomenon of imagining Asia and Asians in hypo- or hypertechnological terms in cultural productions and political discourse" (Roh, et al. "Introduction," 2). David S. Roh, Betsy Huang, and Greta A. Niu note that depictions of Asians and Asian landscapes in Eurowestern science fiction tend to fluctuate between a "premodern-hypermodern dynamic" defined by examples such as Dr. Fu Manchu, the mysteriously brilliant yet technologically challenged villain immortalized in the Fu Manchu novel series and subsequent films throughout the twentieth century, and the hypermodern, Asian-dominated futures visualized in science fiction classics such as the film *Bladerunner* and the TV series *Firefly* (1–2). Many science fiction novels and films embody this juxtaposition of the fascination of Eurowestern cultures with a romanticized notion of "the Orient" explained by Edward Said and an equally potent fear of the "Yellow Peril" introduced in late nineteenth-century writings. Roh, Huang, and Niu explain that the xenophobic anxieties toward Asians that produced the image of the Yellow Peril "found new forms across cultures and hemispheres as Asian economies bec[a]me more visible competitors in the age of globalization and rapid technological innovations" (3). One of the most common places this depiction of a technologized yellow peril emerges is in science fiction.

Eurowestern importing of Japanese popular culture media, most often anime and manga, further complicates discussions of Asian futurism. Danielle Leigh Rich explains in *Global Fandom: The Circulation of Japanese Popular Culture in the US* (2011) that many fans exoticize Japanese culture in their reception and imitation (through fan fiction and cosplay) of Japanese popular culture, a trend that "speaks to Americans' often unquestioned cultural privilege born of uneven economic, cultural and social exchanges between US and other nations (even so-called first world nations such as Japan)" (22). Eurowestern cultures also have the tendency to co-opt and whitewash imported Asian popular culture; one notable example is the choice to cast the white actress Scarlett Johansson in the US film version of *Ghost in the Shell* (2017). The growing popularity of the specific literary and TV science fiction categories of anime and magna may also create issues for Asian and Asian American science fiction authors and artists whose works do not fit the expectations that these imported popular culture forms (and their Western imitations) have created for Eurowestern audiences.

But to limit the definition of Asian futurism to depictions of techno-Orientalism in Eurowestern science fiction would be a disservice to the science fiction authors and Asian futurist critics who are currently shaping visions of Asian futurism to incorporate a non-Eurowestern perspective. As Xin Wang argues in "Asian Futurism and the Non-Other," a critical study of techno-Orientalism

> may be productive for interrogating sci-fi materials with problematic representations of Asian subjects. . . . But this approach might also risk giving these materials more attention than they deserve, unwittingly confining critical reflections on speculative art and literature to the narrow arena of representational identity politics. (9)

Increasingly, Asian American and Asian Canadian science fiction authors are utilizing and reimagining aspects of their cultures to dismantle both Eurowestern perceptions and traditional cultural beliefs. One example is Larissa Lai's *Salt Fish Girl* (2002), which combines the science fiction trope of genetic manipulation with a reworked myth of the goddess Nü Wa to create a non-Eurocentric, non-heteronormative vision of the future. Asian diasporic authors are also forging connections with Asian science fiction through translation; most notable to date is the award-winning Chinese American author Ken Liu's translation of Chinese author Cixin Liu's 2008 novel *The Three Body Problem* which received a Nebula Award in 2015 for the translated version. Liu has also edited two collections of contemporary Chinese science fiction in translation titled *Invisible Planets* (2016) and *Broken Stars* (2019).

Like Afrofuturism, Latinx, Indigenous, and Asian futurism comes from a rich history of these cultures' engagement with the speculative. Cathryn Josefina Merla-Watson and B. V. Olguín note:

> Horror, the gothic, and the post-apocalyptic are not foreign notions to Chican@ and Latin@ subjectivity but rather powerful and enduring structures of feeling.... Horror and related genres are apropos for interpreting Latin@ social life and subjectivity, not only because Latin@s have been continually figured as the monstrous other in US popular culture but also because horror and terror have been endemic to and have textured Latin@ lived experience and history. Indeed, the histories of Chican@s and Latin@s in the Americas have been punctuated by graphic forms of violence, both banal and apocalyptic—the very stuff of horror. (3)

Just as the experience of slavery is frequently linked to the concept of alien abduction by Afrofuturist critics,[21] Latinx, Asian, and Indigenous futurist critics point out that the history of alienation and colonization of Latinx, Asian, and Indigenous peoples in Eurowestern cultures creates possibilities for science fiction authors of color to draw parallels between the fantastic events of science fiction texts and the lived experiences of peoples of color in Eurowestern societies. Díaz frequently compares his immigration from the Dominican Republic to New Jersey to the science fiction trope of time travel:

> As a kid science fiction made perfect sense to someone like me who had lived such extreme reality. I had gone from a 1970s Third World—we're not talking about a 2012 Third World—a 1970s Third World and then suddenly moved to New Jersey. It was as if you had gone in a time machine. It was extraordinary. The US to a kid like me felt like science fiction. For a kid like me who grew up in the shadow of dictatorship, American realistic fiction or realistic stories, and their sitcoms, didn't have any traces of the world I left behind. In science fiction and fantasy I saw a lot of myself reflected. (qtd. in Wolinsky)

Díaz's experience is a literal embodiment of Suvin's cognitive estrangement, one that begins in the very history of colonization of the Dominican Republic.

Afrofuturism, Latinx futurism, Asian futurism, and Indigenous futurism also address a subversive reworking of technology that challenges stereotypes of peoples of color and their use of/access to technology. Merla-

---

21. See works by Kodwo Eshun, Sofia Samatar, and Isiah Lavender III.

Watson explains that "Latin@futurism excavates and creatively recycles the seeming detritus of the past to imagine and galvanize more desirable presents and futures." For the descendants of colonized cultures, the past is a narrative of resiliency; colonized cultures, denied access to newer technologies, must find ways to subvert social systems through the creative refunctioning of technologies and resources. This idea has roots in Afrofuturism and the Black literary tradition, which frequently highlight African and African American cultures' subversive reworking of technology. Nelson, Tu, and Hines explain the significance of repurposed technology for peoples of color in the introduction to their edited collection *Technicolor: Race, Technology, and Everyday Life* (2001):

> While access to technology remains one of the most pressing obstacles for people of color, they have often overcome this challenge by making due with what they have. By "refunctioning" old/obsolete technologies or inventing new uses for common ones, communities in many places have fashioned technologies to fit their needs and priorities. In the process, they become innovators, creating new aesthetic forms (art, music), new avenues for political action, and new ways to articulate their identities. ("Introduction" 8)

One example of recycled hardware is the artwork of Marion C. Martinez, discussed at length in Ramírez's discussions of Chicanafuturism; Martinez's works blend the art of Latinx Santo creation with discarded technological waste. Guillermo Gómez-Peña, a Chicano performance artist, author, and critic, also incorporates recycled technologies into his performances with *La Pocha Nostra*. Examples of Black subversive use of technologies include everything from sampling and dubbing music in hip hop music to "hidden" online communities like Black Twitter. Moya Bailey, digital humanities scholar and "digital Alchemist" for the *Octavia E. Butler Legacy Network* website, notes that recycled technologies include the subversive use of online platforms:

> When I talk about digital alchemy I am thinking of the ways that women of color in particular transform everyday digital media into valuable social justice media magic. We turn scraps into something precious. Like chitterlings, the discarded pig intestines of the internet can be reworked into a delicacy.

Bailey's point demonstrates how peoples of color can use established online platforms, like Facebook and Twitter, for subversive purposes. Science fiction authors of color frequently question the assumption that access to newer technologies makes society better or more advanced; instead, they offer an alternative view that privileges a deliberately creative "misuse" of technology. Finding alternative ways to use and recycle old technologies becomes even more important in postapocalyptic futuristic landscapes, where those who adapt to a loss of "civilization" are best able to survive.

Adapting technology is also not limited to machines; many Afrofuturist and Indigenous futurist critics also explore the impact of newer technologies, such as genetic engineering, on depictions of race in the future. Faucheux and Lavender III examine the incorporation of "trickster technologies" defined as "shapeshifting, bioengineering, and complex forms of machinery that transforms the body, usually to humorous or witty ends" in the science fiction writings of Afrofuturist authors Octavia E. Butler and Nalo Hopkinson (33). Connecting the ideas of "advanced" technologies like bioengineering with the mythology of the trickster figure, Faucheux and Lavender III note how Afrofuturist authors are working to create "a fluid biology" with the potential to undermine fixed, binary notions of racial and gender identity (34). Many figures in African, Asian, Indigenous, and Latinx cultural mythology are represented as plural. From the trickster to deities that embody life and death such as Eshun or the goddess Cihuacōātl, these plural representations challenge the Eurowestern notions of the individual self that often lead to hierarchical systems of thought.

The concept of balance between humans, animals, objects, and spirits is a fundamental idea in many cultures, one that is gaining acknowledgment from Eurowestern scientists. Lynn Margulis's endosymbiotic theory, which argues that cooperation (or symbiosis) at the cellular level forms the basis of evolution, directly challenges Darwinian theories of evolution that focus on a more competitive model. Margulis's theory was rejected when it first appeared in 1967 (Bollinger 34). Laurel Bollinger notes that endosymbiotic theory "calls into question the very notion of a self/other split and reaffirms our connectedness to the natural processes by which life evolves" (36). A symbiotic relationship between all life on Earth decenters the human in depictions of the future; texts such as Celu Amberstone's "Refugees" (2004) highlight the fact that if humanity continues to contribute to climate change without considering the impact, humans may not be present in the future at all.

Like Afrofuturism, Indigenous futurisms highlight native science and technologies not as an alternative to Eurowestern science but as integral to the understanding of science as a whole. As Dillon explains: "Methods that do not resemble western science are not de facto 'primitive'" ("Imagining"

8).[22] Lisa Lopez Levers argues that more Eurowestern doctors and counselors need to incorporate Indigenous scientific knowledge to treat illness successfully:

> Euro-American understandings of indigenous knowledge, in general, and indigenous healing practices in particular, have been limited. However, as the philosophy and history of science literatures have indicated a shifting scientific paradigm, our understandings have been moving gradually away from the hegemony of scientific method and Cartesian logic as the only valid dictum of knowledge. (87)

Indeed, recognition of Indigenous medicines by the World Health Organization (WHO), UNICEF, and the United Nations (UN) is currently leading nations worldwide to rethink the value of Indigenous knowledge (Le Roux-Kemp 274). Many of the authors in this collection, including Celu Amberstone, Tananarive Due, Rivers Solomon, and Nnedi Okorafor, challenge Eurowestern perceptions of technology by incorporating Indigenous practices into their ethnoscapes. These texts demonstrate the limitations of Eurowestern assumptions about Indigenous cultures and argue that Indigenous sciences are necessary for the survival of the human race.

Indigenous science fiction authors are also extremely aware that Indigenous cultures, like African American and Latinx peoples, are living in a "post-Native Apocalypse world" ("Imagining" 10). Experiences of forced relocation, diaspora, and slavery mark many colonized cultures. Critics and authors such as Toni Morrison, Gerald Vizenor, Mark Dery, and Kodwo Eshun note that for these cultures, the apocalypse has already happened.[23] Science fiction authors are thus able to draw on these cultures' experiences with the horrors of colonization to stress the resilience and adaptability of formerly colonized peoples. Afrofuturism, Latinx futurism, and Indigenous futurism each move away from simply documenting the effects of coloniza-

---

22. Dillon is addressing Wendy Makoon Geniusz's *Our Knowledge Is Not Primitive* (2009) when she makes this statement. Makoons Geniusz compares the way in which Anishinaabe botanical knowledge is presented by Western science with how it is preserved in Anishinaabe culture to argue for a decolonization of traditional Anishinaabe knowledge and an opening of dialogue about how scientists can work with Indigenous cultures to gather research in a way that respects Indigenous knowledge.

23. See Morrison's interview with Paul Gilroy in *Small Acts: Thoughts on the Politics of Black Cultures*; Vizenor's *Manifest Manners: Narratives on Postindian Survivance*; Dery's "Black to the Future: Interviews with Samuel R. Delany, Greg Tate, and Tricia Rose" in *Flame Wars: The Discourse of Cyberculture*; and Eshun's "Further Considerations of Afrofuturism."

tion and instead move on to future and alternate worlds where being able to adapt to new conditions becomes paramount to the survival of the human species.

Looking Ahead

At a time when the future of peoples of color in the US is more precarious than ever, science fiction provides a space for authors to warn readers about the equally dangerous rhetorics of racism and racial blindness. Additionally, by writing futures that include people of color in significant ways, science fiction authors are revising the narrative of victimization often imposed on minority ethnic groups by Eurowestern cultures. Science fiction becomes a space where authors of color can address a traumatic cultural past while still imagining what peoples of color can achieve in the future.

Although there is still a stereotyped perception that peoples of color do not read certain popular genres like science fiction and horror,[24] the internet provides science fiction authors of color more ways than ever before to self-promote and fund their work, which is helping these authors work around the perceived "double bind" of being an author of color and an author writing in a popular genre. The large commercial successes of films such as *Black Panther* and *Get Out* and Afrofuturist musicians such as Janelle Monae and OutKast are also creating space for more science fiction by authors and artists of color to come into the public consciousness.

Diverse Futures is my attempt to respond to a growing academic and public interest in science fiction by authors of color. I hope that by drawing attention to the authors who are creating the science fiction worlds they did not have access to as children, these worlds will be available to the next generation of readers, who will not have to question their place in the future.

---

24. Tananarive Due has described her experiences with publishers who do not understand the value of her African Immortals Series, a hybrid science fiction/horror series, and states that they frequently questioned if there was a market for popular writing by authors of color. See Chideya, Farai. "A Conversation with Tananarive Due, Part 1." (2006) https://www.npr.org/templates/story/story.php?storyId=5160333. For additional reading on the intersections of Blackness and horror in literature and film, see Kinitra D. Brooks's *Searching for Sycorax: Black Women Haunting Contemporary Horror* (2017) and Robin R. Means Coleman's *Horror Noire: Blacks in American Horror Films from 1890's to Present* (2011).

CHAPTER 1

Space Travel and First Contact Narratives

Science fiction authors of color are painfully aware of the history of racism in science fiction first contact writing. As Grace L. Dillon (Anishinaabe) explains, "Historically, sf has tended to disregard the varieties of space-time thinking of traditional societies, and it may still narrate the atrocities of colonialism as 'adventure stories'" ("Imagining" 2). The early history of mainstream science fiction writing, which modeled "primitive" alien cultures after societies of color, left little room for equity in human/alien relations.[1] The resulting stories served to impose the same themes of white exceptionalism found in colonized countries onto the landscape of space. This history of racism in science fiction creates a sense of hyperconsciousness for contemporary science fiction authors of color, who must decide how to depict various species and their interactions with humans without reinforcing colonialist ideals. N. K. Jemisin explains that, for her, challenging Eurowestern ideals in her writing is not optional: "Racism, sexism, classism, and the aftershocks of colonialism are part of my daily life. I don't have a choice about ignoring them, even in fictional form" (qtd. in J. Jones). One approach to challenging

---

1. Some examples of early racialized science fiction and fantasy stories include the *Frank Reade* (1865–1939) or *Doc Savage* dime novel series (1933–49), Edgar Rice Burroughs's *Under the Moons of Mars* (1912), and the works of William Murray Gradon, Frank Aubrey, and Fenton Ash, among others. For a critical history of this issue, see John Rieder's *Colonialism and the Emergence of Science Fiction* (2008).

colonialism in the science fiction genre is to create narratives that "transcend the binary nature of the imperial system and question the most fundamental assumptions of the colonial discourse, while giving the voice back to the silenced colonial subject" (Podruczna 265). The authors in this chapter represent a few examples of how science fiction authors can utilize tropes of space travel and first contact to achieve the disruption of the colonial binary Podruczna describes.

To address the binary of "civilized" versus "primitive" culture, the authors discussed in this chapter must make critical decisions about how to depict alien/human relations in their texts. Some employ a stereotypical, othered view of aliens and peoples of color when necessary to draw attention to issues of colonization while others add plot points where alien and human communities are forced to adapt to and learn from one another to survive. I begin by discussing Gina Ruíz's short story "Chanclas and Aliens" (2012), a text that utilizes the familiar stereotype of the alien invader satirically to draw attention to the stereotyping of Chicanx communities. Although this text does not disrupt the stereotypical view of aliens as the invading other, it is a good starting point for the chapter because it demonstrates how an author of color who does not identify as a science fiction author employs a science fiction trope to engage in social commentary. I then discuss Octavia E. Butler's *Dawn* (1987) and Celu Amberstone's "Refugees" (2004) as texts that employ alien/human relations as a vehicle to explore colonial relations. I move on to a discussion of "Refugees" and Rosaura Sánchez and Beatrice Pita's *Lunar Braceros 2125–2148* (2009) which each utilize themes of adaptation to show the resilience of Indigenous and diasporic communities. I end the chapter by examining Butler alongside Ted Chiang's "Story of Your Life" (2010) to demonstrate how these two authors challenge the alien invasion trope to explore potential future relations between Indigenous/diasporic communities and Eurowestern cultures. Ultimately, each author in this chapter utilizes science fiction tropes to draw attention to the power structures between colonizer and colonized and to show the effects of colonization from the view of the colonized. The authors in this chapter also look ahead to new possibilities by demonstrating how acceptance of non-Eurocentric cultural views can potentially lead to the salvation of the human race.

Alien Invasion

Gina Ruíz uses the stereotypical, othered view of the "alien invader" in her short story "Chanclas and Aliens," which was featured in the *Ban This! the*

Bsp Anthology of Xican@ Literature, to critique the stereotyping of Chicanx[2] culture, specifically the "cholo" (feminine form "chola") figure. Playing with the idea of first contact, Ruíz imagines what would happen if the alien's first Earthly encounter is not with the white, male authority, but instead with a doubly-othered ethnic minority. James Diego Vigil explains that the term "cholo" has always implied an "alien" status:

> "Cholo" is a label that Americans and Mexican Americans have used to refer to the poorest of the poor, marginalized Mexican immigrants. The term itself is several hundred years old and was used in various areas of Latin America where Indian populations are concentrated. The label describes an indigenous person who is halfway acculturated to the Spanish ways—in short, a person marginal to both the original and the more recent European culture. (57)

Ruíz's depiction of first contact between aliens and cholo peoples is a deliberate disruption of science fiction's privileging of whiteness and the stereotypical depictions of white peoples heroically overcoming an invasion of "alien" peoples (often modeled on "primitive" cultures of color) that is present in many of the early pulp science fiction writings. Ruíz's narrative also draws connections between the violence of colonization, the present-day policing of cholos as dangerous gang members, and the alienation of Chicanx communities. "Chanclas and Aliens" is therefore a strong example of how authors of color can employ science fiction tropes to draw attention to the inequities faced by peoples of color within Eurowestern countries even if they do not categorize themselves as science fiction authors.

Ruíz's choice to center her story on cholo culture deliberately addresses the consequences of colonization for Chicanx peoples past and present. Many Chicanx peoples have ancestors who were forcefully annexed into the US. The Braceros program,[3] which encouraged millions of Chicanos in the 1940s through the 1960s to come to the US on short-term labor contracts and also encouraged these workers to return illegally after the program was shut down, contributed to issues of illegal immigration that have created misleading narratives about Chicanx peoples. The initiation of Operation Wetback (1954), a mass deportation of Chicanx peoples (Hyman and Iskan-

---

2. For the purposes of this project, I am defining "Chicanx" as referring to all Chicana/o/x peoples. I specifically use this term to discuss Ruíz's work rather than "Latinx" because her setting is specifically focused on the area of Lincoln Park, CA, and the "cholo culture that is very specific to Chicanx peoples living in this area.

3. I will address the Braceros program in more detail in my discussion of *Lunar Braceros* later in this chapter.

der), is one of many examples of how Chicanx peoples are depicted by politicians as outsiders who drain national resources, rather than contributing members of US society, many of whom have ties to the country going back to the nineteenth century. In "Chanclas," Ruíz utilizes the alien invasion trope to add an outside, unbiased perspective of cholos and Chicanx peoples. The aliens' first encounter with the group of cholo men describes them as gods: "The aliens above watched from their strangely shaped ship wondering what manner of creature these tattooed, brown Gods were . . . or so they seemed to the tiny and bent luminescent creatures invading their planet with destruction in mind. To their race, only Gods were tall" (266). This scene takes the cholo figure and reconnects it to its Indigenous history. The cholos are depicted as "gods": tall, proud men of regal bearing. Ruíz's decision to connect depictions of present-day cholos to Indigenous warrior gods also engages with Chicanafuturism. Ramírez notes in her work on Chicanafuturism that these science fiction narratives combat Eurowestern views of Indigenous peoples and peoples of color as premodern:

> As various scholars have argued, the logic of colonialism and racism maintains the existence of a spatial-temporal spectrum, with dark "superstitious," precapitalist peoples occupying one end (the primitive), and white 'enlightened,' capitalist nation-states occupying the other (the modern) . . . By virtue of hailing from, occupying, and/or representing the periphery, Hispanos—especially poor, rural, Catholic Hispanos—have been barred from the present and future and fixed in a racialized past . . . In particular, by virtue of being associated with the preindustrial and predigital, they are often deemed incapable of understanding, mastering, or even living with science and technology, signifiers of the present and future." (63–64)

Cholo culture often engages with technology through subversive reimaginings such as lowrider vehicles and rap/hip-hop music, technologies designed to be "a loud symbol of cultural pride, cruising up against an Anglo world that demanded orderly labor, model minorities, and obedient barrios" (Solis). "Chanclas," therefore, is able to address technological stereotypes of Chicanx peoples as a premodern, exploitable labor force. Ruíz takes an ethnic subgroup often associated with gang violence and employs the aliens as an alternative viewpoint: Rather than seeing the young men as criminals, the aliens are able to see the cholos as powerful.

The only way the human characters in "Chanclas" are able to survive is by bringing together different generations of the local Chicanx community to fight the alien invasion. Specifically, Ruíz makes Chicanas central to the destruction of the aliens. After one of the cholos discovers that his wet chancla (slipper or flip-flop) has the power to wound the aliens, the leader of the cholos calls for the social group most adept at throwing these items—grandmothers. Ruíz takes a well-known cultural reference, the chancla-throwing grandma, and connects this reference to the salvation of the entire planet to provide humor but also to show the value in close-knit Chicanx communities like Lincoln Park, CA. Once the women arrive, the grandma with the strongest throwing arm, Doña Belen, quickly takes over the direction of the battle. Reuben's girlfriend, Smiley, also makes the discovery that her Aqua Net hairspray can dissolve the aliens after she sets one on fire, and she brings this knowledge to the fight. The fact that a can of Aqua Net (a brand best-known for its association with the excess of 1980s big hair) can be used as a weapon connects to the idea of the urban Chicana "ghetto" stereotype and Ruíz's reclamation of this stereotype as a marker of ethnic pride.[4] The Aqua Net hairspray becomes another repurposed technology that highlights the ingenuity of Chicanx peoples. "Chanclas" quickly becomes an intergenerational battle to save the planet as the Chicanx community works together to defeat the alien invaders. These small cultural details, created by Ruíz as inside jokes for Chicanx peoples but which are also understood by many Latinx peoples and other peoples of color, link specific Chicanx and Indigenous cultural references to the survival of the entire planet.

But Ruíz is not interested in creating a utopic story. After the Chicanx community defeats the aliens, the Los Angeles Police Department (LAPD) arrives in Lincoln Park the next day and arrests the cholos for "the purple 'graffiti' all over the park" and "their 'sniffing' of Aquanet to 'get high'" (275). The police completely misinterpret the resulting battle scene due to their biased view of the Lincoln Park Chicanx community. The police also call immigration to deport any cholos who do not have proof of citizenship, because these young men are viewed as a threat to US law-abiding society. Ruíz uses the dominant US cultures' othered view of Chicanx peoples to show how a lack of respect for this culture results in a destructive cycle of misunderstanding. She also highlights specific Chicanx and Indigenous cultural practices, such as a repurposing of technology, an emphasis on community, and respect for the knowledge of elders, to comment on the irony of power structures that refuse to see value in cultures of color.

"Chanclas and Aliens" is an important example of how authors of color can engage with science fiction tropes even if they do not identify as science fiction authors. Ruíz's story also serves as a metaphor for current relation-

---

4. Jillian Hernandez employs the term "sexual aesthetic excess" as a marker of the stereotypical Latina figure who is viewed as "too ethnic, too sexy, too young, too cheap, too loud" and argues that the "Chonga" women who embody this aesthetic be viewed as "indexing ethnic pride, personal confidence, and non-normative sexuality" (66).

ships between authors of color and the science fiction genre. Science fiction has a history of reinforcing Eurowestern colonial thinking, which often leaves authors and readers of color feeling alienated from the genre. And yet because of this alienation, science fiction authors of color are often best suited to provide outside perspectives that challenge current representations of race in this genre. Because of the current barriers for authors of color who engage with science fiction, it is important that science fiction critics and publishers look for authors writing science fiction who may not feel welcome submitting their writing to traditional science fiction venues. Critics of Afrofuturism and Indigenous futurism are currently working to reexamine African American and Indigenous canonical literary works through a science fiction lens,[5] but more work is needed to broaden histories of science fiction so that authors of color can have their works, past and present, included in these histories.

First Contact and Colonial Relations

For Celu Amberstone's "Refugees" and Octavia E. Butler's *Dawn*, first contact becomes an avenue for critiquing the relationship between colonizer and colonized. "Refugees" tells the story of a group of Canadians who are relocated to a new planet by aliens after the destruction of Earth. The refugees refuse to trust the aliens or the Indigenous human population who were previously brought to the planet. The story is narrated by one of the "Indigenous" humans, Qwalshina, who was brought to the new planet, Tallav'Wahir, with the first group of humans to be relocated. Butler's *Dawn*, the first book in her Xenogenesis series, tells the story of Lilith Iyapo, a Black woman who is part of a group of human survivors brought from Earth to a spaceship by an alien group named the Oankali after a nuclear war almost destroys humanity. The Oankali keep the humans in stasis until Earth becomes inhabitable; then they wake the humans and inform them that they are able to manipulate genetic material and intend to mix human and Oankali DNA to create a new species. Both texts complicate the mainstream depiction of colonial relations by blurring the distinction between colonizer and colonized.

Amberstone and Butler each utilize the figure of the cultural mediator to comment on the difficulties faced by women of color trying to survive in

---

5. For examples, see Grace L. Dillon's Indigenous anthology *Walking the Clouds* (2012) and Isiah Lavender III's *Afrofuturism Rising* (2019).

a colonized culture. In *Malinche, Pocahontas, and Sacagawea: Indian Women as Cultural Intermediaries and National Symbols*,[6] Rebecca K. Jager explains that Indigenous female cultural mediators performed important diplomatic functions recognized by their communities as valuable. However, since many of the historical accounts of these women were written by European colonizers, the descriptions of these cultural mediators became problematically associated with white superiority or cultural betrayal. Jager notes that such simplistic myth-making strips the cultural mediator of agency: Historical readers are unable to recognize that female Indigenous cultural mediators were people, often women, facing the dangers of colonization and making hard decisions about whether diplomacy could ensure the safety of their peoples (5). Jager's historical analysis demonstrates that the role of cultural mediation involves a multitude of cultural, social, and economic factors that should not be reduced to a stereotyped victim or traitor description. Amberstone and Butler each respond to myths of cultural mediation by introducing female protagonists who function as cultural mediators, either willingly or unwillingly, and then problematizing these characters and their situations to examine the experience of colonization from the perspective of the colonized.

Amberstone begins "Refugees" with her main character willingly participating in the colonial relationship. At first, Qwalshina does not understand why the new humans doubt the word of the aliens who saved them, named the Benefactors, and tries to reassure the "refugees" that the Benefactors are not going to experiment on them: "Our Benefactors only wish good for us. And, no matter our origin on Earth, we are all one people now, the children of Tallav'Wahir. There has never been any experiment. Please believe me" (65). Qwalshina's people were brought to Tallav'Wahir generations before the arrival of the new refugees, so she has never known a noncolonial relationship. She has never questioned the unequal colonizer/colonized relationship her people were forced to agree to for survival, so she immediately assures the refugees that the Benefactors have no evil intentions. Qwalshina's ancestors also view the Benefactors as having saved them from European colonizers, which Qwalshina learns as part of her oral history. She uses assimilationist language like "one people" because the Benefactors have convinced her that the new refugees need to give up all reminders of their past lives and cultures and learn to embrace life on Tallav'Wahir. Amberstone's plot allows readers to question the costs of colonization by demonstrating

---

6. Although I deeply respect the analysis that Rebecca K. Jager conducts about cultural mediators in terms of gender and cultural context in this work, I have to fundamentally disagree with her choice to use the word "Indian" in the title of this piece.

how colonized peoples are forced to abandon their cultural practices and beliefs to survive.

Qwalshina trusts the Benefactors' intentions at first, but as the new humans push her to think about how the Benefactors control and restrict the human population of Tallav'Wahir, she is forced to question her beliefs. She begins to wonder if Tallav'Wahir was ever her home and whether the Benefactors have been telling the truth about saving her people out of compassion. At one point, Qwalshina becomes angry at the refugees for causing her to question her existence and states, "This new emotion I feel frightens me. What if we are living a lie—what if the people from Earth are right? I hate them!" (178). The refugees' mistrust of the Benefactors' motives causes Qwalshina to examine the relationship between the Benefactors and her people. Being forced to analyze her situation creates confusion for Qwalshina, which she projects onto the new humans by stating that she hates them and wants them to leave. Amberstone portrays Qwalshina as a willing cultural moderator but then creates circumstances that force her to examine her situation from the perspective of a colonized subject. Qwalshina's journey to self-doubt demonstrates the tensions in colonizer/colonized relations by showing the difficulties that arise when one culture or species has complete power over another.

In *Dawn*, Lilith is forced into the role of cultural moderator. She is initially repulsed by the Oankali, who are described as having gray skin and sensory tentacles all over their bodies, but is forced to overcome her fear because if she refuses to help the Oankali, she risks her life and the lives of the other humans being held on the Oankali's spaceship. From the beginning of the series, Lilith's body is manipulated by the Oankali without her consent. She wakes up on the ship to find a scar across her abdomen, and begins to think about her lack of agency: "What had she lost and gained, and why? And what else might be done? She did not own herself any longer. Even her flesh could be cut and stitched without her consent or knowledge" (6). Lilith represents the extreme example of a colonized individual—a slave who has no control over where she lives, what she eats, or what is done to her body. Her position as an experimental subject connects to a long history of Eurowestern coercion of Black slaves and Indigenous peoples in the nineteenth century into invasive and involuntary medical procedures, and a twentieth-century history of peoples of color being tricked into participation in medical research or forced sterilization.[7] Lilith also discovers later

---

7. I provide a detailed explanation of medial experimentation on peoples of color in chapter 2. For an overview of nineteenth- and twentieth-century medical experimentation on African Americans, see Harriet A. Washington's *Medical Apartheid: The Dark*

in the novel that the Oankali have destroyed all traces of human culture on Earth and plan to force humanity to rebuild their culture without the influence of the past. Lilith objects to the Oankali's decisions but is forced to help them to avoid being put back to sleep. The manipulation of her body and her coerced position as cultural moderator helping other humans adapt to an alien presence bring to mind stories of early colonizers using slaves as interpreters.[8]

Throughout *Dawn*, Lilith tries to convince the Oankali to allow humanity to decide its own fate. When she demands to know the "price" for the Oankali's decision to save humanity, one of the Oankali, Jdahya, informs her that humans will be forced to combine their DNA with Oankali DNA. Lilith tries to negotiate for humanity to be left alone, but Jdahya tells her that the Oankali have to "trade" with humanity to survive. Butler's decision to use the word "trade" in this scene recalls the history of European colonizers voiding trade deals and land treaties with Indigenous groups because of their view of these peoples as "savage" and therefore not deserving of equal legal rights. Indigenous and Mexican peoples in the US each endured the consequences of broken treaty promises, which were often justified by US officials through the use of racist ideologies. President Andrew Johnson commented in an address to Congress that the Indian Removal Act "[would] place a dense and civilized population in large tracts of country now occupied by a few savage hunters" (Ferraro). There were even many similarities in the language and enforcement of Indigenous and Mexican land treaties:

> In both cases, the territorial acquisitions were sealed by solemn and idealistic treaties that belied the harsh realities of conquest. In exchange for the transfer of land and sovereignty by Mexico, the Unites States promised

---

History of Medical Experimentation on Black Americans from Colonial Times to the Present (2006). For more information on twentieth-century medical experimentation on peoples of color, see Laura Briggs's "Discourses of 'forced sterilization' in Puerto Rico: The problem with the speaking subaltern" (1998), Susan Reverby's *Examining Tuskegee: The Infamous Syphilis Study and Its Legacy* (2009), and Berthier-Foglar et al. *Biomapping Indigenous Peoples: Towards an Understanding of the Issues* (2012).

8. One good example of a slave as cultural interpreter is La Malinche, a Nahua woman who is rumored to have participated in the Spanish conquest of Mexico, as a way of commenting on historical uncertainty. La Malinche, originally named "Malinalli" or "Ce-Malinalli," lived as a slave among the Chontal Maya and served as a translator for Cortés during his conquest of Mexico. She eventually converted to Christianity and married one of Cortés's officers (Downs 398). The fact that she and Cortés had a child, one of the first Mestizos in Mexican history, makes her a figure linked to historical intermixture and uncertainty.

in the Treaty of Guadalupe Hildago that it would "inviolably respect" the established private property rights of Mexican citizens in the conquered territory and provide them with "guarantees equally ample as if the same belonged to the United States." Indian tribes, in turn, relinquished large tracts of lands in exchange for financial compensation and treaty guarantees that smaller "reservations" of land would be maintained as homelands for the tribes. (Klein 202)

Butler borrows the idea of colonial treaties as forced trade between parties with unequal power relations and uses it as the basis of the Oankali's justification for human conquest. The Oankali claim that they have no choice but to trade; Jdahya tells Lilith without the addition of new DNA into their species, they will not survive. However, Lilith and the other surviving humans have even less choice in the situation: They will be forced to "trade" the way that many Indigenous and Mexican peoples had no real choice but to trade with European colonizers for survival. Butler exposes the forced nature of colonial trade by telling her story through the eyes of the cultural mediator rather than the colonizers'. By creating a black-skinned cultural mediator and making her the first human to be told about the "trade," Butler creates a space where the marginalized experiences of colonized peoples of color become the experience of all humanity.

"Refugees" and *Dawn* also employ alien colonization to critique ideals of "civilization" and the relationship of humans to technologies. Both works use alternate views of technology to deconstruct the notion of technology use as a marker of civilization; this postcolonial viewpoint is described by Homi Bhabha in *The Location of Culture* as "contra-modern" or "contingent to modernity, discontinuous or in contention with it, resistant to its oppressive, assimilationist technologies" (9). In Amberstone's and Butler's texts, aliens control all means of space travel. The ships are described as sentient, living beings, rather than the metal rockets and spaceships found in the majority of science fiction stories. The aliens live in harmony with their advanced technologies, technologies that are denied to humans. In "Refugees," an alien ship eventually kills several humans who try to co-opt it to travel back to Earth. In *Dawn,* when Lilith asks a young Oankali to show her how to open a door in the ship, she discovers that the ship is coded to their biology:

> More programmed reaction to chemical stimuli. No special areas to press, no special series of pressures. Just a chemical the Oankali manufactured within their bodies. She would go on being a prisoner, forced to stay wher-

ever they chose to leave her. She would not be permitted even the illusion of freedom. (56)

Although the sentient ships in both works make it impossible for the humans to escape, they also serve as an alternative depiction of technology that is more symbiotic then Eurowestern science fiction's depictions of technology as machine based. In many Eurowestern cultures, a separation from nature enabled by technology is viewed as a marker of civilization. This limited view of what constitutes technology created many of the Eurowestern colonial descriptions of Indigenous peoples as "primitive," which allowed Eurowestern colonizers to justify the removal of Indigenous peoples from specific lands. Delesslin George-Warren argues that many Indigenous cultures have utilized specific technologies for centuries:

> In 1491, thousands of civilizations existed throughout the Americas with thousands of different technologies for organizing members of those societies. In many indigenous societies, one of the fundamental organizing principles is—though this term is a Western imposition—egalitarianism, a structural technology that facilitated a sustainable relationship to the world.

The sustainability that George-Warren describes becomes evident in Amberstone's and Butler's descriptions of alien technologies, which are more advanced than human technologies because of their apparent sustainability and symbiotic relationship with their creators. In both stories, Eurowestern technologies are also responsible for the destruction of Earth, which creates a view of modern humanity as unable to use technologies responsibly and as self-destructive in nature. "Refugees" and *Dawn* use this stark comparison of human/alien (Eurowestern/Indigenous) technology to demonstrate the consequences of Eurowestern cultures' limited view of technological "progress." In both narratives, the human characters' relationship with and misunderstanding of technology creates barriers to their escape.

Amberstone continues her critique of Eurowestern views of civilization and technology through the interactions of Qwalshina and one of the new refugees, Sleek, a young Canadian girl with Indigenous heritage. In "Refugees," Sleek stereotypes Qwalshina's people as "savages" because she does not see any of the technological devices she understands to be markers of civilization. Qwalshina rebukes Sleek for her limited point of view:

> "We know about the high technologies," I told her quietly. "We use what you would call computers, air cars, and other technical things too. But to

help you make the repatterning, we decided that a simple lifestyle would be best for all of us for a time. There is no shame in living close to the land in a simple way, daughter." (Amberstone 165)

Qwalshina's rebuke serves to contradict Eurowestern cultures' privileging of newer technologies and scientific theories over non-Eurowestern scientific and technological knowledge such as Indigenous scientific literacies,[9] a viewpoint that is often reinforced by mainstream science fiction's depictions of computers, spaceships, and other futuristic machine-based technologies. Sleek lived in a city before she was relocated, and although her life is filled with violence and hardship, she has absorbed the Eurowestern ideal of technology as a marker of civilization. However, the fact that Sleek comes from an Indigenous Earth background also speaks to the legacy of internalized colonization within Indigenous groups:

> Sleek (as well as some of the other newcomers) resorts to the colonial discourse of primitive versus civilised, but what she fails to understand is that, when she calls Qwalshina and her people savage, she effectively calls herself savage as well, repeating the patterns of her own colonial experience as a member of the First Nations. The fact that she feels a certain disconnect between herself and Qwalshina and voices it by pointing to Qwalshina's supposed savagery and backwardness reveals, arguably, the level of internalisation of the colonial discourse that can be observed in some members of the Indigenous communities and points to its insidiousness. What is more, Sleek seems to be completely incapable of recognising that she is, in fact, turning her own history of oppression against those who share that colonial legacy. Thus, the whole colonial paradigm is presented as severely complicated, since everything eludes the binary divide, nothing is as black and white as the colonial discourse would make it seem, challenging in this way the preconceptions perpetuated by the colonial system, and, once again, exposing the system of binary oppositions and the Self-Other dichotomy as severely lacking. (Podruczna 270)

Sleek serves as an embodiment of internalized views of colonization. She has been separated from her Indigenous heritage, although she tells Qwalshina that she remembers seeing her grandmother weave cloth (Amberstone 168). As Podruczna notes, Qwalshina and Sleek's interactions demonstrate the complex effects of colonization on Indigenous communi-

---

9. I discuss the concept of Indigenous scientific literacies further in chapter 4. See Grace L. Dillon's definition of this term in her introduction to *Walking the Clouds* (2012).

ties. Amberstone demonstrates the ways in which Eurowestern colonizers were able to turn Indigenous peoples against each other by removing younger generations from Indigenous communities and training them to think of their peoples as less advanced.[10] Amberstone and Butler both ask readers to rethink their assumptions about civilization and to consider how the contra-modern science fiction landscapes both authors create reimagine the savage/civilized binary in colonized countries. Lilith and Qwalshina each struggle with their roles in the colonial system. Both women also make decisions as cultural mediators that showcase the complexity of experiences within colonized communities. Amberstone and Butler utilize the experiences of these characters to move beyond depictions of colonized peoples as powerless victims and, instead, portray the complex relations and negotiations that have occurred in colonized countries for centuries.

Another way "Refugees" and *Dawn* draw connections between "civilized" cultures and technology is by addressing the ways that modern technologies contribute to the destruction of the environment. Both texts argue that humans' inability to live in harmony with their environment will ultimately lead to the destruction of Earth. This viewpoint is found throughout Indigenous cultural practices, which stress the importance of humanity's relationship to the environment.[11] In "Refugees," Qwalshina frequently gives offerings of her blood to Tallav'Wahir to reinforce her bond with the planet. She also notes that her people are careful not to destroy Tallav'Wahir the same way the humans have destroyed Earth. She describes Earth later on as "a fiery cloud of poisons, a blackened cinder" (162). Qwalshina explains to Sleek that using machine-based technologies in moderation is one way that her peoples are trying to avoid stripping Tallav'Wahir of its natural resources: "Our Benefactors teach us that technology must never interfere with our communion with the Mother, lest we forget the Covenant, grow too greedy, and destroy our new home" (165). The implication in this statement is that humans must learn to live in harmony with the land in order to avoid the disaster that happened on Earth. In *Dawn*, Jdahya tells Lilith that the Oankali will not forbid humans to use machines, but that they will also not provide machines or advanced technology to the humans. This withholding

---

10. The US and Canada both engaged in removal of Indigenous children. For more information, see Mary Annette Pember's "The Traumatic Legacy of Indian Boarding Schools" (2019): https://www.theatlantic.com/education/archive/2019/03/traumatic-legacy-indian-boarding-schools/584293/ and "A History of Residential Schools in Canada" (2008): https://www.cbc.ca/news/canada/a-history-of-residential-schools-in-canada-1.702280.

11. I give a more detailed explanation of Indigenous culture's promotion of balance between humans, other living beings, inanimate objects, and spirits in chapter 4.

of technology is likely a way for the Oankali to maintain control over the human population, the way that Eurowesten colonizers both provided and withheld gun technology to control Indigenous populations.[12] However, this denial is also forcing Lilith and the other humans to readjust their way of life in a way that may be more beneficial to Earth's environment. While the intentions of the aliens in these works are questionable, Amberstone and Butler send a clear message in their works that Eurowestern views of civilization which privilege the superiority of technology must change to ensure the survival of the human race.

Interplanetary Diaspora and Adaptation[13]

Rather than using the theme of space exploration as positive—humans bravely exploring space and "discovering" alien species—"Refugees" and *Lunar Braceros* represent space travel as harsh and human beings as unsuited to their new environments. Amberstone depicts the human refugees as forcibly removed from Earth and "settled" on Tallav'Wahir, a planet which does not have the most compatible environment for human beings. Rosaura Sánchez and Beatrice Pita's *Lunar Braceros* describes a group of humans who travel to the moon to work as contract laborers and later discover that they are actually expendable slaves.[14] *Lunar Braceros* depicts the moon as a harsh

---

12. For more information, see Donald E. Worcester and Thomas F. Schilz's "The Spread of Firearms among the Indians on the Anglo-French Frontiers" (1984): www.jstor.org/stable/1184207.

13. I use the term "adaptation" as a biological term when I am discussing the ability of humans to become more biologically suited to a new environment and "assimilation" as a social or cultural term for humans who adapt their cultural practices to another culture or country's expectations. Because science fiction often involves humans adapting biologically to new planets or alien species as a metaphor for colonization and forced assimilation, it is important not to use these terms interchangeably.

14. Although the concepts of space mining and exploitative labor practices have appeared in many science fiction works, including fiction such as Jack Williamson's *Seetee Shock* (1950) and *Seetee Ship* (1951), Greg Bear's *Eon* (1985), and films such as *Armageddon* (1998), it is interesting to note that Sánchez and Pita's *Lunar Braceros* and Duncan Jones's indie film *Moon*, which were both released in 2009, also look at the psychological aspects of isolation and exploitation. What sets these two works apart, however, is that the leading character in *Moon* is a white man (played by Sam Rockwell) who is cloned without his knowledge so he can be used as an almost immortal worker, reborn every three years, while *Lunar Braceros* addresses the braceros' invisibility as a group. Rockwell's character is one man who never returns home, while the braceros are teams of workers that go missing without any punishment to the corporation that hires them. Considering the fact that the lunar braceros are also a reference to millions of Mexican laborers invited into the US, it is clear that Sánchez and Pita are looking at the effects on an entire population, unlike the more individualistic approach of *Moon*.

environment which takes a physical toll on the human workers, far from the depictions of the Apollo 11 mission as a brave conquering of a serene lunar surface. Both works present an alternate view of space travel linked to the ideas of forced displacement often found in Indigenous and diasporic communities. Amberstone's and Sánchez and Pita's works ask readers to consider interplanetary travel from the viewpoint of humans who are forced to travel and who do not have the agency to decide the terms of their relocation.

One of the reasons that adaptation in "Refugees" and *Lunar Braceros* is so difficult is that the colonizing culture in each text refuses to allow the colonized peoples to have agency or autonomy. In both texts, humans are transplanted to new environments, yet most of the humans and aliens in these two texts are unwilling to give up biological or cultural assumptions or to appreciate the other cultures' values. Helen Addison-Smith argues that biological and social changes are linked in the process of adaptation:

> Taking as its cues scientific discourses such as those of evolution, anthropology, and biological determinism, adaptation to a particular environment is often constructed as a principal determinant of an extraterrestrial's biology and his/her/its socio-cultural formations. . . . It could be expected therefore that a dramatic change in a human's biology to suit a particular environment would also lead to a similar degree of change in their socio-cultural reality. (18, ellipsis added)

Addison-Smith argues that any change in environment should come with a change in social and cultural views. With this view in mind, one could argue that not adapting social and cultural views in a new environment would lead to an inability to adapt to a new environment. *Lunar Braceros* and "Refugees" both take on the connection between environment and adaptation: Each text utilizes the science fiction trope of space travel to demonstrate how unequal power structures between colonizers and colonized or between different colonized groups result in displaced human beings' inability to adapt to their new environments.

"Refugees" highlights the negative consequences of displacement through the inability of the recently resettled human refugees to accept Tallav'Wahir as their home. The first group of relocated humans were Indigenous peoples from Canada, and Qwalshina has been raised to believe that the Benefactors saved her people from extinction at the hands of Europeans. The new group of relocated humans are a random assortment of people from a Canadian city. Amberstone specifically leaves out details about the new refugees' races and ethnicities, although she does note that Sleek has some Indigenous heritage. Amberstone's decision to make the second group of relocated humans a mixed group demonstrates that displacement is not simply an issue for Indigenous peoples; refugees can be any race or ethnicity. Because Qwalshina believes that the new humans should be glad to be on Tallav'Wahir, she is surprised to discover one of the new refugees, Jimtalbot, crying over the loss of his wife and home. When she questions him about why he and the other refugees would want to return to Earth, a planet plagued with social and environmental issues, he replies, "Home is home, no matter how bad it is, and you can't stop caring when it's gone—if it's gone!" (70). Jimtalbot's attachment to his home culture and his suspicion of the Benefactor's motives leaves him unwilling to assimilate into the culture of Tallav'Wahir. His experience echoes the experience of many diasporic peoples,[15] who often choose to create ethnic enclaves within another country or spaces where immigrants of the same culture group together to preserve cultural practices.[16] The human refugees are suspicious of the Benefactors and frequently question whether Earth has really been destroyed. This doubt and their dislike of life on Tallav'Wahir results in fights between several humans and the eventual decision of a group of humans (from both the first and second relocated groups) to attempt to take over an alien ship and return to Earth. The refugees' unwillingness to be forced into assimilation allows readers to recognize the injustice of forced assimilation for Indigenous and diasporic groups. Amberstone's text also demonstrates the negative consequences of forced assimilation; for example, the Benefactor's refusal to allow the human refugees to return to Earth and their insistence that the humans assimilate into Qwalshina's culture creates a negative social situation that results in the deaths of both humans and Benefactors.

In "Refugees," the original human group relocated to Tallav'Wahir are also not perfectly attuned to their environment. Qwalshina and her people were originally members of an Indigenous peoples on Earth. She and her peoples attempt to adapt their Indigenous practices to Tallav'Wahir but are ultimately unsuccessful. One of Qwalshina's first comments in the text is

---

15. Although it is common to discuss diasporic and Indigenous peoples as separate groups, for the purposes of my work, I choose to depict both groups as displaced peoples. This definition is in keeping with Fourth World Theory. For more information on Fourth World Theory and "Refugees," see my article in *Extrapolation* titled "Interplanetary Diaspora and Fourth World Representation in Celu Amberstone's 'Refugees'" (2017).

16. In "The Physical and Cultural Attributes of Ethnic Enclave: A Basis for Conversation" (2014) Bakri et al. argue that ethnic enclaves help immigrant communities maintain a strong connection to their home culture through physical aspects (location) and cultural aspects (common food, cultural practices, and language).

about her blood being an "alien color on this world" (161). Shortly after, she explains that her people need the new refugees to replenish their gene pool: "Tallav'Wahir is kind, but there is something in this adoptive environment that is hard on us too. We aren't a perfect match for our new home, but the Benefactors have great hopes for us" (163). Amberstone's alien planet is not simply a different environment that humans need to adjust to; it is a harsh, alien environment that is having negative biological effects on the humans currently residing there. Qwalshina and her people continue to try to adapt to the planet Tallav'Wahir throughout the story, symbolized by Qwalshina's blood offerings to the planet. Podruczna notes the importance of Qwalshina's repeated blood ritual as a symbol of diasporic people's attempts to locate their cultures in foreign spaces:

> It is the ritual, then, grounded in body, blood and earth, as opposed to technology (which carries clear undertones of the Indigenous-Western dichotomy), which facilitates self-identification of the members of the diaspora, faced with colonisation and displacement, and which grounds the colonial subject and allows for access to the ancestral heritage in order to search for something that would resemble home. (268)

Qwalshina's blood offerings represent her people's attempt to adapt to their new environment through the maintenance of rituals, a form of identification denied to the new refugees. The fact that the new refugees are being forced to adapt without maintaining cultural connections represents the eventual attempts of most colonizers to assimilate Indigenous and diasporic groups into the dominant culture. Amberstone's choice to link the new human refugees' survival to their ability to adapt to an Indigenous/alien culture speaks to Eurowestern colonizers' inability to accept non-Western cultures as valid. "Refugees" further critiques this colonizing practice by suggesting at the end of the story that adaptation to a foreign environment comes at great cost and may even be impossible. Such a view contradicts popular stereotypes of Indigenous peoples as "naturally" attuned to their environments,[17] as well as Eurowestern narratives about civilized humans being able to "tame" nature.[18] The fact that Qwalshina and her community,

---

17. This Indigenous stereotype is found in Eurowestern writings from the colonial times to the present day. Clare Bradford gives a detailed accounting of Eurowestern myths about Indigenous peoples being attuned to nature in chapter 3 of *Unsettling Narratives: Postcolonial Readings of Children's Literature* (2007).

18. M. Ruth Noriega Sánchez argues in *Challenging Realities: Magic Realism in Contemporary American Women's Fiction* (2011) that magical realism is well equipped to expose

former Indigenous Earth peoples, continue to try to adapt to their new planet despite the seemingly hopeless situation highlights the ability of Indigenous groups to adapt to different locations, an ability learned as a result of their experiences with colonization. Amberstone's description showcases the resilience of Indigenous groups while also destabilizing the stereotype that all Indigenous peoples are perfectly attuned to their environment.

In *Lunar Braceros*, the imported human population is also physically unable to assimilate to the moon's harsh conditions. The braceros, who work in manual labor and technology positions, must endure extreme temperatures and long workdays. "Braceros" is a title stemming from the informally named bracero program of Mexican migrant workers in the US during and after World War II,[19] positions that were mostly manual labor on farms and that were also highly exploitative. *Lunar Braceros* is set in a dystopic future where corporations control most of the world's resources. People who cannot find work are forced to live on reservations and work for free, creating a cycle of poverty that is impossible to escape. The braceros consist of Black, Latinx, and white disadvantaged people looking to avoid the reservations or jail; instead, they choose to become contract workers for corporations that are dumping nuclear waste on the moon or mining for moon minerals. In return, the corporations promise to deposit salaries that the braceros can access when they return to Earth, which would allow the lunar braceros to free themselves from the reservations. Several braceros describe the work as

---

the myth of the American Western frontier, which she describes as "the confrontation between European civilisation and 'others,' exoticised or objectified as savages, and which is symbolised by that imaginary line that allows a superior civilisation to tame nature and the wilderness" (140).

19. The reference to braceros specifically refers to the working conditions of contracted (and, later, illegal) Mexican workers between 1942 and 1964. The braceros program began with a series of agreements between the US and Mexico that allowed workers to be contracted out and hired by US planters in need of manual labor during WWII. Mexican workers had come across the border to help US farmers during WWI, and the Mexican workers brought to the US during WWII were depicted as helping the war effort through their support of US agriculture. During the early braceros programs, the braceros made up only 5 to 10 percent of agricultural labor, much less than contemporary undocumented workers in the US today. Eventually, the braceros program lost traction when former braceros, who knew how to find work in the US, came across unofficially (encouraged by US farmers, who wanted to hire them without the hassle of federal paperwork). Deteriorating economic conditions in Mexico encouraged more workers to migrate, despite strengthened border patrols and regulations in the US and Mexico. In 1954 alone, one million undocumented workers crossed into the US, leading to US roundups. For more information about the Mexican braceros of the twentieth century, see Deborah Coen's *Braceros: Migrant Citizens and Transnational Subjects in the Postwar United States and Mexico* (2013).

dangerous and highly physical. The moon's fourteen-hour days and harsh weather conditions mean that the braceros must work when the conditions allow and live in underground bunkers for long periods of time (Sánchez and Pita 43). The braceros are also monitored by audio and video equipment at all times, making the moon environment akin to the reservations most of them were trying to avoid. Sánchez and Pita link the situation of the moon braceros to the condition of twentieth-century migrant workers in order to demonstrate how physically and psychologically scarring it can be to come into a harsh, restrictive environment not by choice, but by economic need. Sánchez and Pita's decision to use the word "braceros" to describe the contracted moon workers links the situation of the lunar braceros to a history of exploited US labor and, as described by Lysa Rivera, "US consumerism's demand for invisible—and therefore easily disposable—forms of intense physical labor" (426). Sánchez and Pita utilize the trope of space travel to combat the idea, reinforced in much science fiction literature, that future human societies will find ways to overcome issues of racism.

Because the corporation that employs the braceros views them as disposable, the administrators are ordered to kill the braceros at the end of their contract to bypass labor costs. The inability of the corporation, and through them the administrators, to see the braceros as human results in a conflict that turns the moon into a prison and forces the braceros to fight for their right to live. Sánchez and Pita challenge stereotypes of braceros as a nonskilled labor force through the depiction of the main character, Lydia, who is highly skilled with computers. Yet access to and mastery of technology does not protect the braceros; as Chabram-Dernersesian notes, "Being part of a specialized technological migrant workforce does not guarantee social mobility, adequate remunerations for one's painstaking labor, or economic well-being" (193). In fact, Lysa Rivera describes the impact of technologies on the Mexican and Chicanx workforce as creating cyborg laborers, people forced to become low-paid, menial workers who also engage with technologies designed to dehumanize the workforce, such as factory machinery.[20] After Lydia and Frank discover the bodies of the former bracero team,

---

20. The figure of the cyborg is most often associated with Donna Haraway's groundbreaking social-feminist work "A Cyborg Manifesto" (1984), which defines the cyborg as a synthesized, hybrid creature with the ability to disrupt distinctions between human and animal, man and machine, and the physical and nonphysical. However, Rivera is using Lavín's definition of the cyborg figure as colonized subject from his article titled "Reaching the Shore" (1994) as the basis of her reading of Mexican and Chicanx laborers. She explains the distinction between the two definitions in her article: "Lavín recasts the futuristic cyborg as a colonized subject, one whose labor is extracted by US capitalism at the expense of Fragoso's very humanity. Lavín's colonized cyborg clearly departs

believed to be back on Earth, stuffed into waste containers on the moon, they both see a mirage of Frank's dead brother while driving on the moon's surface. When Lydia discovers that the mirage is being transmitted by the com system, or communication implants, she realizes that the technology the braceros are implanted with can also be used to manipulate their minds and bodies. She tells Frank, "Someone's messing with our minds" (Sánchez 67), indicating that their bosses are using the implant technology as a form of psychological control or manipulation. The technologies of space travel and implant technology each serve to keep the braceros in a colonized position. This depiction of technology as restrictive rather than liberating, a depiction described by Rivera as "the ways in which mass-media technologies simultaneously criminalize and police brown bodies," is reflected in the works of many authors of color, such as the performance pieces and writings of Guillermo Gómez-Peña and the film *Sleepdealer* (2008) directed by Alex Rivera.

The braceros eventually discover that implant technology is also being used to maintain social order on the moon. After they overpower the supervisor who has been monitoring them, he suffers from a seizure caused by an implant in his head. The supervisor admits that he is being coerced into helping the corporation monitor and dispose of the braceros, but he also notes that he has come to enjoy his small amount of control, even though he will never be allowed to leave the moon. The social order of the moon mirrors that of a territory or colony, with the social order of an absent corporation being enforced by lower-level bureaucrats who are themselves coerced into compliance. Colonial states were often defined by contradiction; for a colony to be economically successful, a relatively peaceful social order needed to be maintained. However, this social order was often enforced using violence and coercion because in order to be profitable, the colony also needed a cheap labor source (Frederiksen 1274). The corporation running the moon operation in *Lunar Braceros* retains a peaceful order through promises of wages, but when the illusion of peace is broken, they resort to violence to control their employees. Sánchez and Pita take the colonial economic system to an extreme by creating literal "disposable" labor: Once the moon workers have completed their contract, the organization kills them to avoid having to pay wages. Like "Refugees," *Lunar Braceros* uses a colo-

---

from Donna Haraway's more utopian vision of the cyborg as that which can subvert the 'informatics of domination,' a new form of power that I read as decentralized transnational capitalism that has replaced 'the comfortable old hierarchical dominations' under colonialism; ("Cyborg Manifesto" 161; Rivera 421).

nial social order to demonstrate the negative effects on all humanity when humans recreate unequal social relations in new environments.

The braceros in *Lunar Braceros* eventually manage to commandeer a company ship and fly it back to Earth. The corporation then attempts to assassinate the braceros to keep them from revealing the truth about moon labor, so the braceros decide to seek refuge in a Latin American Indigenous community named Chinganaza. The Chinganazan people have isolated themselves to avoid the influences of the New Imperial Order (NIO) and the Cali-Texas state. Lydia explains that Chinganaza's resistance to being incorporated into the political and economic monopolies that control the novel's future world is what has allowed the Indigenous community to thrive:

> It was the growth of the Indigenous movement throughout the 21st century that allowed the Amazonian populations to limit the incursions planned by transnational mining, oil, and natural gas enterprises that kept them from destroying all the biodiversity of the area and from displacing thousands of Indigenous villagers. This movement is what enabled the general autonomy of Chinganaza and its maintaining certain traditions and the Chinganaza commons, while other Indigenous cantones took the road of so-called modernization. Economic equity has been achieved within this commons although not yet in other Amazonian sites. Nevertheless, these political changes have—believe it or not—enabled Chinganaza to survive. (21)

Unlike the Indigenous peoples in "Refugees" or the braceros, the people of Chinganaza have managed to maintain their land rights and autonomy, which is why they are able to act as a site of refuge for the braceros. Through isolation, the maintenance of cultural traditions, and resistance to "so-called modernization," the Chinganazans are able to create a community separate from the new world order. "Refugees" and *Lunar Braceros* both critique the costs of cultural assimilation for Indigenous and diasporic peoples and the consequences of these cultures' refusing to adapt. The Chinganazans are forced to isolate themselves and limit their trade to avoid being colonized by the corporations. If the corporations and governments acting as a colonizing force in the novel were to adjust their assumptions about Indigenous communities and agree to treat these communities as equals, the people of Chinganaza might have chosen to adapt their Indigenous culture to the new state, or at least to participate in trade relations. The conflict between the people of Chinganaza and governmental/corporate interests brings to mind the history of land conflicts and assumptions of white cultural superiority that continue to affect relations between Indigenous and Eurowestern peoples in countries with histories of colonization.[21]

Amberstone and Sánchez and Pita each imagine space travel and life off-world as harsh, hostile environments that have negative physical and psychological effects on humans. The humans' struggle in these environments mimics the experiences of Indigenous and diasporic groups trying to adapt, but not assimilate, to a new country or region. Both texts also include social hierarchies that keep the relocated humans from adapting to their new environments. Amberstone and Sánchez and Pita suggest that when groups bring unequal social relationships of colonizer/colonized into a new environment, whether it be another country or another planet, there is little chance for successful adaptation to new environments.

Decentering the Human

The authors discussed in this chapter who utilize alien characters all choose to create alien races that avoid the science fiction trope of human-based aliens[22] to address issues of xenophobia and alienation. Octavia Butler and Ted Chiang examine the idea of difference even more intensely by creating alien races with alternate social values that conflict with Eurowestern cultural views of embodiment and communication. In *Dawn* and "Story of Your life," humans are forced to compromise their core beliefs or values and adapt to an alien group's non-Western values to survive. In *Dawn*, Butler challenges the idea of an essential human body by depicting humans who are forced to share and combine their genetic material with an alien species. In "Story of Your Life," Chiang creates a technologically advanced

---

21. One recent example of Eurowestern/Indigenous tension in the US is the recent demand by South Dakota Governor Kristi Noem that the Cheyenne River Sioux and Oglala Sioux tribes remove highway checkpoints designed to limit travel to their reservations during the COVID-19 crisis. For more information, see "South Dakota Governor Demands Tribe Leaders Remove Checkpoints Set Up to Prevent the Spread of COVID-19" (2020): https://time.com/5834749/south-dakota-governor-native-american-tribes-coronavirus/.

22. Brooks Landon discusses the tendency of early science fiction authors to pattern alien races after cultures of color considered "primitive" in "Dime Novels and the Cultural Work of Early SF" (2009). Much of the visual side of this trope also comes from limitations in CGI technologies for early science fiction films and TV shows. Early science fiction films and shows like *Star Wars* and *Star Trek* featured humanlike aliens with slight differences in skin color and additions of body parts. Even contemporary versions of these works as well as newer science fiction films like *Guardians of the Galaxy* (2014) include alien races that are humanlike beings, often actors of color with painted skin.

alien species who use a nonlinear language and perception of time/history that humans must learn in order to communicate. In both texts, humans are forced to alter their views about the centrality and individuality of humanity to survive an alien encounter.

It is no accident that Butler and Chiang each choose a tentacled alien description. Ryan Britt explains the logic behind the often-employed science fiction trope of the tentacled space alien:

> The presentation of more "realistic" aliens with tentacles in science fiction is probably based on this line of thinking: Life as we know it would have evolved in an ocean. Things that live in the ocean have tentacles and seem "alien" to humans.

The idea that tentacled aliens have become more "realistic" to science fiction creators than human-based aliens demonstrates a human anxiety about the idea of encountering truly "alien" species. Cephalopods, which include the octopus, squid, cuttlefish, and nautilus species, are some of the most intelligent and long-lived species on the planet, which is perhaps another reason science fiction creators would choose to base alien races on these species. Jules Verne captivated readers with his fictional account of a tentacled sea creature and fantastic underwater vessel, the *Nautilus*, in *Twenty Thousand Leagues under the Sea* (1870). Since then, tentacled aliens have appeared in novels such as H. G. Wells's *War of the Worlds* (1898) and H. P. Lovecraft's Cthulhu novels (1928–37)[23] and in films like *Alien* (1979), *Independence Day* (1996), and *Arrival* (2016), a film based on "Story of Your Life." One thread that links these examples is the amazement and horror that the tentacled aliens evoke from the human characters. Tentacled aliens, therefore, have become a symbol of the monstrous, othered alien whose strangeness evokes fear.[24]

In *Dawn* and throughout the Xenogenesis series, the Oankali's insistence that humans allow the alien species to manipulate their DNA and participate in the human reproductive process challenges the idea that an essen-

---

23. It is important to note that many members of the science fiction and fantasy communities are speaking out about Lovecraft's racism and anti-Semitism. See author Nnedi Okorafor's reaction to winning the World Fantasy Award, which at the time featured a bust of Lovecraft: https://nnedi.blogspot.com/2011/12/lovecrafts-racism-world-fantasy-award.html.

24. There is a selection of science fiction that also depicts consensual or forced relations with tentacled creatures, commonly referred to as "tentacle-porn." For academic research on this topic, see the works of Danielle Talerico, Katherine Harmon Courage, Susanna Paasonen, and Dagmar Van Engen.

tialized human body is what defines humanity.[25] When Jdahya explains to Lilith that within one generation, the Oankali will manipulate human DNA to the point where the human body will cease to be the biological organism she knows, she immediately has a negative reaction to the news:

> "I think I wish your people had left me on Earth," she whispered. "If this is what they found me for, I wish they'd left me. Medusa children. Snakes for hair. Nests of night crawlers for eyes and ears." (43)

Lilith's reaction stems from her inability to accept the idea of the human body as a biological organism separate from an essentialized "self"; for her, combining human and Oankali DNA would mean the extinction of the human race. Her fear of the Oankali's otherness, represented by her references to the Greek monster Medusa[26] and her description of the monstrous future children she will be forced to have, represent the xenophobic views of colonizing cultures, who often discuss race in terms of pureness and who see othered races as a contamination of the colonizing culture. Butler loves contradiction; having her Black female protagonist express a fear of otherness through an alien "attack" on the essentialized human body conflates race and humanity, a move that highlights the need for all peoples to accept racial and cultural difference.

Butler also problematizes the Oankali's offer of "trade" by putting humanity in a situation where they are forced by the Oankali to combine their genetic material. Because the Oankali must incorporate genetic material to survive, they are not willing to give humanity a choice about whether they wish to share their genetic material. The Oankali could take human genetic material without forcing the humans to change their genetic makeup, but Jdahya explains to Lilith that the Oankali believe humans are genetically flawed and must be modified to save them from destroying Earth again. If what Jdahya says is true, then modifying the human genome would actually save humanity. Furthermore, if humanity believes in an inherent "self" separate from the physical body, then modifying the human genome should not result in human extinction; the change could be

---

25. See my discussion of Sherryl Vint's connection between the physical body and identity in *Bodies of Tomorrow* in the introduction. For additional perspectives on the Xenogenesis trilogy and genetic essentialism, see the works of Nancy Jesser, Cathy Peppers, and J. Adam Johns.

26. Original Greek myths about Medusa did not always depict her as monstrous. She was also represented as a beautiful woman who was the victim of rape and endowed by Athena with the power to enact revenge on men (Hastings).

viewed as a new stage of evolution.[27] The fact that the Oankali are forcing the humans to change their view of humanity is a form of colonization, but it could also be viewed as Butler's commentary on the need for humanity to embrace people who don't fit societal "norms," or future technological advances that could enhance the human body, such as genetic modification or artificial organs. Butler employs a technologically superior alien race to challenge essentialized views of the human body that are as damaging to humans today who do not fit into Eurowestern society's narrow views of personhood[28] as the Oankali's forced trade is to Lilith and the other human survivors in the series.

Chiang's "Story of Your Life" examines alternate forms of communication by introducing an alien species that one of the characters names "heptapods," a combination of the Greek prefix "hepta," or seven, and scientific class cephalopoda. The heptapods land ships around the globe, but because humans cannot communicate with the aliens, they do not know the heptapods' intentions. Like the Oankali, the heptapods look nothing like humans: They are described as "radially symmetric" with seven limbs, "lidless eyes," and no distinct joints (96–97). Two of the humans tasked with attempting to communicate with the heptapods, linguist Louise Banks and physicist Garry Donnelly, attempt to relieve their anxiety about meeting the aliens by referring to the tent that houses the alien communication device as the entrance to a circus freak show. Louise also states that she "jumps" when the aliens enter the tent for the first time (96). Although both scientists are excited about the idea of learning to communicate with another species, it is clear that they both also view the heptapods as utterly alien. Louise names the two heptapods she interacts with "Flapper" and "Raspberry," names more likely to be used for pets than for human counterparts. While Louise eventually learns from the heptapods how to move outside human systems of linear thinking, her initial interactions with the alien species treat them as simplistic, potentially threatening beings despite their obviously advanced technologies.

Chiang uses multiple references in "Story" to examine the connection between a culture's language and its degree of civilization. Louise recalls an

---

27. See Damien Broderick's *The Spike: How Our Lives Are Being Transformed by Rapidly Advancing Technologies* (2002).

28. Sherryl Vint also suggests in *Bodies of Tomorrow* (2007) that Western culture's attachment to an idea of the self as disembodied has had and is currently having negative effect on relationships between humans and between humans and the environment (6–7). She also notes that other critics who have commented on the relationship between the physical body and identity formation include Bruno Latour, Donna J. Haraway, and Mark Dery, among others.

anecdote about Captain Cook mistaking the word "kangaroo" for the animal when the word really means "What did you say?" (99). Louise reveals later in the scene that the anecdote is actually historically inaccurate. This reference to a historical tale and its inaccuracies serves as a metaphor for "civilized" cultures' tendency to make assumptions about "primitive" races and the fact that the histories of these encounters are often convoluted. Later in the story, Louise states that the heptapods' writing "was reminiscent of primitive sign systems," and she is confused because she believes that the alien's advanced technology could not be possible if they used a rudimentary language to express themselves (106). Eventually, she learns that the heptapods are using a nonlinear, visual syntax. This language system is the polar opposite of English, which the linguist expresses by stating, "[The heptapod language] didn't follow the pattern of human languages, as expected, but it was comprehensible so far: free word order . . . in defiance of a human language 'universal'" (113). Chiang's examples ask readers to remember that a failure to understand the context of another culture's language can result in misunderstandings that range from humorous to disastrous. Because humanity has accepted the notion of a universal standard of language, the narrator has a hard time imagining that alternate forms of language could be equally sophisticated.

As her language skills become more advanced, Louise finds her thoughts mimicking the heptapod's language system:

> I found myself in a meditative state, contemplating the way in which premises and conclusions were interchangeable. There was no direction inherent in the way propositions were connected, no "train of thought" moving along a particular route; all the components in an act of reasoning were equally powerful, all having identical precedence. (127)

Chiang employs the heptapods' nonlinear language, which treats all parts of language equally, as a metaphor for cross-cultural communications. The military general in the story is constantly questioning how much information the narrator is giving the heptapods because he is concerned that they have come to invade Earth. Chiang reverses the alien invader trope to question if it is possible for a technologically advanced species to visit a planet and not invade. The heptapods do not view themselves as superior to humans. They have come to trade, but unlike the Oankali, they do not force humanity to give more than they choose. Instead, they learn human languages and exchange gifts of information. Once they have completed their exchange, they leave. The heptapods represent an ideal cultural exchange, where neither species plays the role of colonized or colonizer, one that Chiang also links to the mathematical concept of the "non-zero-sum game."²⁹ One species' or culture's gain does not necessarily mean the other's loss; in "Story," this concept equates to an ideal cross-cultural exchange.

As Louise learns the heptapods' language, she begins to understand that humanity and heptapods have chosen two radically different ways of perceiving time, which has led to two vastly different ways of perceiving history and free will. Humanity views time as linear and sequential; the actions of the past lead to the reactions of the present in a cause/effect relationship. The future is, therefore, unknowable because free will means that any number of paths can occur based on humanities' decisions. Heptapods, however, view time as simultaneous and, as a result, "experience all events at once," which allows them to perceive an underlying purpose to every choice they make (134). Louise explains, "What distinguishes the heptapods' mode of awareness is not just that their actions coincide with history's events; it is also that their motives coincide with history's purposes. They act to create the future, to enact chronology" (136). Heptapods have knowledge of what will happen in the future, a knowledge that Louise inherits from learning their language, yet this knowledge does not make them wish for a different outcome. The future is simply one direction in the multidirectional timeline of all events. This philosophy is why Louise is able to accept her daughter's birth and death as equally valid occurrences. Knowing that her daughter will die at twenty-five does not make Louise want to try to change the future, because her simultaneous mode of awareness allows her to understand that these two events are connected to a larger purpose.

The heptapod vision of time and history is reminiscent of many Indigenous cultures' views of time as ongoing and cyclical. Waktole Tiki et al. explain the connection between the Borana African culture's oral timeline and perceptions of time and history:

> The Borana *gada* timeline is based on the systems of social organization and transfer of power between the five patri-classes called gogessa (also called luba), into which the society is divided. Power is transferred from one gogessa to another in regular sequence after fixed terms of eight years ... so that each gogessa returns to power every 40 years. ... According to

---

29. A non-zero-sum game in game theory is defined as a "situation where one decision maker's gain (or loss) does not necessarily result in the other decision makers' loss (or gain). In other words, where the winnings and losses of all players do not add up to zero and everyone can gain: a win-win game" ("Non Zero Sum Game).

> Legesse,[30] *gada* is a socio-political concept that 'incorporates all history and the total cognitive framework in which historical processes unfold.' This suggests that the *gada* system serves as a societal memory of the past and that it 'predicts' the future. (36)

By understanding time and history as a series of ongoing, cyclical events and by relegating the memory of historical time periods to specific peoples and groups, the Borana have created a detailed oral history whose knowledge they can draw on to predict upcoming "major environmental, social, political and economic disturbances" (Tiki et al. 36). Chiang utilizes a similar cyclical, non-linear view of time and history to challenge Eurowestern narratives of forward "progress."

Rather than referencing a specific Indigenous belief system, Chiang uses the notion of teleology to complicate Eurowestern science and its dismissal of purpose, a dismissal that often distinguishes Eurowestern science from non-Eurowestern cultural knowledge. The main principle that Chiang builds his story on is the idea that according to Fermant's principle, a traveling light wave needs foreknowledge of its end-point to arrive in the least amount of time. When Louise tells Gary that this theory does not "sound like a law of physics," Gary explains that Fermat's principle has been a debated philosophical question in Physics for centuries (123–124) because of its teleological implications. The philosophy of whether scientific laws are present for a specific purpose places teleology and Eurowestern science at odds; however, like the heptapod view of science, Indigenous scientific literacies move away from a causal view of science and "reflect *relational* reasoning about perspectival relations among living things and their environments" (ojalehto 3). The heptapod view of science depicts time and history as ongoing processes, an idea which aligns with many Indigenous knowledge systems.[31]

Indigenous authors frequently draw on Indigenous views of time to create "Native slipstream" literature, a concept defined by Dillon as texts which "[view] time as pasts, presents, and futures that flow together like currents in a navigable stream" to "[replicate] nonlinear thinking about space-time" ("Imagining" 3). While Native slipstream texts like Gerald Vizenor's "Custer on the Slipstream" utilize time distortion and alternate realities to challenge Eurowestern historical accounts, Chiang employs a non-chronological story line and non-linear view of time to examine the ways that Eurowestern

---

30. Tiki, et al., are referencing A. Legesse's *Gada: Three Approaches to the Study of African Society* (1973). They do not include a page number for this quote in their report.

31. Heather Goodall argues that Traditional Environmental Knowledge (TEK), in particular, should be viewed as "a process rather than an archive" (355).

and non-Eurowestern cultures interact. "Story of Your Life" ends with the heptapods presenting gifts of knowledge to humanity and leaving without exploiting the human population; one could argue that Chiang is utilizing science fiction tropes to present an ideal example of cultural exchange, yet this ideal also serves to critique the history of Eurowestern expansion and colonization, which appear ignorant and violent by comparison.

Is Decolonization Possible?

Addressing the consequences of colonization can be difficult because of the long-lasting psychological effects on the colonized culture. Aimé Césaire explains that "it must be clearly understood that the famous inferiority complex in the colonized, which some take pleasure in pointing out, does not come about by chance. It is a result sought by the colonizer" (140). In order to rebuild a colonized culture, there must first be an acknowledgement of the political, economic, cultural, and social issues created by colonization. Grace L. Dillon notes that Indigenous futurisms, many of which involve post-colonial perspectives, are attempting to examine the effects of colonization on both a personal and communal level:

> It might go without saying that all forms of Indigenous futurisms are narratives of *biskaabiiyang,* an Anishinaabemowin word connoting the process of 'returning to ourselves,' which involves discovering how personally one is affected by colonization, discarding the emotional and psychological baggage carried from its impact, and recovering ancestral traditions in order to adapt in our post-Native Apocalypse world. This process is often called 'decolonization,' and as Linda Tuhiwai Smith (Maori) explains, it requires *changing* rather than *imitating* Eurowestern concepts. ("Imagining" 10, emphasis in original)

The "post-Native Apocalypse world" that Dillon describes demonstrates the severe consequences of colonization on communities of color. Often, cultural practices and identities lost through the process of colonization cannot be recovered. While it is unclear if colonized groups will be able to rebuild or recover lost heritage, it is perfectly clear that without the acknowledgement from the colonizers of the harm they have caused and continue to cause, such a rebuilding or recovery becomes much more difficult. Dillon's stress on the need for Indigenous communities to advocate for change in Eurowestern colonial views and practices is directly addressed in the themes of adaptation discussed in the texts above. Each author discussed in this chapter imagines what a decolonized society could look like if members are willing to move beyond the effects of colonization and adapt to the new needs of their communities. The history of exploitation of Indigenous and diasporic peoples, especially peoples of color, at the hands of European colonizers cannot be erased; however, the authors in this chapter work to find ways to both express their experiences and move towards new representations of cultural interaction.

It may seem obvious that colonized peoples need to address issues of internalized racism and accept that former iterations of their cultures may be lost. However, these accomplishments take cross-cultural dialogues between colonized and colonizer, and between different generations and cultural groups within colonized cultures. Such conversations can be difficult, especially when complicated by a legacy of mistreatment and distrust. Podruczna argues that the nuances of colonization can also lead to conflicts within diasporic communities about how to address the effects of colonization: "It would seem, then, that it is possible to observe in the diasporic communities a certain longing for the past and the lost home, but also a realization of the fact that it is impossible to go back and that this imagined home of their ancestors does not exist anymore, changed forever by the colonial discourse" (269). This sentiment also applies to Indigenous cultures. Author Deborah A. Miranda (Esselen and Chumash) notes the discrepancy between the need for Indigenous cultures to adapt to many new systems, and the consequences for those Indigenous peoples who successfully adapt in her memoir *Bad Indians* (2013): "Those who will not change do not survive; but who are we, when we have survived?" (Location 104). Miranda's statement of confusion is shared by many colonized peoples, and I would argue that the works discussed in this chapter are each authors' answer to this difficult question of cultural identity and even, for those who have been dehumanized by the practices of colonization, human identity. Gina Ruiz uses the alien invasion trope to comment on the dehumanization and criminalization of contemporary Cholo culture. Amberstone and Butler each use the relations between humanity and a colonizing alien race to comment on the tensions colonized cultures faced when forced to adapt to a colonizing culture. Chiang uses themes of translation and non-Eurowestern scientific thought to comment on the difficulty of forging relations when two cultures do not have the same priorities or values. This chapter ultimately demonstrates that science fiction is a vehicle of change, one that can help authors create worlds that teach lessons about the past and present, while also imagining a future where adaptation can exist alongside cultural rebuilding.

CHAPTER 2

Race, Genetics, and Science Fiction

George Schuyler's 1931 satire *Black No More: Being an Account of the Strange and Wonderful Working of Science in the Land of the Free, A.D. 1933–1940* imagines a world where a Black man, with the help of a scientific procedure, becomes white. The rest of Schuyler's work discusses the consequences of the change in skin color on the "passing" Black man and the African American community in general.[1] Schuyler's work is an important reminder of the legacy of scientific racism used to justify the institution of slavery in many Eurowestern countries.[2] The fact that early scientific theories of evolution were used to mark peoples of color as inferior creates a link between Eurowestern science and social theories of race that exists to this day. Matthew Desmond and Mustafa Emirbayer explain in "What Is Racial Domination?"

---

1. Many "passing" novels in the nineteenth century addressed the growing social anxiety that light-skinned Black peoples would pretend to be white. This anxiety led to laws such as the "one-drop" rule, which proclaimed that people with even one "drop" of Black blood would be considered Black. For more information on the history of racial passing, see Allyson Hobb's *A Chosen Exile: A History of Racial Passing* (2014).

2. The argument that humans of different races have separate origins (polygenism) and thus different levels of intelligence has been used since the seventeenth century to justify slavery practices (Marks 448). For a comprehensive history of scientific racism and its impacts, see Jonathan Marks's "Scientific Racism" section of the *Encyclopedia of Race and Racism* (2013).

that the naturalization of race, specifically attributing negative behavioral characteristics to peoples of color, forms the foundation of institutional racism in many Eurowestern nations (339–45). *Black No More* is an example of an early science fiction text which utilizes an imagined scientific experiment to disrupt the notion of race as inherent and natural. The science fiction authors discussed in this chapter continue Schuyler's dialogue about racial and ethnic identification by questioning how the manipulation of genes could affect the ways in which societies identify and label race and ethnicity.

As a genre with the ability to imagine new technologies or to extrapolate the direction of scientific discoveries based on current scientific achievements, science fiction authors have the unique ability to examine the connection between skin color, racial and ethnic identification, and cultural influence. Many of the authors discussed in this chapter utilize the science fiction genre to question how much of a person's identity is dependent on the color of their skin or defining features through the depiction of genetically engineered characters. This use of genetic engineering destabilizes essentialized notions of humanity; however, such destabilization also has the potential to undermine views of race, ethnicity, and cultural belonging. Science fiction authors of color are therefore often working to balance challenges to scientific racism with stories that demonstrate the value of non-white, non-Eurowestern races and cultures. By breaking down the human body into its DNA sequences or using genetic modification to create hybrid human-animal or human-alien characters, the science fiction authors discussed in this chapter test the limits of humanity while also commenting on the alienation of peoples of color in Eurowestern-dominated environments.

This chapter centers on three specific tropes of genetics utilized in the texts discussed: genetic experimentation, genetic mutation, and genetic engineering. Each of these subcategories of the science of genetics has historical significance for peoples of color living in Eurowestern countries. I begin my discussion with Nnedi Okoroafor's *The Book of Phoenix* (2015) as an example of genetic experimentation that speaks to the history of medical experimentation on the bodies of peoples of color in Eurowestern countries. Okorafor's genetically created main character has the phoenix-like ability to return from death, which evokes the ongoing cycle of violence through slavery and colonization that Eurowesten countries often dismiss. I then move to a discussion of N. K. Jemisin's Broken Earth series (2015–17), a series that draws on the history of genetic mutation and race in science fiction to recognize the dehumanization of peoples marked as "uncivilized" or "other." I end the chapter with a discussion of Larissa Lai's *Salt Fish Girl* (2002) and Octavia E. Butler's *Fledgling* (2005) as examples of genetic engineering. These texts demonstrate how views of race and genetics have the ability to harm peoples of color through rhetorics of racial essentialism while also offering Butler and Lai an opportunity to dismantle the idea of naturalized racial difference.

Do Genetic Differences Matter?

Advances in genetics and genetic modification are reviving arguments about whether genetic differences between humans are significant. Reactions to Darwin's *On the Origin of Species* (1859) and *The Descent of Man* (1871) led scientists throughout the nineteenth and early twentieth centuries to create the Social Darwinist concepts of eugenics and scientific racism.[3] The newly discovered science of genetics helped the movement gain momentum as scientists and politicians attempted to justify anti-immigration laws and efforts to control population growth, including forced sterilization (Kevles 45–46).[4] One British geneticist even suggested growing fetuses created from the gamines of "superior" men and women in glass jars (46). The tools available to eugenicists at the time did not allow for such practices (though the suggestion sparked a number of science fiction writers' imaginations),[5] but contemporary medical practices such as in-vitro fertilization and advances in genetic engineering are leading to more arguments about the ethics of using genetics to create "normal" humans.[6] The contemporary view in sci-

---

3. In "Social Darwinism: From Reality to Myth and from Myth to Reality" (2011), Daniel Becquemont explains that nineteenth-century scientists created a variety of arguments about how Darwin's theory of evolution impacted theories of human culture. A few of the theories argued that theories of evolution demonstrated the necessity of socialism, while others argued that Darwin's theory applied to primitive man, but that the creation of civilizations negated the notion that humans must compete for survival (13). While theories of eugenics are not the only Social Darwinist theories, they are the theories that most impact the subject of this chapter.

4. "The History of Eugenics" by Daniel J. Kevles chronicles the history of eugenics movements, which included contests to identify families with strong "hereditary merit" and the encouragement of women from upper-class families to give birth to more children (45–46).

5. Examples of genetic engineering in science fiction from the period include Olaf Stapledon's *Last and First Men* (1930) and Aldous Huxley's *Brave New World* (1932).

6. In fact, genetic modification of embryos has recently experienced a breakthrough. In July 2017, researchers at the Oregon Health and Science University, aided by researchers in California, China, and South Korea, reported a successful editing of genes in embryos, an editing that repaired a mutation that causes a common heart condition. If this new technology can successfully edit cell mutations, it has the potential to prevent more than 10,000 inherited conditions (Belluck). However, scientists also acknowledge

entific communities for the last few decades has stressed that people of different races do not demonstrate any major genetic differences;[7] however, the concept of genetic differences between races and ideals of genetic essentialism have persisted and continue to affect both the ways that people identify with a specific race or ethnicity and the amount of racism they experience. Today, genetic mapping efforts such as the Human Genome Project and personal genetic testing, which stress genetic differences between humans, are heavily impacting the way society views racial difference.

In "Genetic Essentialism: On the Deceptive Determinism of DNA," Ilan Dar-Nimrod and Steven J. Heine explain that media representations of the connection between genetics and human difference largely impact public opinions about both genetics and specific ethnic groups:

> We propose that people's understanding of genetics with relation to life outcomes is shaped by their psychological essentialist biases—a process termed *genetic essentialism*—and this leads to particular consequences when people consider the relations between genes and human outcomes. At the same time, we argue that this genetic essentialist tendency is, in turn, reinforced by the representations of genes in public discourses. (800)

Dar-Nimrod and Heine's arguments demonstrate the dangers of humans applying essentialist terminology to the science of genetics. The implication that *all* humans should have a specific genetic makeup could lead to the belief that humans with genetic differences are somehow less than normal or are abnormal. Nicholas Wade's *A Troublesome Inheritance: Genes, Race, and Human History* (2014) is one example of how contemporary authors are using genetic advancements to revive claims that specific ethnic groups are more genetically predisposed to certain behaviors. Wade begins his work by noting that evolution is an ongoing process. He then divides humanity into three principal groups—Africans, Asians, and Caucasians—and argues that in addition to physical changes such as skin color, these groups also demonstrate distinct differences in brain function. He also argues that there is a biological component to race and cites recent gene mapping efforts to prove his point (4). He even goes so far as to argue that if one race is found to be genetically more intelligent, this fact would not impact views of the other

---

that this technology could be used to modify genes not related to life-threatening conditions, which raises questions about ethical use and access to this treatment.

7. Ilan Dar-Nimrod and Steven J. Heine note in "Genetic Essentialism: On the Deceptive Determinism of DNA" (2011) that the majority of the scientific community agree that there is no biological foundation for the idea of racial difference (804).

races (8). Wade's text is a good example of the ways that advances in genetic testing and engineering can be used to create arguments that reinforce essentialist views of race through the implication that slight differences in DNA have led to major differences in ethnic groups over time, a view that exaggerates current scientific findings to suit essentialist ideals.

One of the recent trends in accessible genetic testing, the personal DNA test, is a good example of the benefits and complications of genetics in relation to race and ethnicity. Although there are several genetic testing companies offering to provide personalized genetic heritage testing for a small fee, I will use one site, *AncestryDNA*, as an example of the ways genetic heritage testing is being marketed to the public. Using examples of three individual "success" stories, the site explains in a question tab titled "Why would I take the Ancestry DNA test?" how their service "combines advanced DNA science with the world's largest online family history resource to predict your genetic ethnicity." ("Top questions"). *AncestryDNA* and many similar sites use a narrative of connection to sell their products; peoples who provide DNA will be able to learn important facts about their genetic history and will have the ability to connect with lost family members. But because these companies are privatized, the exact science behind the DNA results is not available for peer review, which has led some geneticists to question the certainty of ancestry results, especially when linked to specific countries of origin (Kolata). *AncestryDNA* and other genetic testing sites personalize DNA by selling a narrative of using science to revise lost cultural connections or family histories.

Genetic testing sites stress that DNA results should be used in conjunction with family history research, but one of the stories posted on the *AncestryDNA* home page, from a man named Kyle, raises the question of how people will react to the results of their genetic heritage results. Kyle explains that he grew up identifying as German and participating in German cultural practices. However, when he discovers through the site that his ethnic heritage is actually Scottish, he decides to "[trade] in my lederhosen for a kilt" ("Kyle"). This testimonial seems to imply that discovering your genetic heritage negates the cultural connections made within ethnic communities; once a person is discovered to be genetically of a different ethnicity, they will simply replace one ethnic identity with another. The site also has a dedicated question responding to queries about Native American heritage. The site explains that specific tribal affiliations will not be included in test results and that *AncestryDNA* results "cannot be used as a substitute for legal documentation" ("Top question"). The implication of this question is that people may attempt to claim tribal affiliation using their genetic results. The website's statement raises questions about how genetic heritage testing could modify census data, which directly affects how much government aid is available to specific ethnic groups. For example, if a large number of Americans are found to have some percentage of Native American DNA (a good possibility considering the history of Native American tribes gifting Native American women to European men to act as cultural mediators),[8] these numbers could skew data on how many Native Americans attend college, which would affect the scholarship money available to Native Americans. If Rachel Dolezal, a woman outed as passing for Black despite having white parents, is found to have any percentage of African DNA in her genetic heritage, does this information negate the fact that she benefited from adopting an ethnic identification many activists argue that she had no claim to?[9] The implications of advancements in genetic modification and personalized genetic testing are numerous, and I argue that the works in this chapter show how science fiction authors are responding to and challenging assumptions about the connections between DNA and racial, ethnic, and cultural identifications.

Genetic Experimentation and *The Book of Phoenix*

In Harriet A. Washington's *Medical Apartheid: The Dark History of Medical Experimentation on Black Americans from Colonial Times to the Present,* she notes that the medical treatment of Black peoples in the US has always been intrinsically linked to the justification of and enhancement of slavery:

> Despite their claims of unique expertise, the shoddy research that southern physicians conducted into black health consisted of an untested nucleus of mythology about the biological nature of blacks. . . . There certainly was no provision for removing ethnocentric bias—this "science" was the *embodiment* of ethnocentric bias. This science also served a critical political purpose, for it provided a biological and ethical rationale for enslavement. (31)

This circular logic of white doctors ignoring facts in favor of medical conclusions that would paint Black peoples as lazy, inferior beings has

---

8. Rebecca K. Jager discusses this practice in detail in *Malinche, Pocahontas, and Sacagawea: Indian Women as Cultural Intermediaries and National Symbols* (2015).

9. For more information about Dolezal, see Kirk Johnson, Richard Pérez-Peña and John Eligon's "Rachel Dolezal, in Center of Storm, Is Defiant: 'I Identify as Black'" (2015), https://www.nytimes.com/2015/06/17/us/rachel-dolezal-nbc-today-show.html.

negatively influenced both white physicians' views of peoples of color in medical research and peoples of color's willingness to ask for medical assistance when needed. The addition of overlooked medical experimentation on peoples of color from James Marion Sim's gynecological experimentation on Black female slaves in the nineteenth century to the Tuskegee Syphilis Experiment on African American men from 1932 to 1972,[10] the forced sterilization of Puerto Rican women from 1930 to 1970,[11] experimentation on Canadian Indigenous children from 1942 to 1952,[12] and the use of Africa as a site for Eurowestern clinical drug trials in the 1990s[13] demonstrates centuries of violence and mistreatment against peoples of color in the US and other Eurowestern countries, all backed by views of scientific racism supported by scientific experimentation.

Okorafor utilizes the science fiction trope of genetic experimentation in *The Book of Phoenix* as a metaphor for the history of Eurowestern experimentation on peoples of color. The main character, a genetically engineered being named Phoenix, is one of several "speciMens" or peoples subject to "advanced and aggressive genetic manipulation or cloning" (8). Phoenix explains in chapter 1 that speciMens are "invented, altered, or both" and describes herself and the other genetically manipulated peoples as "abominations" (8). Okorafor's choice to use the words "advanced" and "aggressive" in the same sentence immediately align the scientists of LifeGen Technologies, also called the "Big Eye" for their surveillance abilities, with colonial aggression and violence. Phoenix's description of herself and the other speciMens as "abominations" shows her indoctrination into Eurowestern racial hierarchy, where peoples of color are abducted and experimented on by LifeGen without fear of recourse because these peoples are viewed as disposable. As Phoenix begins to reveal the story of her creation and imprisonment in Tower 7, the LifeGen facility in charge of genetic experimentation, it is clear that Phoenix is a modern-day slave. She describes herself as an accelerated organism who "was like a plant they grew for harvesting" (9). Again, Okorafor's terminology links the science of genetically

---

10. For more information on the Tuskegee experiment, see Susan Reverby's *Examining Tuskegee: The Infamous Syphilis Study and Its Legacy* (2009).

11. See Laura Briggs's "Discourses of 'Forced Sterilization' in Puerto Rico: The Problem With the Speaking Subaltern" (1998).

12. See Noni E. MacDonald et al.'s "Canada's Shameful History of Nutrition Research on Residential School Children: The Need for Strong Medical Ethics in Aboriginal Health Research" (2014), https://www.ncbi.nlm.nih.gov/pmc/articles/PMC3941673/.

13. See Stephanie Kelly's "Testing Drugs on the Developing World" (2013), https://www.theatlantic.com/health/archive/2013/02/testing-drugs-on-the-developing-world/273329/.

modified organisms (GMOs), most often modified crops and farm animals, to the history of slaves being treated as animals and used to harvest crops.

Phoenix is viewed as a dangerous and valuable piece of property, not as a human being. After she escapes Tower 7, she is able to explain why the Big Eye scientists allowed her to read extensively:

> I was nothing to worry about or fear. They saw me as they saw the African made slaves during the Trans-Atlantic Slave Trade hundreds of years ago. They saw me as many Arabs saw African slaves over millennium and how some see Africans today. The Big Eye didn't think they needed to put a leash on me because my leash was in my DNA. (136)

Phoenix's words demonstrate the connections between scientific racism and the science fiction trope of genetically created individuals being used as slaves.[14] The reference to the "leash" in her DNA posits whether humans can be created or modified to have specific traits, such as docility.[15] The reference to reading is also a reminder of the early technologies of reading and writing, which were considered dangerous for slaves to learn. Eventually, Phoenix is able to access a critical piece of information denied to her in captivity: the name of the woman who gave birth to her. When Phoenix visits this woman, named Vera, she learns that Vera wanted to raise her but was not allowed:

> They come back when they knew it was safe. Took you from me! They promised me I could raise you! That you'd be mine. . . . They classified you as a "dangerous non-human person." That's how they justified taking you from me. (205–6)

The separation of slave children from their mothers and descriptions of the heartbreak these mothers felt are recorded in numerous slave autobiographies.[16] To make the metaphor even more direct, Okorafor has Vera

---

14. I will discuss one example of a genetically engineered human being enslaved through the addition of animal DNA in Larissa Lai's *Salt Fish Girl* later in this chapter.

15. One example of this idea in science fiction is Bacigalupi's *The Windup Girl* (2009), a novel whose main character is hinted to be genetically engineered with dog DNA that makes her docile. However, Bacigalupi has come under criticism for utilizing Orientalist stereotyping of Asian women in his novel, which is one of several reasons why Bacigalupi's text is not included in this chapter.

16. There is at least one scene of child separation in two of the most prominent US slave autobiographies, *Narrative of the Life of Frederick Douglass, an American Slave* and *Incidents in the Life of a Slave Girl*.

describe the LifeGen scientists as "modern day slavers!" (205). Dehumanization is one tactic that allowed Eurowestern slave owners to justify their actions; LifeGen continues this tactic through their classification of Phoenix and the other speciMens as "non-human." Vera dies during Phoenix's visit, and as Phoenix mourns the death of the mother she never knew, she states, "Let them watch. Let them see how human beings are supposed to treat one another" (206). At this point, Phoenix overcomes the propaganda of the Big Eye scientists and is able to view herself as a "human being" rather than an "abomination." The LifeGen scientists' experimentation at the expense of Phoenix and the other speciMens is indicative of the history of exploitation of peoples of color in Eurowestern societies.

The Book of Phoenix also employs scenes of extreme torture and coercion to demonstrate how the genetically engineered and modified peoples in the novel are dehumanized, which allows the Big Eye workers to justify their captivity and treatment. Phoenix describes the many ways the LifeGen scientists tested the limits of her power to endure and create heat:

> Before I started to heat myself, they would place me in a heated room and watch me sweat and wheeze for hours. In my second year of life, they started burning me. With hot needles, then larger broader instruments. On my face, belly, legs, arms, they burned every part of me. I knew the smell, sound, and sight of my cooking flesh. (66)

Okorafor's description of Phoenix's torture is laced with references to the treatment of African slaves. Washington notes that "wheezing" was a common health condition for slaves: "Enslaved African Americans were more vulnerable than whites to respiratory infections, thanks to poorly constructed slave shacks that admitted winter cold and summer heat" (28). The burning of slaves in myriad ways as a cause of punishment and death was also popular among Eurowestern slave owners.[17] The fact that Phoenix's power is linked to heat and destruction combines Indigenous mythology with scientific experimentation. The Phoenix is best known in Eurowestern cultures as part of Greek mythology, but this legend originated in Egypt and Arabia.[18] The fact that Phoenix's first "death" is combined with an explo-

---

17. In *The Black Jacobins: Toussaint L'Ouverture and the San Domingo Revolution* (1989), C. L. R. James notes that burning wood was often applied to sensitive areas of slaves bodies as punishment, and also states that hot wax and other heated materials were used to punish or kill slaves. Burning at the stake was also allowed (12).

18. For more information on the origins of the Phoenix, see Joseph Nigg's *The Phoenix: An Unnatural Biography of a Mythological Beast* (2016).

sion compared to an atomic bomb highlights the US's history of scientific experimentation for destructive purposes. However, Phoenix's ability to be reborn is mix of a blessing and a curse: She will always be hunted by the LifeGen scientists, yet she also has the ability to use her power to free others. Phoenix's powers and story become like the legend of the Phoenix itself—an ongoing cycle of destruction and rebirth which serves as a powerful metaphor for the experiences of enslaved peoples of color.

As Phoenix and two of the other speciMens who escaped their captivity in Tower 7 attempt to free the captives of the other six towers, they continually encounter evidence of LifeGen's human experimentation. When Phoenix infiltrates the main Big Eye facility, Tower 1, she discovers rooms full of human cyborgs who have had cybernetic parts grafted onto their bodies. She also frees a trapped alien whose body is made of a smokelike substance. Later, Phoenix and two of the other speciMens work together to free the captives of a different LifeGen tower, Tower 4, one of which is a woman named "HeLa," a black-skinned woman born in India who was captured by the Big Eye and whose blood has immortal properties. HeLa is named after Henrietta Lacks, the African American woman whose "immortal" cells were harvested unknowingly in the 1950s and used in many scientific advances. Phoenix learns that HeLa's blood is being harvested by LifeGen and sold to wealthy men for profit. Okoroafor creates the HeLa character to reference how people of color worldwide have been used for centuries to build the wealth and success of Eurowestern societies. When groups of humans are targeted and dehumanized, their bodies can then be used for labor and harvested for scientific gain.

The end of Okorafor's novel is a powerful critique of Eurowestern societies' reliance on written and recorded historical narratives as "truth," despite the fact that the voices of colonized peoples are rarely accurately included in this narrative.[19] Phoenix warns the man who finds and listens to her recorded story to be careful to faithfully record the recounted events. But when the man writes Phoenix's story for others, he changes it to suit his beliefs. Eventually, his "Great Book" is so convincing, people believe that it is true. The Epilogue of the novel is narrated by a man named Sola, a white man who describes himself as privileged and who states that most of his words are lies. Nevertheless, he explains that the man who rewrites Phoe-

---

19. One example of Eurowestern influence on historical narratives is the difficulties some Indigenous cultures are having at finding noncolonized narratives of Indigenous knowledge. Wendy Makoons Geniusz (Anishinaabe) details these difficulties for Anishinaabe cultural preservation in *Our Knowledge Is Not Primitive: Decolonizing Botanical Anishinaabe Teachings* (2009).

nix's story is "a victim of his own environment" and notes that the man's community "was a wounded people, so these ideas were wounded too" (231–32). The "Great Book" that Okorafor describes, and its effects, calls to mind the Bible and how it was used to justify the enslavement of peoples of color. The oral story that becomes twisted by its future storyteller demonstrates how Eurowestern cultures have often controlled the narratives of colonized cultures by writing historical narratives. The "wounds" that are referenced could be viewed as linked to issues of internalized racism that are often a result of colonization. When given the truth in an oral storytelling, the storyteller cannot reconcile this truth with the history that he has been raised with. The result is a twisted narrative that modifies cultural knowledge to reinforce learned narratives of superiority and inferiority. Okorafor's ending seems to suggest that until peoples of color can take control of their own narratives, they will continue to be victims of the historical amnesia often located in Eurowestern historical narratives.

The Book of Phoenix is a powerful condemnation of centuries of experimentation and exploitation inflicted on peoples of color living in Eurowestern-colonized countries. Recounting this history, one that most Eurowestern cultures would rather bury in descriptions of the historical past, can be difficult for authors of color; however, Okorafor is able to skillfully craft a science fiction narrative that links the history of human experimentation of peoples of color to the ethics of genetic experimentation, a much-debated contemporary topic that has already been cited for abusive practices.[20] With a genius Black female character who holds great power, Okorafor is able to take historical atrocities and tell these stories in a new light, one that links past and present to highlight the ways peoples of color have been manipulated in Eurowestern historical and cultural narratives.

Genetic Mutation

Genetic mutation gained popularity in science fiction writings in the 1950s as authors began to address anxieties about exposure to chemicals and radiation brought about by the atomic age. Marvel comics creator Stan Lee took up this premise in 1963 for the first edition of the *X-Men* comic series, which

---

20. Examples include the collection of Henrietta Lacks's cells and the use of those cells without permission and the CRISPR baby scandal. For more information on these cases, see Rebecca Skloot's *The Immortal Life of Henrietta Lacks* (2010) and Ed Yong's "The CRISPR Baby Scandal Gets Worse by the Day" (2018): https://www.theatlantic.com/science/archive/2018/12/15-worrying-things-about-crispr-babies-scandal/577234/.

he states was both an easy way to give characters powers and a metaphor for racism and bigotry:

> I wanted to spotlight a group of innocent people who were feared and shunned and later hated and persecuted. . . . I wanted to show how anyone, no matter how blameless, can be victimized if the fates so decree. (qtd. in Martin 27)

When the *X-Men* series was revived in 1975, new characters were introduced; one of the most significant additions was the character Storm, a Black woman with the power to control the elements. The series also included Indigenous and Asian characters. This revived run made the metaphor for mutants as peoples of color blatant. Since then, Marvel has created hundreds of *X-Men* characters and has produced multiple *X-Men* comic series, a TV series, and several blockbuster films. The series includes characters of various races and ethnicities and is constantly pushing the boundaries to add more-diverse character offerings; one newer addition is a burka-clad *X-Men* character named Dust. Although there are some criticisms about making a direct parallel between mutants and peoples of color as well as issues with nonwhite characters being written off or "whitened,"[21] the *X-Men* series effectively utilizes the trope of genetic mutation to tackle issues of racial representation and the consequences of xenophobia in Eurowestern cultures.

Stan Lee favored the trope of genetic mutation because it was a plausible explanation for why mutants would develop their differences at a specific time: puberty. Until then, mutants are indistinguishable from the rest of humanity. This idea of human mutants being indistinguishable from the rest of humanity serves as a metaphor for racial passing and the "one drop" rule that enslaved many peoples who would otherwise be viewed as white. Schuyler understood the absurdity behind the idea of having to "pass" for another race and used parody and invented scientific procedures in *Black No More* to mock the "science" behind scientific racism. However, science fiction authors have mostly tended to utilize the mutant trope as either a commentary on the effects of radiation on humans, animals, and the environment, a horror tactic where genetically mutated creatures are treated as monstrous, or a broad metaphor for oppression, rather than specifically

---

21. For one example, see Mikhail Lyubansky's "The Racial Politics of X-Men" (2011), https://www.obv.org.uk/news-blogs/racial-politics-x-men. P. Andrew Miller also notes in "Mutants, Metaphor, and Marginalism: What X-actly Do the X-Men Stand For?" that many of the non-European characters within the series were either written off or given European features or heritages (286–87).

linking this trope to race and ethnicity.[22] Mutation is also often viewed as negative and linked to genetic conditions,[23] which may cause science fiction authors of color to avoid a representation of inherent genetic difference that, used incorrectly, could reinforce issues of genetic essentialism and scientific racism.

N. K. Jemisin's *Broken Earth* trilogy (*The Fifth Season*, 2015; *The Obelisk Gate*, 2016; *The Stone Sky*, 2017)[24] proves that the trope of genetic mutation can be a powerful tool for addressing themes of alienation, enslavement, racial passing, and xenophobia. In this series, humans with a specific genetic mutation are known as "orogenes" or by the derogatory term "rogga." Orogenes can manipulate various forms of energy; they are viewed as dangerous because some of them cannot control their abilities. Non-orogenes fear orogenes and frequently choose to kill them before they fully develop their abilities. Although Jemisin creates new ethnicities in her series, which leaves readers to discover which races are considered "favorable" as the novel progresses, readers learn in the first chapter of *The Fifth Season* that the main character, an orogene woman who changes her name three times (Damaya, Syenite, Essun) as she attempts to escape enslavement, is "unpleasantly ocher-brown" with locks and "enough Sanzed in them to show, not enough to tell" (10). The most powerful orogene in the series is ironically named Alabaster, though the first description of him refuses to mention race; Syenite simply describes his hair as "dense, tight-curled stuff" (*The Fifth Season* 67). Jemisin utilizes the science fiction and fantasy element of world building to create new ethic designations, and slowly reveals characters' skin colors and features to make the impact of her racial allegory more powerful. Readers of the series are introduced to Jemisin's world through the eyes of a brown-skinned female character, and they may think of Alabaster as default white or mixed-race before they read the description of his dark skin color later

---

22. Examples of mutation as a result of radiation exposure include Wilmar H. Shiras's *Children of the Atom* (1953) and films like *Total Recall* (1990); these two works epitomize the two results of mutation—either humans with enhanced abilities or class oppression of mutants as "othered" peoples. Examples of monstrous mutants include characters in Suzanne Collins's *Hunger Games* trilogy (2008–10) and the *Teenage Mutant Ninja Turtles* cartoon series (1980–present).

23. The University of Utah's Genetic Science Learning Center notes in an article titled "What Is Mutation?" that many gene mutations do not cause health issues, but simply cause slight variations in genetic makeup which result in differences like blood type or eye color. For more information, see https://learn.genetics.utah.edu/content/evolution/mutation/.

24. I have to note here that this series is not only groundbreaking in its themes; it is also the first science fiction series to win the Hugo Award for Best Novel in three consecutive years. No other author to date has equaled Jemisin's achievement.

in the series. These choices in when to reveal a character's skin color allow Jemisin to empower characters of color while also not making race their only defining feature.

Jemisin admits that the *Broken Earth* trilogy is motivated by allegories of race, but she also refuses to allow critics to categorize the allegories as only pertaining to African Americans or US slavery. Although Jemisin has not explicitly stated that the term "rogga" is a metaphor for a specific racial slur, she does note that the term is intended to be derogatory:

> It's hopefully obvious that I meant for "rogga" to be an ugly word, and hopefully obvious that I'm deliberately exploring some real-world allegory through this story. But then, it's not like this is the first time I've done so. I feel. . . . like I did what I intended to do? ("Hi, r/Fantasy")

Jemisin also states in an interview with *Wired* magazine that the *Broken Earth* trilogy was influenced by issues of race both in the US and worldwide:

> I didn't set out to write big heavy themes. I did not set out to write an allegory for slavery and caste oppression. I set out to write a world in which people who are powerful, who are valuable, are channeled into systems of self-supported and externally imposed oppression. It's about how you keep people who can throw mountains from throwing mountains—and running the world. ("World Shaker")

Jemisin's work thus becomes an allegory for many colonized peoples of color, who are forced to survive in Eurowestern-dominated societies that justify their enslavement or class status through themes of genetic essentialism and scientific racism. At the same time, I would also argue that the fact that the word "rogga" is given a two-syllable, double-*g* consonant sound immediately links it to a historically derogatory term for African Americans in particular. If Jemisin, an African American author, notes that she intended to create a "real world" allegory of race based on her views and experiences, then it is accurate to say that the novel is both an allegory of the historical treatment of African Americans in the US and a broader allegory of the effects of colonization worldwide. Like Okorafor, who highlights the history of colonial violence both within the US and in Africa in *Who Fears Death*, Jemisin creates a series with multiple layers of allegory that ties the specific experience of African Americans to a larger global history of Eurowestern violence against peoples of color.

The majority of the *Broken Earth* series focuses on Essun, an orogene who hides her abilities in order to "pass" and live in a community, or "comm," and her orogene daughter Nassun. The first novel, *The Fifth Season*, opens with Essun grieving the loss of her two children, one of whom has been killed by her husband after he discovers that the child is an orogene, and Nassun, who is abducted by her father who attempts to "cure" her of being an orogene. The entire series draws attention to the history of African Americans' being forced into racial passing and the dangers of unchecked xenophobia. In a flashback from Essun's past, readers learn that Essun's birth name was Damaya. When a Guardian, an enhanced human tasked with keeping orogenes in check and overseeing their training, named Schaffa comes to claim her, he finds that her family has locked her in a barn out of fear. When Schaffa confronts Damaya's mother about the treatment, she responds, "Ordinary people can't take care of . . . of children like her. . . . She almost killed a child at school. . . . And it's any citizen's duty, isn't it?" (*The Fifth Season* 32, ellipsis in original). Damaya's mother is afraid to keep her at home because anyone caught harboring an orogene faces expulsion from their community (36). Later in the novel, when the head of the town Essun has lived in for ten years discovers she is orogene and lets her leave instead of killing her, he puts himself in danger of being labeled a "rogga lover" (54). These scenes clearly set the stage for a comparison of orogenes to other racial groups that had to be hidden for their own safety, such as Jewish peoples in Nazi cultures[25] or Black slaves in the US.

Jemisin draws parallels between the treatment of Essun/Damaya and the cycles of violence and enslavement faced by Black slaves throughout her series. The Fugitive Slave Acts of 1793 and 1850 allowed slave hunters to capture and return runaway slaves ("The Fugitive Slave Acts"). However, since slave hunters only needed to affirm that the captured African American was a runaway slave, with no need for corroborating documents, these laws created a situation where freed Black slaves or Black non-slaves could be captured and sold into slavery. The laws also made it illegal to harbor or aid a runaway slave and included punishments ranging from fines to imprisonment ("Fugitive"). The social situations described in Damaya's imprisonment by her own family take the history of exploitative racial laws in colonized settings and extrapolates a future where mutation will lead to families "turning in" their own children. Damaya's mother has been raised with stories of orogenes as monstrous, and her belief causes her to almost

---

25. For more information, see Eva Fogelman's "Rescuers of Jews During the Holocaust," https://www.writing.upenn.edu/~afilreis/Holocaust/rescuers-article.html.

kill her own child. She also knows that the laws of her community would expel her and her family from the comm if they were found guilty of harboring an orogene, which would essentially be a death sentence. Essun's husband has even killed his own child because he believes that orogenes are "monstrous abominations," a term that has been used to justify racial or ethnically motivated atrocities like ethnic cleansing.[26] The use of the term "rogga lover" as a derogatory term is linked to the history of white peoples in the US disparaging peoples who demonstrated racial tolerance toward African Americans. The use of the term "citizen's duty" also calls to mind the propaganda and death threats imposed on communities by the Nazis, who often equated xenophobia with citizenship. Jemisin uses Essun's childhood flashback and the actions of her adopted community after she is no longer able to "pass" to comment on the history of xenophobia both within the US and abroad.

Jemisin makes her allegory of slavery even more explicit during Damaya's time as an apprentice at the Fulcrum, an orogene training center where orogenes learn to manipulate kinetic and geothermal energy. After she successfully completes her training, Damaya renames herself Syenite in the tradition of orogenes taking the names of rocks or minerals. She believes that the Fulcrum and its Guardians are helping her until she is ordered to breed with a ten-ring orogene named Alabaster. Alabaster tells her that orogenes who are not bred in the Fulcrum are labeled "feral" and explains why the Fulcrum applies this negative label to orogenes born outside its walls: "That's how they think of you. A wild mutt to my domesticated purebred. An accident, to my plan. . . . What it actually means is that they couldn't *predict* you. You're the proof that they'll never control us, not really. Not completely" (*The Fifth Season* 72). Alabaster's "planned" creation calls to mind early eugenics programs or slave breeding, and the Fulcrum's distaste of "feral" orogenes references xenophobic views of ethnic purity. The Fulcrum wants to control orogenes because they charge comms money for orogenetic services. In *The Obelisk Gate*, Schaffa even admits to Nassun that the guardians have spread exaggerated rumors about orogenes and their destructiveness to create fear in the comms and to encourage citizens to kill or turn over orogenes (149). Jemisin's description of the Fulcrum's control of orogene labor is a reference to the history of forced labor or slavery experienced by African slaves and other racial and ethnic groups.

---

26. Examples of ethnic cleansing range from the Nazi Holocaust to the killing of Tutsis and moderate Hutus in Rwanda. For a definition of ethnic cleansing, see the United Nations webpage on genocide prevention: https://www.un.org/en/genocideprevention/ethnic-cleansing.shtml.

Schaffa's explanation of Fulcrum tactics is also reminiscent of the use of scientific racism to justify the enslavement and imprisonment of peoples of color.

Some of the most exploitative processes that the Fulcrum initiates to control orogenes is the creation of the Guardians and node maintainers. When Alabaster takes Syenite to a "node," one of the stations that uses orogenetic ability to stabilize the planet, she learns that Fulcrum orogenes who cannot learn to control their abilities pay a horrible price:

> The body in the node maintainer's chair is small, and naked. Thin, its limbs atrophied. Hairless. There are things—tubes and pipes and *things*, she has no words for them—going into the stick-arms, down the goggle-throat, across the narrow crotch. There's a flexible bag on the corpse's belly, *attached* to its belly somehow, and it's full of—ugh . . . She focuses on all this, these little details because it helps. Because there's a part of her that's gibbering, and the only way she can keep that part internal and silent is to concentrate on everything she's seeing. Ingenious, really, what they've done. She didn't know it was possible to keep a body alive like this: immobile, unwilling, indefinite. (139–40, emphasis in original).

The node maintainer description takes the concept of slavery to its most extreme level. The orogene in the chair becomes a living battery, a body with no autonomy whatsoever. Alabaster tells Syenite that some citizens even pay to sexually assault the immobile node maintainers. Jemisin employs a dystopic setting and extreme coercion to highlight the dehumanizing effects of xenophobia by depicting orogenes who face varying levels of slavery. Alabaster and Syenite are controlled by the Fulcrum, forced to work and even to procreate, but they are also allowed to travel and eventually manage to escape Fulcrum control (albeit at a high price). The node maintainer scene forces readers to confront the atrocities of xenophobia by showing the horrors that become possible when social and political systems ignore the exploitation of vulnerable racial and ethnic groups.

Jemisin creates a bleak setting and society in the *Broken Earth* series, but she does not leave her readers without any hope for change. At the end of the series, Nassun decides to give humanity another chance when she uses the obelisk gate to restore the moon's orbit and stop the seasons. She had originally intended to use the machine to kill humanity and end the suffering of all orogenes. But when Essun sacrifices herself trying to stop her daughter, Nassun decides to honor her mother's wish to save humanity. Afterwards, in a conversation with a stone eater named Hoa, a being who is part of a long-lived people made of stone, she expresses her fear that humans will decide to kill all orogenes once they realize that the seasons are over. She argues, "People killed us and hated us when they *needed* us. Now we don't even have that" (*The Stone Sky* 395, emphasis in original). Hoa points out that without the need for protection from the seasons, orogenes have the power to retaliate and kill all non-orogenes. He also notes that the treatment of orogenes was not a necessary evil, but a deliberate choice to force a minority group to become a source of exploited labor: "Imprisonment of orogenes was never the only option for ensuring the safety of society. . . . Lynching was never the only option. The nodes were never the only option. All of these were choices. Different choices have always been possible" (395). Jemisin makes a direct reference to lynching to highlight how people of color were devalued as human beings even after they were "freed." She makes it clear that the rhetoric of difference that allows peoples of color to be portrayed as inherently inferior and forced into exploitative labor practices is a deliberate choice made to maintain white superiority. While Okorafor is focused on highlighting the cyclical nature of violence against peoples of color, Jemisin leaves room for her society to make different choices, to choose to acknowledge the violence and make amends. Okorafor and Jemisin each use genetic tropes and refences to unresolved historical trauma to draw attention to the legacy of silence that continues to affect cultures with histories of slavery and oppression.

The science fiction trope of mutation as the origin of powerful abilities can be used as an equalizing tool for science fiction authors. Since anyone can be born with mutated genes, genetic differences such as skin color are not the only factors that determine which peoples are oppressed. And yet mutation can also be a powerful metaphor for the lived experiences of peoples of color. Jemisin utilizes the trope of genetic mutation in the *Broken Earth* series to highlight the ways Eurowestern cultures use fear of difference to justify the oppression of peoples of color. At the same time, her decision to world-build new races and racial hierarchies allows readers an estranged view of racism and xenophobia where it is not clear at first which characters are which races, or which races are deemed inferior in Jemisin's world. The experience of being in Essun's head and living through the horrors she has faced as an orogene and a woman of color draws attention to both the historical and the ongoing violence against peoples of color in Eurowestern societies. But it also demonstrates the strength and adaptability it takes for peoples of color to survive in a society that is actively working to enslave and control them.

Genetic Engineering

Debating scientific ethics is a popular topic for science fiction authors. Science fiction critics often cite Mary Shelley's *Frankenstein; or, The Modern Prometheus* (1818), with its famous reversal of the "noble scientist perusing truth for the common good" stereotype and its critique of scientific ethics (Evans 28), as a foundational text of the genre. Therefore, it is not surprising that science fiction authors frequently critique the sciences of their times, often by extrapolating potential futures where scientific advances have had a major effect on society.[27] Debates about the ethics of genetic engineering, or the manipulation of one or more genes in an organism ("Genetic"), have once again gained national consciousness with the advent of technologies such as in-vitro fertilization (1977), the Human Genome Project (1990), and the Clustered Regularly Interspaced Short Palindromic Repeats (CRISPR) gene-editing method (2013).[28] The ethical scandal of the CRISPR-edited babies, where scientist He Jiankui claimed to have successfully modified the genes of three embryos which were then implanted and birthed (Cyrenoski), has led to debates over the potential for future uses of gene-editing technologies to significantly alter the human population. Scientists argue that if cosmetic genetic engineering were legalized, this choice could usher in a new eugenics movement.

Many science fiction authors have noted the potential benefits and consequences of altering human beings. David A. Kirby notes that the trope of genetic control over future populations has been envisioned and debated for almost a century:

> The idea of direct genetic control started with the publication of evolutionary geneticist J. B. S. Haldane's "speculative science" book *Daedalus, or Science and the Future* (1924), which offered the vision of a "new" eugenics that relied on technological breakthroughs and avoided selective breeding. Haldane outlined a process he called "ectogenic creation" that involved direct intervention into the human genome. Many people found the idea of directly manipulating hereditary material for the "betterment" of humanity

---

27. A prime example of this science fiction trope is the idea of the takeover of artificially intelligent robots or computers in texts like Karel Čapek's "R.U.R" (1921), William Gibson's *Neuromancer* (1984), and Daniel H. Wilson's *Robopocalypse* (2011) and films such as the *Terminator* series (1984–19) and *Slaughterbots* (2017).

28. For more information on the discovery and timeline of CRISPR, see John R. Christin and Michael V. Beckert's "Origins and Applications of CRISPR-Mediated Genome Editing" (2016), https://www.ncbi.nlm.nih.gov/pmc/articles/PMC5319590.

unpalatable, and Haldane's vision was sharply satirized in Aldous Huxley's *Brave New World* (1932). (194)

Huxley's terrifying vision of a future where a person's value is decided at birth is an iconic science fiction text that has influenced many contemporary science fiction authors. Contemporary fear about the ethics of genetic engineering in science fiction include texts such as Greg Bear's *Blood Music* (1985), Octavia E. Butler's *Xenogenesis* trilogy (1987, 1988, 1989), Nancy Kress's *Beggars* trilogy (1993, 1994, 1996), and films like *Jurassic Park* (1993), *The Fifth Element* (1997), *Gattaca* (1997), *Avatar* (2009), and *Jupiter Ascending* (2015).

One of the largest fears for critics of genetic engineering is the debate over who will decide what aspects of humanity are "superior" and how genetically engineered peoples will be viewed by their communities. The two texts I examine for this section, Larissa Lai's *Salt Fish Girl* (2002) and Octavia E. Butler's *Fledgling* (2005), take very different approaches to the depiction of their genetically engineered main characters. *Salt Fish Girl* includes two genetically engineered main characters: One (Evie) is a clone with 0.03% carp fish DNA, and the other, Miranda, is a woman whose genes have been modified by a durian fruit implanted with human genes. Lai's human/animal and human/plant hybrid characters examine the potential for genetic engineering to bring back slavery by creating human beings who have enough "foreign" DNA to be considered nonhuman property. *Fledgling* takes a more positive approach: Butler's story of a genetically engineered human/Ina (vampire) hybrid and her eventual acceptance by the majority of the Ina peoples argues for the potential of genetics to create dialogues of reconciliation in Eurowestern cultures.

If cosmetic genetic engineering becomes legal and people are able to change their future children's physical attributes like skin, hair, eye color, height, and facial features, then, scientists note, one side effect of this practice could be a loss of racial diversity as societies begin to decide which physical attributes are "desirable" (Kirby 196). Considering the influences of scientific racism ingrained in many Eurowestern societies, it seems plausible that whiteness would become the literal "default" race as families with means attempt to give their children yet another advantage in a society that values whiteness. Kirby notes that for this real-life *Gattaca*[29] scenario to happen, societies would have to accept the notion of genetic essentialism, or that

---

29. The film *Gattaca* is based on a society where genetic makeup determines which people are defined as "in-valid," or genetically inferior, and which "valid" members are given opportunities and resources.

humans are the literal sum of their genetic makeup (197). This reductionist tendency leaves communities of color vulnerable to being labeled, once again, as inherently inferior.

Lai utilizes the reductionist narrative of genetics to extrapolate a world where human beings are enslaved or ostracized because of their genetic differences. Evie and her clone sisters, the Sonias, are genetically engineered to possess 0.03% carp fish DNA, which allow them to be legally used as a disposable labor force. The only marker of Miranda's genetic difference is that she smells like durian fruit; however, this slight genetic difference is enough to put her life and the lives of her family members at risk. Though Lai stresses genetic difference as the marker of otherness for Evie, the Sonias, and Miranda, the fact that these characters are all women of color is significant. Evie and the Sonias are rumored to be descended from "a woman called Ai, a Chinese woman who married a Japanese man" (160).[30] Malissa Kurtz notes that Lai uses this hinted racialization of her cloned characters to connect the science of genetics to the history of using physical characteristics like race to justify colonial practices:

> This genetic indicator marks Evie as a biological other and provides the reason Nextcorp can exploit the labor of women of color—where early colonialism used phenotypic characteristics to indicate the inherent inferiority of people of color, Nextcorp uses genetic difference to assert that Sonias are sub-human. In *Salt Fish Girl*, race *is* technology, not only because it is purposely and culturally engineered, but also because the supposedly neutral scientific field of genomics establishes race. (122, emphasis in original)

Scientists, like historians, are not immune to the influences and assumptions made by their cultures. This point is beginning to surface in scientific discourses that advocate for "decolonizing" Eurowestern scientific practices.[31] Kurtz's point about race being a form of technology in science fiction,

---

30. While Lai does not explicitly state the ethnicity of characters in *Salt Fish Girl*, her choice to set part of the novel in China, her critical writings on Asian cultures in Canada, and her interest in Canadian immigration laws demonstrate her interest in issues of immigration and assimilation for Asians and other peoples of color. For examples, see "Corrupted Lineage: Narrative in the Gaps of History" (Lai 2001), "Asian Invasion vs. the Pristine Nation: Migrant Entering the Canadian Imaginary" (2000), and "Political Animals in the Body of History" (1999).

31. I discuss the argument for scientific decolonization further in chapter 4. For examples of texts advocating for a decolonizing approach to science, see Wendy Makoon Geniusz's *Our Knowledge Is Not Primitive* (2009), Robin Wall Kimmerer's *Braiding Sweetgrass: Indigenous Wisdom, Scientific Knowledge, and the Teachings of Plants* (2013), Kim

which she adapts from Beth Coleman's work in media studies, demonstrates how authors like Lai can expose the ways that scientific study continues to racialize specific groups, and how these assumptions can harm peoples of color by reinforcing ideals of genetic essentialism. Lai's inclusion of human clones with animal DNA also speaks to Eurowestern cultures' fear of genetic impurity and these cultures' tendency to animalize races that they desire to control and exploit as a cheap labor source.

While Evie and Miranda are able to "pass" for non-engineered or altered citizens at times, each character is vulnerable to exploitation because of her genetic differences. Evie and Miranda are each hunted and victimized by Dr. Flowers, the man responsible for genetically engineering Evie and her clone sisters. Rita Wong reads these scenes of exploitation in *Salt Fish Girl* as "informed by Lai's witnessing of the immense gap between the discourses of acceptance and compassion that circulate in the name of the nation and the systemic violence of incarceration that meets those who are extra-legal— that is, who may be undocumented or structurally unable to gain access to the privileges required to enter through the nation's front door" (111). Wong relates exploitation in *Salt Fish Girl* to the experience of undocumented immigrants, which would certainly be the case for Evie who is a clone with no legal status or rights. However, I would argue that the majority of peoples of color, documented or not, living in Eurowestern cultures find themselves subject to systemic racism and violence. Like these peoples, Miranda's status as citizen is unable to save her from being assaulted and taken advantage of because she is not considered of value to the dominant society.

Evie and Miranda are subject to exploitation because of their genetic differences, but it is also important to note that their position as sexually fluid women of color living in patriarchal, heteronormative settings adds additional layers of metaphor to Lai's narrative. Jemisin and Lai each normalize non-heteronormative relations in connection to Indigenous culture or myth to critique Eurowestern cultures' privileging of heteronormative relations. Their depictions are an important reminder that race and sexuality are not mutually exclusive in science fiction. Sylvie Bérard explains the potential of science fiction to address the alienation of queer identities in Eurowestern cultures:

> To me, science fiction has always been about identifying with the green man, and a great part of my pleasure, as a science fiction reader, is to look

---

TallBear's *Native American DNA: Tribal Belonging and the False Promise of Genetic Science* (2013), and Alondra Nelson's *The Social Life of DNA: Race, Reparations, and Reconciliation after the Genome* (2016).

for new metaphors for queer identities, to finally feel at ease in a genre where not everything is a matter of familiar genders and sexualities. Not every piece of science fiction (intentionally) breaks the common (binary) patterns, but it is always there as a potential. (386)

Many science fiction critics note that science fiction is the literary genre of the not-yet-realized, which makes it ideal for portraying a non-Eurowestern-influenced vision of races and sexualities. Samuel R. Delany in particular is known for creating narratives with sexually fluid multiracial characters. Authors like Jemisin and Lai are building on Delany's legacy by inventing worlds that also celebrate non-heteronormative sexuality in non-white relationships.

In the *Broken Earth* series, Syenite and Alabaster both engage in a three-way relationship with an Indigenous pirate named Innon. Syenite questions the relationship at first because it goes against the norms of the culture she was raised in, but Innon's Indigenous culture accepts the relationship without question (*The Fifth Season* 372). The choice to make an Indigenous culture more accepting then a Eurowestern one speaks to Indigenous acknowledgment of a multiplicity of genders and sexualities. Roger M. Carpenter notes in "Womanish Men and Manlike Women: The Native American Two-Spirit as Warrior" (2011) that European colonizers in North America chronicled the existence of "two spirit peoples" in many Indigenous cultures: men or women with fluid gender identities whose sexuality ranged from asexual to bisexual. They also noted that polyamory was often present in Indigenous cultures and could include young men or boys raised to act and dress in "feminine" manners (Carpenter 148–51). While the acceptance of two-spirit peoples varied by tribe, Carpenter notes that European colonizers often influenced tribes through their promotion of ideals of masculine dominance (153). Emasculation of Indigenous men was a common tool for Eurowestern colonizers looking to justify taking control of Indigenous populations, which creates a link between race and sexuality in colonial discourse. Since science fiction is heavily influenced by the colonial and scientific discourses of its time,[32] it comes as no surprise that much of it still relies on male protagonists and heteronormative relations. Jemisin is never hesitant to critique the racial politics of the Eurowestern cultures that now dominate science fiction

---

32. For a full explanation of the connections between colonialism and science fiction, see John Rieder's *Colonialism and the Emergence of Science Fiction* (2012).

authorship,[33] and the addition of the Syenite/Innon/Alabaster relationship is one such critique.

Lai interweaves the story of Evie and Miranda with a story of two women lovers (suspected to be the original Evie and Miranda) in 1800s South China. The two parallel past/future storylines highlight Lai's intent to critique the treatment of women in Asian and Asian diasporic cultures. It becomes clear as the story unfolds that whether the women in Lai's novel live in the 1800s or in 2044, they are persecuted for their failure to conform to heteronormative cultural expectations. In one of the chapters of the novel set in the 1800s, an unnamed narrator falls in love with a girl who sells salt fish. Both girls are forced to run away after the salt fish girl's father attacks the narrator for pursuing a relationship with his daughter (Lai 56). Evie and Miranda's relationship in 2044 is similarly interrupted by Dr. Flowers. Evie is Dr. Flowers's adopted daughter; when she disobeys his wishes, he sends her to live and work in a factory with other female clones of her line to remind her of her disposable nature. After Dr. Flowers finds and kills the Sonia clones Evie has helped to escape, she goes to Dr. Flowers' office with Miranda to kill him. Miranda ends up stabbing Dr. Flowers as he physically overpowers Evie, and the two women escape his office before security can catch them (254–57). The main female characters of *Salt Fish Girl* spend most of the novel trying to overcome the oppression of the patriarchal societies that continually attempt to control their bodies and desires. Lai moves between past and futuristic settings to highlight the ongoing cycle of mistreatment and control of women, especially women of color, in patriarchal societies.

The end of *Salt Fish Girl* finds Evie and Miranda at the heart of the clone processing facility, which is designed by an Indigenous artist to mimic a curled, fetal shape. The women leave the cabin, and the story ends with Miranda giving birth in a hot spring after she and Evie revert to their original, snake/fish goddess forms and interlock their tails. In this scene, Evie and Miranda become a representation of the power of the female body; the genetic experimentation that causes these characters to be viewed as less-than-human also allows two women to create a baby. This depiction of female creation caused by genetic accident is fused with the story of Nü Wa, a creation goddess, to challenge the notions of patriarchal institutions that attempt to control procreation and colonial institutions that suppress local beliefs. Lai fuses Chinese mythology with reproductive technologies

---

33. See Jemisin's Hugo Award speech in 2018, https://www.barnesandnoble.com/blog/sci-fi-fantasy/read-n-k-jemisins-historic-hugo-speech/.

to create a cyborg narrative in the spirit of Donna Haraway's description of cyborg gender roles:

> The cyborg is a creature in a post-gender world; it has no truck with bisexuality, pre-oedipal symbiosis, unalienated labor, or other seductions to organic wholeness through a final appropriation of all the powers of the parts into a final unity. In a sense, the cyborg has no origin story in the Western sense.... An origin story in the "Western," humanist sense depends on the myth of original unity, fullness, bliss and terror, represented by phallic mother from whom all humans must separate, the task of individual development and history, the twin potent myths inscribed most powerfully for us in psychoanalysis and Marxism.... The cyborg skips the step of original unity, of identification with nature in the Western sense. (292)

Lai's Eastern mythological perspective demonstrates how the use of specific cultural references can overcome the dominant Eurowestern mythology that Haraway describes to "challenge conceptions of science fiction that privilege a version of Western modernity in which scientific progress and rational thought occlude all other possible modernities and genealogies" (P. Lai 167). Through the fusion of Eurowestern sciences, Indigenous art, and Eastern mythology, Lai creates a cyborg narrative that challenges the influence of Eurowestern patriarchal thinking on the science fiction genre.

Fledgling and the Potential of Genetic Engineering

So far, the depictions of race and genetic modification discussed in this chapter have been dystopic portrayals designed to highlight the rejection of peoples viewed as other and the dehumanization of peoples of color in Eurowestern cultures. While these depictions address concerns about the ethical use of genetic engineering and its very real consequences, it is also important to note that genetic advances have the potential to help peoples affected by slavery or forced immigration to reclaim a lost cultural history. In *The Social Life of DNA: Race, Reparations and Reconciliation after the Genome* (2016), Alondra Nelson explains that many African Americans are participating in genetic genealogy testing in the hopes of educating the public about the history of slavery in Eurowestern cultures and, ultimately, achieving racial reconciliation. She also argues that "the social power of DNA is being similarly leveraged to raise awareness of Blacks' past experiences and, in doing so, contribute to today's racial politics, which are too often marked by historical amnesia" (6). Nelson understands the fraught history of DNA testing and peoples of color in Eurowestern cultures,[34] yet she also argues for the value in using genetic research responsibly as a means of educating Eurowestern cultures about the far-reaching effects of colonization and restoring some pieces of lost cultural history for the descendants of peoples of color who were enslaved. I argue that Octavia E. Butler's *Fledgling* depicts genetic engineering through a more positive lens by examining the potential of genetics to question views of genetic essentialism and create dialogues of reconciliation in Eurowestern cultures.

Butler's *Fledgling* is a clear example of the science of genetic engineering being utilized as a science fiction trope to disrupt notions of racial essentialism. Butler has stated in several interviews that the idea for her novel *Kindred* (1979) came from her fascination with how later generations of African Americans would survive in the time of slavery.[35] If this novel demonstrates her fascination with the past, *Fledgling* shows her fascination with the future of human identity and the politics that often accompany it. Butler is known for being an avid reader and researcher; in 1976, she wrote herself a reminder to "speak and write only of things you've earned the right to speak and write about through experience and/or study" (qtd. in Schalk 165). Her personal notes at the Huntington Library include multiple references to genetics and symbiosis.[36] Butler's fascination with genetics and human essentialism is clear throughout her *Xenogenesis* series (1987–89), but in *Fledgling* (2005) she deviates to specifically examine the impact of genetic engineering on views of race. Her protagonist, Shori, is a genetically engineered character created to explore the connections between skin color and racial/ethnic identification. Shori is a young, female Ina, a vampire-like race, who has been genetically engineered, through the addition of human DNA, to have black skin. She originally appears to be a helpless child with amne-

---

34. The examples that Nelson references are the Tuskegee syphilis study (82), as well as the practice of police in the US collecting DNA from peoples arrested for minor offenses (82) or even collecting DNA before charging individuals with a crime (108).

35. In an interview with Lisa See, Butler states, "I also had this friend who could recite history but didn't feel it. . . . So I wanted to write a novel that would make others feel the history: the pain and fear that black people had to live through in order to endure" (40).

36. For example, in her archived papers, Butler makes several notes to herself to copy information on exons and chromosomes from two different sources and makes a note that "viruses 'reassort' or swap genes." She then writes the question, "What makes us human?" She also writes an idea for a story titled "Transhumance" that involves symbiosis between humans and aliens (OEB 598).

sia. However, as the novel progresses, readers discover that the manipulation of Shori's genes has made her a powerful transgenic figure.[37]

Shori embodies the advantages of both the Ina and human species. Fittingly, the human advantage that Shori gains is black skin, which allows her to walk in daylight, a direct challenge to views of black skin as inferior. Butler is not the first author to utilize a Black vampire figure; Jewelle Gomez's *The Gilda Stories* (1991) depicts a young Black girl who is turned into a vampire by another vampire. The *Blade* film series (1998–2004) also features Wesley Snipes as Blade, a half-vampire, half-human Black man whose mother is attacked by a vampire. Blade gains "daywalker" abilities from the attack and uses these abilities to becomes a vampire hunter. However, neither of these characters is created through genetic engineering, and these depictions of Black vampire characters, while important, do not directly challenge racial representation in their works. Shori's position as a person who literally embodies the genes of two different species and who utilizes the advantages of both species to help Ina and humans overcome cultural bias demonstrates how Butler uses the idea of genetic engineering to complicate views of racial and genetic essentialism.

Shori's black skin gives her advantages over other Ina, such as being able to tolerate sunlight, yet it also causes her to become the target of racism. Shori and her companions assume that she is a target because of her black skin; however, Butler complicates the Ina's reaction to Shori by conflating their views of race and humanity. The Ina need a symbiotic relationship with humans in order to survive; however, some Ina view humans as inferior and describe Shori's mix of human/Ina genes as a contamination of their species. Butler conflates Blackness and humanity, so that at times the Ina are discussing Shori as more human, while at other times she is specifically referred to as Black. During the trial against the Ina responsible for the death of Shori's family, Milo Silk refers to Shori as a "clever dog" (238) and when sentenced to banishment for murder, he cries out, "Murdering black mongrel bitch . . . What will she give us all? Fur? Tails?" (300). Both references point to the dehumanization of Black peoples historically used to justify slavery. The Ina/human relationship is described as symbiotic and mutually beneficial by the Ina, yet it is often conflicted and parasitic because the chosen humans are not allowed autonomy or viewed as equals by all Ina, much like the historical relationship between Black slaves and white slave owners. The idea of Black peoples as less-than-human has informed many of the laws and

---

37. "Transgenic organism" is the scientific term for an organism that has been modified through the addition of DNA from a different organism.

social relations of Eurowestern cultures, and Butler uses the Silks' reaction to Shori's presence as a metaphor for the persistence of racist views in present-day Eurowestern societies.

Butler's choice to complicate Shori's human identification represents a more complex version of racial identity that she links to the survival of the human and Ina species. Shori is an Ina/human hybrid, yet she also represents the creation of a new species (as evidenced by her ability to pass on her human genes to her offspring) that marks a space for positive depictions of Blackness. Ali Brox notes that while Shori could be read as a biracial figure, discussing her only in terms of a racial binary is misleading: "While readers may perceive Butler's heroine, Shori, in biracial terms, the hybrid figure proves valuable for discussing Shori's identity and expanding the conversation beyond a rigid binary of black and white, vampire and human" (391). Butler's use of genetic engineering to give Shori human DNA complicates the notion of race and culture. The fact that Shori's human DNA gives her noticeable advantages over the "pure" Ina forces the Ina to question their essentialist views of race. This situation mimics the situation of many Eurowestern peoples, who may discover through genetic testing that their DNA is not as "pure" as they thought.

Acceptance of hybridity in *Fledgling* is consistently linked to survival. Gregory Jerome Hampton argues, "To be identified as a hybrid in Butler's fiction is, often times, synonymous with becoming a survivor and a signifier of the future" (192). The humans and Ina who cannot accept Shori are depicted as fanatics who will destroy the chance of true mutualistic relations between their species. Butler thus depicts a world where, in order to survive, humans and Ina will have to accept new racial and species identifications. The Ina's eventual acceptance of Shori creates a positive depiction of a genetically engineered being, one that allows readers to consider how real-world genetic advances could lead to a greater acceptance of racial intermixture and a rejection of white, Eurowestern rhetorics of supremacy.

Looking Ahead

Although no one can say for sure how advancements in genetics will affect views of race and race relations for future generations, the authors discussed in this chapter demonstrate a variety of ways that genetic engineering will lead either to heightened views of genetic essentialism and xenophobia, or to a greater understanding of race and racial intermixture. Lavender III notes, "The tremendous potential of genetic science to discredit racism (and even the notion of race itself) as completely inconsistent with the biological reality of human existence is a noteworthy dream. Although we certainly like to think that scientific progress pushes prejudice and discrimination to the side, science fiction suggests otherwise" (*Race in American* 50). None of the authors in this chapter are arguing that genetics will create a "race-blind" future; in fact, all of the genetically altered characters in this chapter have their lives threatened because of their differences. But the depiction of genetic engineering in science fiction texts does open interesting conversations for how genetics may allow specific groups to challenge long-held views about race or to reclaim a lost history. One fact that the texts in this chapter highlight becomes clear: An adjustment to views of racial essentialism is necessary to avoid continuing the cycle of oppression currently affecting many peoples of color in Eurowestern cultures.

CHAPTER 3

The Apocalypse Has Already Come
Post-Apocalyptic Landscapes

In "Reading Hurricane Katrina: Race, Class, and the Biopolitics of Disposability," Henry A. Giroux argues that the aftermath of Hurricane Katrina exposed a "biopolitics of disposability," a term that builds on Michel Foucault's concept of "bio-power"[1] to explain how the results of poverty are compounded for peoples of color by governmental and public reaction to crisis, particularly through stereotyped media coverage of Black peoples as criminals:

> It must be noted that there is more at stake here than the resurgence of old-style racism; there is the recognition that some groups have the power to protect themselves from such stereotypes and others do not, and for those who do not—especially poor blacks—racist myths have a way of producing precise, if not deadly, material consequences. Given the public's preoccupation with violence and safety, crime and terror merge in the all-too-familiar equation of black culture with the culture of criminality, and images of poor

---

1. In "Right of Death and Power over Life," Michel Foucault explains the concept of bio-power, a term he creates to explain the regulation of the human body in politics. Foucault then moves to a discussion of modern government and the notion of biopolitics, noting that the system of sovereign rule has been "supplanted by the administration of bodies and the calculated management of life" (262).

blacks are made indistinguishable from images of crime and violence. . . . This [criminalization] becomes particularly dangerous in a democracy when paramilitary or military organisations gain their legitimacy increasingly from an appeal to fear and terror, prompted largely by the presence of those racialized and class-specific groups considered both dangerous and disposable. (Giroux 176–77)

The authors discussed in this chapter address this tension between peoples of color as "both dangerous and disposable" through the use of post-apocalyptic landscapes, one of the most recognizable tropes of science fiction. Science fiction and fantasy texts ranging from Mary Shelley's *The Last Man* (1826) to screen-adapted popular works such as *World War Z* (2006) and *The Hunger Games* (2008–10) portray the end of the world as an unforgiving environment where only exceptional white humans can survive. As authors and scholars begin to consider what role race plays in the end-of-the-world scenario, contemporary authors of color are writing post-apocalyptic works that center the narrative voices of peoples of color. As Lavender III notes in the introduction to *Black and Brown Planets: The Politics of Race in Science Fiction* (2014), in order to move forward to a more racially inclusive science fiction, authors and critics must "[lift] blacks, indigenous peoples, and Latinos out from the background of this historically white genre" (6). The works discussed in this chapter are a small sample of the contemporary voices of color emerging in post-apocalyptic science fiction.

Each of the authors discussed writes their story from the perspective of a character of color to address the tensions of living in a post-apocalyptic world that is still predominantly defined by white, Eurowestern culture. The characters in Sabrina Vourvoulias's *Ink* (2012) and Gabby Rivera's "1.0" (2019) live under constant surveillance by the state, which utilizes narratives of emergency to justify the denial of rights to specific groups. Stripping these peoples of their rights as citizens allows the state to use their bodies for labor and reproduction and dispose of them once they are no longer useful. Both pieces also use the theme of sickness, real and imagined, to comment on the portrayal of peoples of color as contaminating. The contemporary zombie apocalypse narratives of Colson Whitehead's *Zone One: A Novel* (2011) and Ling Ma's *Severance* (2018) speak to the dangers of capitalism in a nod to George Romero's classic horror film *Dawn of the Dead* (1978), but they also specifically address the ways that people of color are often forced to assimilate to white Eurowestern cultural beliefs for survival.[2] The main characters

---

2. One example of contemporary forced assimilation is the conversation surrounding #BlackInTheIvory. Many Black US academics in 2020 used this hashtag to discuss

of these texts downplay their abilities and overlook racist and sexist behaviors to appease the white majority. The zombie-like figures in Whitehead's and Ma's works also speak to Eurowestern fear of racial contamination. All of the texts in this chapter challenge the notion that in the face of disaster, humans will put aside racist ideologies and work together for the good of humanity. However, these texts also demonstrate the resilience of peoples of color who have collectively survived centuries of racism and violence.

Ink and "1.0": Narratives of Citizenship and Surveillance

Surveillance of Black and brown bodies and narratives of contamination both connect to belief in the superiority of Eurowestern "civilization" and the desire to exploit peoples of color to gain land and other natural resources. Eurowestern colonizers justified their colonization of peoples of color by employing a rhetoric of criminality. Samson explains that in nineteenth-century India, the British colonial government created laws based on the argument that certain races and ethnicities were more prone to criminal behaviors:

> Later on, legislation such as the Criminal Tribes Act of 1911 would classify particular ethnic groups as possessing inherently criminal cultures, authorising the jailing of individuals simply for belonging to one or other of the so-called "criminal castes." This type of interpretation was similar to that involving "martial races." Both were part of a process in which Europeans assumed the right to define various groups, to codify them using names of their own choosing, creating hierarchies in which some groups were favoured over others. Anthropological speculation could both explain and justify imperial expansion and control. (Samson 71)

Colonizers were thus able to use the science of their times to label specific peoples of color as criminal by nature. The label of "criminal" allowed colonizers to justify the control and containment of specific ethnic groups and the denial of the privileges of full citizenship to these groups. The results of criminalizing peoples of color in colonial times can currently be seen in contemporary narratives in the US and other Eurowestern nations address-

---

how they were forced to assimilate to their predominantly white programs and workplaces and the negative backlash associated with refusing to do so.

ing police brutality against peoples of color as well as current immigration narratives depicting refugees of color as a contaminating, criminal force.[3]

One tool governments use to subvert legality against specific groups of peoples within a nation-state is the invocation of a "state of emergency," or a situation in which the government suspends regular protocol for access to permissions and funds, thereby allowing for a prompt response in emergency situations, such as natural disasters. States of emergency are designed to be used only when local and national governments are facing an "imminent threat" to its citizens (Barber). However, Giroux argues that the US employs a "permanent state of emergency" as a tool for privileging some lives over others, mainly based on racial and class factors (181). Though Giroux was writing about the Bush administration, the same rhetoric is consistently being used today by the Trump administration to justify the criminalization of Latin American and Central American asylum seekers and aggressive military and economic practices in the Middle East and Asia.[4] Such rhetoric is also being employed by UK government officials to discuss the influx of refugees from Syria and Iran.[5] Eurowestern governments' invocation of permanent states of emergency have the potential to create oppressive government systems that depend on the criminalization of certain citizens and the use of fearful rhetoric against those citizens to maintain its power. Vourvoulias and Rivera each imagine such a future in their post-apocalyptic writings.

Sabrina Vourvoulias's *Ink* and Gabby Rivera's "1.0" discuss the criminalization and detainment of peoples of color in their stories to highlight how Eurowestern governments employ narratives of emergency to justify control and detainment of specific peoples of color. *Ink* is set in a near-future US where all immigrants and permanent residents are branded with a tattoo that literally marks their immigration status in US society. The lowest people in this system have black tattoos; these peoples are temporary

---

3. For a more detailed explanation of the criminalization of peoples of color in the US, see D. Marvin Jones's *Dangerous Spaces: Beyond the Racial Profile* (2016), Tanya Maria Golash-Boza's *Immigration Nation: Raids, Detentions, and Deportations in Post 911 America* (2011), and Patrick J. Buchanan's *State of Emergency: The Third World Invasion and Conquest of America* (2006).

4. See *The Washington Post* (2019), "Trump's most insulting—and violent—language is often reserved for immigrants"; *The Guardian* (2018) "US imposes sanctions on China, stoking fear of trade war"; and *NPR* (2020), "Trump administration announces more economic sanctions against Iran."

5. See *BBC News* (2018), "Chanel migrants: Home secretary declares major incident"; and *New York Times* (2019), "Brexit and the U.S. shutdown: Two governments in paralysis." .

laborers devoid of any privileges of citizenship. All marked peoples are labeled "inks," and, as Vourvoulias's story progresses, the government systematically strips inks of more and more rights until the country reaches a moral breaking point after being confronted with pictures of ink children in shackles. *Ink* is a blueprint for "the legislative steps by which democracy is transformed into totalitarianism, steps that initially target only the most marginalized so that society slowly reaches the boiling point without most of the frogs recognizing that the pot is no longer safe" ("Don't").

Gabby Rivera's "1.0" begins in a world where IMBALANCE, "a sentient bacterium that [preys] on white-supremacist greed," has ravaged the planet, killing off 40 percent of the world's population and affecting "areas that never even knew of inconvenience let alone catastrophe" (228, 232). One effect of the bacterium is that humans can no longer procreate.[6] So when Mala Lafayette-Santana and her partner Orion conceive, they hide this fact for as long as possible to keep from being noticed by the oppressive Federation that monitors the lives of all citizens. Once discovered, they find their every move and word being controlled by the Federation, a government structure desperate to use Mala and Orion's pregnancy to sell its citizens a narrative of hope. Mala and Orion eventually go on the run to avoid having their baby consumed by the Federation and its citizens. Rivera proves in "0.1" that even when white supremacy has been eradicated by a sentient virus, governments may still employ state-of-emergency rhetoric to justify the detaining of specific individuals for the good of society.

Both texts create narratives where peoples of color are labeled as unfit or criminal and, as a result, are stripped of citizenship rights and subjected to detention or extreme surveillance. The label "ink" allows the US government in Vourvoulias's narrative to create laws that first dehumanize ink immigrants and citizens alike, leaving them open to exploitation and violence, and eventually criminalize inks through narratives of illness. Mari is a

---

6. It is worth noting that in Michel Foucault's discussions in *Society Must Be Defended: Lectures at the Collège de France, 1975–1976,* he discusses the shift in thinking about illness from isolated incidents to global epidemics, which he links to issues of capitalism and biopolitics: "These were illnesses that were difficult to eradicate and that were not regarded as epidemics that caused more frequent deaths, but as permanent factors which—and that is how they were dealt with—sapped the population's strength, shortened the working week, wasted energy, and cost money, both because they led to a fall in production and because treating them was expensive. In a word, illness as phenomenon affecting a population" (243–44). Rivera plays with the idea of the "cost" of the epidemic by assigning a specific percentage to the total deaths and by discussing Mala's more personal grief over the loss of her parents. In the world of "1.0," all humans have become a commodity because of the decline in population and issues of infertility caused by the virus.

citizen, yet because her mother was Guatemalan, she is forced to wear a blue tattoo marking her as a permanent resident. Her tattoo makes her a mark for ink trackers, or citizens who have taken it upon themselves to deport inks. The trackers are similar to the border vigilantes who police the US-Mexico border. Mari attempts to enforce her citizenship when she shows the trackers her blue tattoo, but the trackers dismiss her tattoo as fake. When she tells the head tracker that she is as American as he is, he states, "You don't see me having to wear a tattoo, do you? So not quite as American" (81). The trackers view her tattoo as marking her as less than human; while one tracker views her with disgust, stating, "I don't fuck Ink" (87), another tracker views her as available for consumption and rapes her (90). Like many slaves in Eurowestern colonies, Mari is dehumanized by the trackers to justify their violence. The trackers eventually let Mari go after they discover that her tattoo is real, but the lead tracker also makes a point to show her that the other captured inks have fake black tattoos. The trackers use this fact to justify their violence against all inks, using a rhetoric of fairness and national security to justify "dumping" the ink children and Mari's injured friend in the Canadian wilderness where they will all likely die. Vourvoulias writes this scene to show the humanity of the captured inks, women and children who are trying to survive a cruel system that has labeled them as unworthy and criminal. The current state of immigration at the US-Mexico border clearly demonstrates the rhetoric of criminalization the US government employs to justify violence; the Trump administration has separated and detained more than 5,400 families after this administration adopted a "zero tolerance" immigration policy in 2018 which labeled all immigrants and asylum seekers coming from Mexico and other Central/Latin American countries as breaking US laws ("More"). The Trump administration employed a rhetoric of national emergency and narratives of white supremacy to justify the denial of rights to specific populations of color. The fact that public outrage was not strong enough to deter this new immigration policy demonstrates that many citizens in Eurowestern countries are willing to accept the suspension of rights for peoples they view as "other." *Ink* shows how Mari's experiences of detainment and violence, common for many Latinx asylum seekers and citizens, can quickly escalate to the detainment of all peoples the government views as dangerous to national security.

In "1.0," Rivera uses the term "free" to create irony-filled labels of citizenship. Mala and Orion live within the "Federation of Free Peoples," a government created by three queer Black children of a Nuyorican government official. Key Desmond and his twin siblings, Ayima and Trent, create the Federation to be a space of shared resources and compassion for all:

No longer divided by borders and politics, we insisted on being Free People. Everyone who agreed on their own, without coercion or blackmail, signed our pact. Formally known as the 2066 Pact of the Free Peoples. It was originally a pledge between me and the twins. We promised each other compassion, the type that shares food, resources, and provides care for all. (237)

The irony in the name "Free Peoples" is referenced throughout the narrative: first, when Mala and Orion fear that the Federation will "keep hold of us forever" (228), and later, when the Federation begins to control the narrative of the birth of "Offspring 1," nicknamed "Baby Free" by Federation citizens (231). The Federation Care Team coaches Mala on which details of the birth of her child are "appropriate for mass consumption" and plans to broadcast the birth of the child for all citizens to watch. Mala describes the desires of Federation peoples to consume the story of Baby Free as increasingly invasive:

They wanted Orion Lafayette-Santana, our baby—the one the Feds called 0.1, the one the people nicknamed "Baby Free"—and me, Mala Amelia Santana; they wanted every second of the new world growing inside of Orion. The Federation encouraged me to consider the feelings of the entirety of Free Peoples and what a birth meant to our planet.

Something had to give, and as hard as I tried, it had to be us. And so I offered a tiny piece of us to the world. (231)

The Federation is able to control its population through the influence of mass media; the story of Baby Free becomes a product for consumption in the same way that advertisers convince consumers to buy into specific lifestyles or products.[7] It is "selling" a story of hope, but to succeed in its message, the Federation must execute control over the peoples involved. At first, the Federation sequesters Mala and Orion; when they allow them to return home because of public protest, they continue to monitor them. The Federation is also monitoring every one of its citizens, a fact that readers discover when Mala reveals that the personal information she shares with Federation citizens boosted the "Global Happiness Meter" by 48 percent (232). Rivera's narrative exposes the ways in which the Federation citizens give up their privacy and freedom for the protection and resources the Federation sup-

---

7. For more information on the influence of consumer capitalism, see Jess Benhabib and Alberto Bisin's "Advertising, Mass Consumption and Capitalism" (2002), http://www.econ.nyu.edu/user/benhabib/pomo10.pdf.

plies. "0.1" references contemporary arguments surrounding government surveillance and the ways this monitoring suspends citizens' right to privacy in the interest of national security.[8]

Rivera's choice to use the descriptor "free" to describe the citizens of her post-apocalyptic narrative also speaks to the irony of concepts of "freedom" for peoples of color in Eurowestern countries. D. Marvin Jones explains that in the nineteenth century, the concept of the "free black" created a sense of anxiety for US slave-owning states like South Carolina, where white slave owners were outnumbered by black slaves. The result of this racial anxiety was the creation of laws that criminalized all Black peoples and created "an illicit linkage between race and crime, skin color (appearance) and social disorder." (40). Such laws allowed white citizens to keep Black peoples, free and slave, under control either on plantations or in jail. Either way, the result was control through surveillance and containment, which Jones connects to the idea of a "police regime":

> At the root of the injustice here is this: slavery itself is a police regime. A police regime is a regime of "law" that comes into being when a society feels it is in a state of siege. All individual civil rights are suspended or simply ignored. A police regime does not focus on individuals at all. The goal of a police regime is to control dangerous populations. The issue in each individual's case is whether they are a member of the class to be controlled. (40)

In Rivera's work, race and sexuality are not entirely the defining factors in the Federation's decision to limit their rights as citizens; however, the fact that the main characters are both queer women of color may make it easier for the Federation to classify them as "dangerous" or unfit and therefore liable to increased surveillance. Rivera takes the concept of the police regime to its extreme by creating a society where the virus IMBALANCE has created a permanent state of emergency, one which allows for the surveillance and control of all "free" citizens in an attempt to bring "order" back to a society that has lost 40 percent of the world's population.

When Mala and Orion flee from Federation control, Key describes the Federation reaction as one of fear and anxiety:

---

8. For more insight into the relationship between national security and privacy, see Ido Sivan-Sevilla's "Complementaries and Contradictions: National Security and Privacy Risks in U.S. Federal Policy, 1968–2018" (2019).

Baby Free must survive. But first they had to be born. And, dammit, there'd been a whole plan, developed in conjunction with the birth family and the Federation. The entire Federation was predicated on commitment to agreements, and if at the first sign of new-ness that commitment faltered, well then, how? How were we supposed to remain calm and not start an inter-Federation hunt for 1.0?

HOW? (239)

In this scene, Key describes a precarious government system where the defiance of two citizens has the ability to dismantle the entire system. His anxiety echoes the anxiety of slaveholders, who limited slaves' access to information and ability to travel in an attempt to limit uprisings. Jones explains that white anxiety after the abolishment of slavery has created a more subtle surveillance of Black bodies that includes racial profiling, stop-and-frisk programs, and the labeling of urban "ghettos" as high-crime areas (41–50). Though he acknowledges that the current state of racial affairs is better than slavery, his contemporary examples of white racial anxiety leading to the surveillance and criminalization of populations of color in Euro-western countries demonstrates how peoples of color in these countries have never been truly "free." Rivera goes further and strips her future society of narratives of white supremacy to argue that even in a "race blind" future, humans will continue to find ways to alleviate public anxiety through the control and surveillance of specific populations.

Ink and "1.0" both utilize pregnancy narratives to address the effects of surveillance and criminalization of peoples of color on their children. Mitchell Travis notes in "We're All Infected: Legal Personhood, Bare Life, and The Walking Dead" (2015) that pregnancy often results in women being legally declared "unfit" or in a suspension of their legal status as people/citizens if the state decides that their decisions are not in the best interest of the fetus, whose life takes precedence (791). The many legal arguments surrounding abortion also demonstrate the global conversations surrounding pregnancy and women's rights. These legal conversations demonstrate how pregnancy makes women even more vulnerable to being labeled as unfit to exercise their rights as citizens.[9] Ideals of fertility and citizenship have also been linked in Eurowestern cultures for centuries through histories of colonization. Eurowestern countries have frequently attempted to control the fertility and reproduction of peoples of color, who were labeled as either breeding

---

9. See Jacqui Wise's "Global Abortion Rate Stalls while Proportion of Unsafe Abortions Rises" (2012) and Allotey-Reidpath, et al., "Nine Months a Slave: When Pregnancy Is Involuntary Servitude to a Foetus" (2018).

animals or unfit to reproduce, through forced breeding of slaves, eugenics projects, and sterilization. Sasha Turner notes in *Contested Bodies: Pregnancy, Childrearing and Slavery in Jamaica* (2017) that Eurowestern slaveowners began buying young slave women to breed with their mostly male slave population in the late eighteenth and early nineteenth centuries because of new restrictions on the importation of African slaves. To curtail abolitionist narratives of sexual exploitation, the slave owners furthered a narrative of slaves being naturally promiscuous and licentious (64–65). By criminalizing slave women, slaveowners were able to strip them of their humanity and justify rape and enforced breeding. *Ink* and "1.0" make pregnancy a central part of their narratives to demonstrate how pregnancy can affect women's ability to exercise their rights as citizens and to highlight how these issues are compounded for women of color.

Many women of color in Eurowestern countries also find that birthright citizenship is not guaranteed for their children. The continually shifting policies on citizenship for children born to US citizens abroad highlights the ways Eurowestern governments can choose to deny birthright citizenship to peoples of color by linking citizenship to "responsible" behavior, particularly the heteronormative ideal of marriage: "Heightened citizenship guidelines for the out-of-wedlock children of US national fathers, therefore, allow biology and gendered stereotypes about parenting to become proxies for xenophobia, despite the children's and fathers' longstanding residency and social ties to the United States. . . . these decisions make explicit how national borders are literally mapped onto women's bodies" (Oliviero 12). In *Ink*, this mapping is literal as Mari's blue residency tattoo becomes a brand that jeopardizes her son, whose father, Finn, is a white, male citizen. Finn's citizenship, however, is not enough to save his future child from ink laws, even if he marries Mari; in the text, Finn's sister reminds him of this fact, stating, "What happens if you get married, have kids? Have you thought what it'd be like to see your children tattooed and monitored like all the other inks? Because at a quarter ink, they'd still be subject to it" (63). When Finn dies, his obituary lists him as a single father and names his sister, Francine, as guardian to his son, Gus, in an effort to save Gus from being tattooed (394). However, if the government discovers his marriage or that Mari is Gus's mother, Gus will be subject to ink laws. The example of Finn and Mari's relationship links ink status to past US racial laws, such as the "one-drop rule," which excluded African Americans from full citizenship status in the early twentieth century.

When Mari is eventually placed in an "inkatorium," a detention facility that is disguised as a public health center, Gus is taken from her and adopted by citizens. Eventually, Mari and Finn's friend, Abby, hacks the paperwork on Gus's adoption, and Finn is able to regain custody of his son. However, Oliviero explains that the practice of adopting out the children of immigrants and asylum seekers is not uncommon for the children of undocumented peoples in the US:

> The detention of parents often leads to the preliminary placement of children in foster care, and removal processes conflict with child social-welfare assessments. Parents frequently lack counsel and are commonly relocated to detention facilities without adequate communication to lawyers or child welfare advocates. These communication barriers combine with the physical separation created by detention to impede parents' ability to attend court dates and otherwise meet requirements to regain custody of their children. The combined obstacles therefore increase the likelihood that parental rights will be terminated and children will be adopted—thus making family fragmentation permanent. (17)

Mari's parental rights are superseded by the government's need to label her as dangerous and contaminating. Oliverio describes this situation as "a familial state of emergency" and explains, "The social, economic, and emotional vulnerabilities created by family separation—a familial state of emergency—are dismissed as accepted casualties of the immigration state of emergency" (17). The fact that the inkatoriums are making a profit from selling ink babies to rich families that can afford to falsify citizenship paperwork demonstrates that the officials in charge of the inkatoriums understand that the inks are not a public health risk, yet they are still willing to use the national emergency rhetoric for profit. Vourvoulias uses an example of extreme governmental control to highlight the real horrors being faced by peoples of color seeking asylum and citizenship in Eurowestern nations. *Ink* uses a fictional dystopic narrative to demonstrate the potential results of labeling immigrants and asylum seekers as imminent threats to justify a continued state of emergency.

"0.1" utilizes its pregnancy narrative and post-apocalyptic setting to highlight how peoples of color, particularly those who do not adhere to the state-sanctioned heterosexual narrative for families, find themselves struggling to assert their familial and citizenship rights. LGBTQ couples who cannot marry find themselves subject to restrictions on citizenship for children born outside the US. Tanya Maria Golash-Boza also notes that US immigration laws often force families of color to choose between citizenship and family unity. She explains that this choice creates a tension between "human rights and citizenship rights" and keeps many citizens of color from being able to enjoy "full citizenship," which she defines as "feeling a sense of belonging" and "the realization of civil, political, social, and cultural rights" (112). Oliverio notes that for LGBTQ peoples, the US government's privileging of heteronormative marriage and families creates additional barriers to belonging. As a result, LGBTQ peoples and families find themselves cast as "undeserving, or at the very least illegible" in the consciousness of their own government (21). This status often leads to LGBTQ peoples facing barriers to the creation and maintenance of their family unit, which includes marriage recognition, adoption, and access to healthcare benefits for spouses/children.[10]

The precariousness nature of the post-apocalyptic setting also gives Rivera a space to explore the connections between citizenship and family agency for LGBTQ peoples of color. Initially, the Federation quarantines Mala and Orion to "protect" their family unit. Key, a federation official, explains that this decision created the first "sequestering" of a Free person (member of the Federation) since IMBALANCE (240). Eventually, the Free Mothers, a citizens'-rights group, begin advocating for the release of Mala and Orion because their being held violates their right to privacy. Key cannot understand why the group is being so adamant; when confronted with protesters, he states, "Their signs made it seem as if chaos should be honored, as if the life of [B]aby Free should be left to fate, all things that kept me lying awake at night mourning a generation that hadn't been born yet and could possibly die if we didn't intervene" (240). Although Key is a queer man of color working to create an equitable government, he still gives in to fear and reverts to a rhetoric of emergency to justify the Federation's decision to sequester citizens. His use of the words "chaos" and "fate" creates a sense of danger and uncertainty while also casting Mala and Orion as unfit to make parental decisions for their unborn child. Key feels that the Federation has the right to intervene to protect the safety of the child. These ideas echo US deportation rulings, which often claim to be acting in the interest of protecting children while also simultaneously undermining familial unity (Oliverio 14). Key further notes that the Federation has "bargained for the rights to the birth," which he describes as the right to broadcast the birth at a secure Federation location (241). However, Mari and Orion's decision to become fugitives and their fear that the Federation would "keep hold of them forever" demonstrates that Key and other Federation officials likely

---

10. For examples of discrimination against LGBTQ families see Kari M. Haines, et al., "'Not a Real Family': Microaggressions Directed toward LGBTQ Families" (2018).

have the ability to detain Mala, Orion, and the baby indefinitely, a direct violation of their rights, in the interest of national security (228). The Federation is not interested in seeing Mala and Orion as individuals, and it is also not taking into account that they may want to make familial decisions that differ from the Federation's guidelines for the promotion of health and well-being. The fact that the Federation labels them as fugitives once they stop agreeing to Key's terms speaks to the narrative of marking peoples of color as criminal to alleviate the fear of the majority.

Rivera utilizes the invocation of the Free Mother's prayer (recited twice in "1.0") to advocate for the protection of all families. One of the lines of this prayer states, "Bless all families in spirit and reality. For all deserve to be fed, cared for, raised to thrive. Provided with housing and education, embraced as full and free people" (234, 246). Rivera's use of the words "full and free people" speaks to the citizenship challenges peoples of color still face in Eurowestern countries. Because peoples of color have not yet achieved "full" citizenship, these peoples and their families will be similarly limited in a governmental system that has the discretion to execute and enforce laws on a case-by-case basis. Golash-Boza uses the example of prosecutorial discretion in Deferred Action for Childhood Arrivals (DACA) cases to explain how Eurowestern governments categorize immigrants as both exceptional and criminal:

> Prosecutorial discretion and DACA generate the needed flexibility to alleviate some of the vulnerabilities that our immigration laws create for migrants. Their relief, however, recreates binaries of redeemable and criminal noncitizens. Such dichotomies reflect the exceptionalist thinking within immigration law and its state of emergency presumptions. An American citizenry that imagines itself to be a diverse nation of immigrants, although from its founding has viewed some migrants as a source of national threat, positions immigrants as both external to, and defining of, its national body-politic. The uncertain legal situation created by discretionary relief and DACA reflects this liminality. (22)

The US government reserves the right to create, rescind, and enforce immigration laws as they see fit, and the rules frequently change according to which administration is in power. The Trump administration's decision to end DACA in 2017, which was overturned by the Supreme Court in 2020, demonstrates the government's power to decide who is worthy of citizenship. The US Citizenship and Immigration Services website enforces the "discretionary" nature of immigration law in its statement about DACA:

Deferred action is a discretionary determination to defer a removal action of an individual as an act of prosecutorial discretion. Further, deferred action under DACA does not confer legal status upon an individual and may be terminated at any time, with or without a Notice of Intent to Terminate, at DHS's discretion. ("Deferred")

The discretionary nature of DACA allows the government to decide which people get to enjoy full citizenship while simultaneously labeling others as dangerous and undeserving. The fact that the government can terminate the agreement at any time leaves many families of color living in a constant state of anxiety. White Eurowestern fear of the other as contaminating is translated into laws that leave undocumented immigrants with little hope of maintaining family unity.

The fact that the Federation labels Mala and Orion's baby "Baby Free" while they simultaneously restrict their family's rights speaks to the binary of a "nation of immigrants" that labels some immigrants as exceptional additions and others as criminal trespassers. If, as Golash-Boza argues, full citizenship entails both the enforcement of rights and a sense of belonging to one's country, peoples of color, citizen and immigrant, in Eurowestern countries will never be free to enjoy full citizenship without the elimination of racist ideologies. Rivera enforces this idea in "1.0" when Mala states that her parents killed themselves because "IMBALANCE also killed the American Dream they'd believed in all their lives. It was too much" (229). Mala's parents viewed themselves as citizens, but IMBALANCE taught them that the majority of their business associates and friends did not view them as equal human beings. Rivera uses Mala's explanation to point out the hypocrisy of the American Dream, which advocates for immigrants to assimilate and achieve success through hard work, yet also often denies these peoples full citizenship and equal opportunity. DACA recipients, often referred to as "Dreamers," are currently facing the possibility that the only country they know may choose to label them as trespassers and deport them without notice or mercy. "1.0" exposes the hypocrisy underlying the "American Dream" and "Land of the Free" US mythology, where US immigrants and citizens of color are extended legal rights that can be circumvented at any time through prosecutorial discretion.

Rivera and Vourvoulias each reference Indigenous cultural values and practices as a potential solution to the post-apocalyptic effects of racism present in their works. Rivera's choice to refer to the sentient virus that destroys white supremacy as "IMBALANCE" connects to certain Indigenous cultures' beliefs that balance between all living beings on the planet is necessary for the survival of all species. Grace L. Dillon (Anishinaabe) notes that the concept of imbalance is frequently found in Indigenous post-apocalyptic writing:

> Native Apocalypse is really that state of imbalance, often perpetuated by "terminal creeds," the ideologies that Gerald Vizenor warns against in advocating survivance in the face of invisibility. Imbalance further implies a state of extremes, but within those extremes lies a middle ground and the seeds of bimaadiziwin, the state of balance, one of difference and provisionality, a condition of resistance and survival. ("Imagining" 9–10)

Dillon's reference to Gerald Vizenor's (Anishinaabe) theory of survivance[11] highlights the choices and compromises Indigenous peoples have had to make to survive in a "post-Native Apocalypse" environment (10). Rivera's work demonstrates the similarities between the treatment of immigrant and Indigenous cultures,[12] who have each been subjected to narratives of contamination, criminality, and disposability in the histories of many Eurowestern nations. "1.0" makes it clear that overcoming "IMBALANCE" will involve Eurowestern countries acceptance of previously marginalized peoples, particularly LGBTQ peoples and peoples of color.

The concept of restoring balance through acceptance is also located in George Manuel (Shuswap) and Michael Poslun's vision of a "Fourth World" in *The Fourth World: An Indian Reality* (1974, reprinted in 2019).[13] Manuel and Poslun argue in this work that European colonizers and Indigenous peoples worldwide will need to overcome a history of violence and create a new, decolonized society. They explain:

> We cannot become equal members in *your* society. We can become a member of a new society in which everyone chooses to share. But that cannot happen until you begin to reconsider and reformulate your understanding, and your view of the world, as we have begun to reformulate ours. (location 4778, par. 5)

---

11. See Vizenor's *Survivance: Narratives of Native Presence* (2008).
12. Guillermo Gómez-Peña explains the connections between Indigenous and diasporic communities and these groups' relation to Fourth World Theory in *The New World Border: Prophecies, Poems & Loqueras for the End of the Century* (1996).
13. See a more detailed explanation of Fourth World Theory and Indigenous post-apocalyptic literature in my article "Interplanetary Diaspora and Fourth World Representation in Celu Amberstone's 'Refugees'" (2017).

Manuel and Poslun argue that as long as white citizens hold the majority of power in a Eurowestern nation, peoples of color will continue to suffer from the systemic effects of racism. What is needed is a new world where all peoples work together to build equality into their cultures and societies. Here is where science fiction can make an invaluable impact; Dillon explains that works of Indigenous futurisms, including Indigenous science fiction,[14] can aid decolonization efforts by helping authors and readers visualize what a decolonized world could look like:

> It might go without saying that all forms of Indigenous futurisms are narratives of *biskaabiiyang,* an Anishinaabemowin word connoting the process of "returning to ourselves," which involves discovering how personally one is affected by colonization, discarding the emotional and psychological baggage carried from its impact, and recovering ancestral traditions in order to adapt in our post-Native Apocalypse world. This process is often called "decolonization," and as Linda Tuhiwai Smith (Maori) explains, it requires *changing* rather than *imitating* Eurowestern concepts. ("Imagining" 10, emphasis in original)

Peoples of color have suffered for centuries from the racism of European and Eurowestern colonizers. Science fiction is one avenue where authors can highlight the effects of these views by creating dystopic or post-apocalyptic worlds where the effects of racism have become even more extreme. However, science fiction also offers a space for imagining the Fourth World, a world where all peoples would truly be equal, where no life is viewed as disposable, and where all peoples would enjoy the advantages of full citizenship.

Vourvoulias and Rivera each provide hope for the eventual creation of a Fourth World at the end of their works. In *Ink,* public outcry at televised footage of ink children being deported in shackles, heightened by a picture of Mari's that Finn's editor runs on the front page of the Hastings *Gazette,* finally causes state and federal politicians to begin creating "non-compliance and ink restoration laws" that mark the beginning of restored humanity for ink peoples. Mari explains, however, that the laws will not create peace for inks:

---

14. The definitions of Indigenous Futurisms and Indigenous science fiction are often used interchangeably; however, Elizabeth LaPensée (Anishinaabe) explains in "Indigenous Futurisms in Games" (2020) that Indigenous Futurisms can take "many forms in areas of focus as well as types of expression" ("Indigenous").

> The "Ink Incidents," as our undeclared war comes to be called, limps along. . . . The faces at the top switch, the circumstances morph, and the words start seeming less like acid on broken skin. But the heart changes more slowly, and it'll be years before we know peace or understand the scope of our losses. (442–43)

The consequences Mari describes echo the language of decolonization practices and the evocation of the Fourth World. This scene argues that changing laws is not enough to overcome the effects of racism in Euro-western countries; each person must truly be open to changing their views of othered peoples of color to effect lasting change. Conversely, the inks must also be willing to forge a new relationship with their former colonizers, a feat that can be accomplished only through assessment of loss and the acknowledgement of victims' accounts.

Rivera creates a scene at the end of "1.0" where Key and his siblings change their views about the commodification of Baby Free. As the baby is born, they storm into the room, set to detain Mala, Orion, and the baby. However, once they see the baby in the flesh, crying and alive, Key and his siblings begin to see the baby and her parents as individuals. They recite the Free Mothers' Prayer together, an experience Rivera describes as "a meditation on survival" (244). Key calls off the manhunt, which places his position of authority at risk with other Federation officials who threaten to overthrow him. The group is all set to help Mala and Orion escape when Trent checks her phone and discovers that another pregnancy has occurred. This discovery takes the pressure off Mala and Orion and allows them to return to their lives. In "1.0," Rivera gives an example of the change of heart Vourvoulias calls for in *Ink*. Everyone in the room, Federation officials, the Lafayette-Santana family, and their doula, are each committed to upholding the tenets of the prayer that call for the protection of life and the fair treatment of all families. Rivera writes this scene to help readers visualize the possibilities available when governments treat all peoples as individuals deserving of equal rights and freedoms.

Ink concludes with a scene that goes beyond institutional change and highlights the importance of decolonizing nations by hearing and honoring the stories of the victims of colonization, particularly those of Indigenous peoples. Mari returns to the Guatemalan village where she was born. There, she encounters the twinned animal spirits of the massacred villagers. Her animal twin tells her *"you're not here to tell stories . . . but to listen to them"* (460, original italics). Mari is tasked with hearing the forgotten stories of not just her family, but every member of the village who died in "the undeclared war" resulting from Spanish colonization, as well as the stories of the kaibiles, dwarfs that serve the evil of the world. As Mari hears the stories of evil, she states, "As much as I'd like to set those takes aside, I cannot. Every story holds some small fragment of what is true, a trace of spirit that gives us life" (461). Vourvoulias writes this scene as a guide for decolonization. Mari is a member of the community who takes on the responsibility and emotional labor of bearing witness to the stories of her peoples. She is not imposing her own narrative on the site; instead, she helps her peoples find peace by hearing and remembering their stories. Her efforts are similar to those of Indigenous cultures trying to document and revitalize their cultural stories and practices. Decolonization efforts are therefore a possible solution to the biopolitics of disposability. Documenting the stories of peoples of color and exposing systemic racism in Eurowestern countries helps combat narratives of peoples of color as criminal. Making the stories of peoples of color public also ensures that these people become less disposable. Governments cannot quietly erase history if the public has knowledge of past injustices.

Many peoples of color living in Eurowestern countries are present because of a history of colonization. Vine Deloria Jr. explains in the introduction to the reprinted edition of *The Fourth World* that as George Manuel, an Indigenous activist and coauthor of this text, spoke with Indigenous peoples of New Zealand, Australia, and Africa, he found similar narratives of racism that affected these groups' ability to exercise their legal rights and continue their cultural traditions (location 126, par. 2). Racism stemming from colonial rule continues to affect peoples of color in Eurowestern countries worldwide, whether immigrant or citizen. Vourvoulias and Rivera's dystopic and post-apocalyptic works challenge narratives of peoples of color as criminal peoples unfit for citizenship. Their works speak to the many authors, critics, and activists worldwide calling for an end to the narratives of racism that treat peoples of color as both an immediate threat and a disposable commodity.

Zone One and *Severance*: Zombie Novels as the Final State of Emergency

While Vourvoulias and Rivera attempt to resolve the racist states of emergency underlying their dystopic and post-apocalyptic narratives, both Whitehead and Ma push this narrative to the brink of human extinction to highlight the adaptability and resilience of peoples of color. The zombie is not only a disposable other; it is one that can be killed without reason or regret. As such, it is the truest representation of Giorgio Agamben's concept of *"homo sacer* (sacred man), who *may be killed and yet not sacrificed"* (8, original italics).[15] Agamben's figure of a man existing outside of politics is frequently applied to peoples of color and used to explain the justifications of Eurowestern governments' decisions to withhold aid to peoples of color both within and outside Eurowestern nations. Giroux and Gerry Canavan each note that in times of natural disaster (Hurricane Katrina and the 2010 Haitian earthquake), narratives of criminalization of Black peoples allowed the US to justify allocating funds away from humanitarian aid and toward national security efforts (Giroux 176; Canavan 448). The victims of these natural disasters, legally stripped of their right to aid and left to die, become examples of bare life. Like many science fiction figures, including aliens and cyborgs, zombies make racial conversations about bare life literal. Instead of passively killing peoples of color by denying assistance to those who cannot afford to evacuate disaster zones, people regard zombies as figures that can be killed in the open because they are no longer considered to be "human" or "alive." Canavan notes that contemporary zombie narratives thus become a way for Eurowestern cultures to fantasize about violence against the racial other, a desire born of the racial views expressed through colonization, without directly engaging with the reality and effects of this violence on the racialized other (439). Many contemporary zombie science fiction narratives become an outlet for the racial anxiety of white peoples who feel overwhelmed by the growing number of peoples of color in Eurowestern countries; however, Whitehead's and Ma's novels demonstrate the opposing side of this narrative: the anxiety of peoples of color who have to navigate racism to avoid becoming the object of white anxiety.

One popular theme in contemporary zombie apocalypse narratives is the effects of capitalism. Canavan explains:

> When our computers are compromised by hackers or viruses, they become zombie computers, and when our financial institutions fail, it is because they are zombie banks. Remorselessly consuming everything in their path, zombies leave nothing in their wake besides endless copies of themselves,

---

15. I am not the first scholar to make the connection between the zombie figure and bare life. Gerry Canavan makes several references to Agamben's theory in "'We Are the Walking Dead': Race, Time, and Survival in Zombie Narrative" (2010). Other examples include Jon Stratton's "The Trouble with Zombies: Bare Life, and Displaced Peoples (2011) and Mitchell Travis's "We're All Infected: Legal Personhood, Bare Life, and *The Walking Dead*" (2015).

making the zombie the perfect metaphor not only for how capitalism transforms its subjects but also for its relentless and devastating virologic march across the globe. (432)

The horde of undead figures swarming a group of surviving humans, made famous by George Romero's *Night of the Living Dead* horror film series, has become one of the hallmarks of the zombie narrative, one that many critics have linked to the costs of a capitalist system that rewards an ever-smaller number of peoples at the expense of many.[16] Leif Sorensen expands on critiques of zombies as the effects of capitalism by examining the post-apocalyptic narrative as a response to capitalist crisis. He explains in "Against the Post-Apocalyptic: Narrative Closure in Colson Whitehead's *Zone One*" that as a vision of the most extreme form of crisis, the literal almost-end-of-humanity, post-apocalyptic narratives attempt to impose order on an irrational event by imagining a future after the apocalypse, which he argues "normalizes the open narrative form of late capitalism" (563).[17] Sorensen notes that whether the zombie narrative concludes with a return to "normalcy" or a permanent change to society, the majority imagine a future where some of humanity survives.[18] Some semblance of order is restored, which allows humans to return to political and economic normalcy.

Whitehead and Ma each address the effects of capitalism in their narratives; however, each author also adds specific examples that bring together themes of labor and race. Leah Richards notes that as a figure rooted in slavery, zombie narratives provide a space through which to critique capitalism's effects on workers: Like slaves, the oppressed workers "live" only to work and consume (657). Although I agree that in this metaphor, workers are connected to the history of Eurowestern reliance on black slave labor, I also argue that Whitehead and Ma add a contemporary racial element by highlighting the additional labor that peoples of color must go through to

---

16. For an in-depth analysis of capitalism and social disparity, see Robert B. Reich's *Saving Capitalism: For the Many, Not the Few* (2015).

17. For a more detailed definition of late capitalism, see Fredric Jameson's *Postmodernism, or, the Cultural Logic of Late Capitalism* (1989, 1991).

18. One interesting exception to this trend is M. R. Carey's *The Girl with All the Gifts* (2014), a narrative where only one human, the teacher Miss Justineau, survives. The main zombie character, or "hungry," is an intelligent, second-generation zombie girl-child named Melanie. At the end of the novel, Melanie tricks a human into using a flame-thrower on the fungus causing the zombie virus, which will cause all humans to become infected zombies. If Melanie is correct, Miss Justineau will become the only noninfected human on the planet, which will force her to choose between becoming a zombie or dying. Either way, this novel imagines the transformation of humanity into a new, zombie species.

navigate predominantly white corporate and civil work environments. The main characters of *Zone One* and *Severance* fit the description of a proletarian worker: Both worked in office environments before the apocalyptic event where they engaged in repetitive, meaningless labor and were barely noticed by their white officemates and superiors. When Mark Spitz is attacked in an office at the beginning of *Zone One*, he imagines the three female zombies as middle-class white women[19] working in HR and compares the women to the exacting head of HR in his first job in the mailroom of a payroll company:

> The only downer was the ogre head of Human Resources, who'd been relentless about Mark Spitz's paperwork, downright insidious about his W-this, W-that, the proper credentials. She served the places where human beings were paraphrased into numbers, components of bundled data to be shot out through fiber-optic cable toward meaning:
> "Your check can't be processed without complete paperwork." How was he supposed to know where his social security card was? . . ." You're not in the system. You might as well not exist. Where was The System now? (21)

The corporate insistence on workers' having the "proper credentials," such as a Social Security card, speak to both the tracking of Eurowestern citizens through paperwork and the exclusion of peoples likely to not have access to this paperwork, typically poor and undocumented citizens of color. A lack of ability to access citizenship documents can lead to barriers in receiving public assistance or healthcare and can keep Eurowestern citizens from exercising their right to vote. Donald Moynihan and Pamela Herd explain that US administrative restrictions, often referred to as "red tape," have a large effect on which peoples are able to exercise citizenship rights:

> Administrative activities play a crucial part of the policy feedback process by shaping access to basic citizenship rights that are central to democracy. Red tape, and administrative actions more generally, may affect not only the ability to participate via political and social rights but also the capacity

---

19. Although Whitehead's description of the skel HR "ladies" does not include their race, Mark Spitz notes that one of the women wore a popular hairstyle called "The Marge" which was favored by young women who watched a popular sitcom featuring the actress Margaret Halstead. This reference draws parallels to "The Rachel" haircut popularized by Jennifer Anniston in the 1990s sitcom *Friends*. This reference and the fact that the US Bureau of Labor Statistics notes that female HR employees are predominantly white (over 70 percent of managers and workers) drive my assumption that "The Marge" and her coworkers are white ("Labor").

and desire to participate. Second . . . red tape disproportionately weakens political and social rights for certain groups. This raises the question of whether the negative effects of red tape are not accidental but represent a deliberate policy design choice to limit access to political and social rights for specific groups of citizens. (655)

Although Moynihan and Herd focus their research on poor and disabled citizens, peoples of color are also a specific group that is often disadvantaged by targeted administrative policies. Karina Moreno Saldívar notes that US policies and red tape targeting Latinx peoples, implemented to protect "national security," may be linked to variations in Latinx political participation and distrust/disillusionment in the Latinx community's ability to exercise rights as citizens (70). Lack of access to political and social rights in Eurowestern countries is compounded for new or undocumented immigrants, who may not have assistance to complete paperwork or the funds to pay high naturalization fees.[20] The assertion that Mark Spitz, a US citizen, does not exist without the proper paperwork highlights the precarious nature of citizenship for peoples of color in Eurowestern countries, even those who are citizens. Whitehead uses the zombie trope to bring this precariousness out into the open: The fact that the HR zombie attacks Mark Spitz just as he is nostalgically thinking about the return of "normalcy" or "The System" is Whitehead's warning about the desire for reconstruction of racist political and economic systems the post-apocalyptic narrative exposes.

Ma recreates Romero's mall-as-capitalist-sanctuary from his zombie film *Dawn of the Dead* (1978) to highlight the effects of global capitalism on Eurowestern immigrants of color. Directly after Candace and the group of survivors occupy a suburban mall, choosing various stores to serve as living quarters and communal spaces, Candace is imprisoned by Bob. Another survivor, Evan, discloses to Bob that Candace is pregnant, and Bob decides to confine Candace to her mall kiosk to keep her from attempting to escape with the baby. Like Mari and Orion, Candace has been declared "unfit" to make decisions because she is pregnant; as a representative of the law or state, Bob gets to decide what is best for the baby at the expense of Candace's autonomy and personhood. As Candace sits in her kiosk, she has flashbacks of her parents' immigration from China to the US. Wali and Renzaho note that immigrants from non-Eurowestern countries often struggle to adjust to the more individualistic, isolated lifestyle of Eurowestern countries. When

---

20. See Alex Shashkevich's "High cost of naturalization prevents low-income immigrants from becoming citizens, Stanford study finds" (2018), https://news.stanford.edu/2018/01/17/low-income-immigrants-face-barriers-u-s-citizenship/.

interviewing immigrants from a number of non-Eurowestern countries, they note that these peoples describe the families they left behind as their "capital" and note experiencing a loss of this capital after immigrating (8). They also describe the pressure to send money home to their families, who often depend on this money to survive (7). When Candace's mother feels isolated and fights with her husband about returning to China, he uses America's economic prosperity to convince her to stay. Candace explains, "Her homesickness eased in department stores, supermarkets, wholesale clubs, superstores, places of unparalleled abundance. The solution was shopping" (177). Candace follows her mother's example when she gets an unfulfilling job designing Bibles; she passes time by spending money on luxury goods like "Shishedo facial exfoliants, Blue Bottle coffee, [and] Uniqlo cashmere" (11). Later in the novel, Candace honors her parents by performing a Chinese ceremony of mourning and ancestral worship. She burns spirit money and pictures of luxury items her parents would enjoy in the afterlife (104–6). She also continues to send her Chinese relatives money and luxury goods the same way her mother did. Ma uses these scenes to demonstrate the conflicting feelings experienced by immigrants of color, particularly those coming from non-Eurowestern cultures. As first-generation immigrants, Candace's parents feel obligated to portray themselves as successful and happy to their relatives, despite their struggles with social isolation and financial difficulties. Candace inherits this tension between the desire for a familial connection and an obligation to present herself as a successful US immigrant. Though she daydreams about returning to China, she risks her life to remain in post-pandemic New York City because her job offers her a lucrative contract. By the end of the novel, Candace is rich in capital in a world where money has become meaningless. Like Whitehead, Ma utilizes the post-apocalyptic zombie narrative to comment on capitalism as a system that rewards individuality and competition at the expense of meaningful social and cultural relationships. The fact that Mark Spitz and Candace are peoples of color further complicates the post-apocalyptic narrative: Both characters fantasize about a return to political and economic "normalcy" while also being aware of how the restoration of these systems would also restore pressures to conform to white Eurowestern cultural beliefs.

Vourvoulias's and Rivera's narratives focus on surveillance and containment of peoples; they each reference past deaths, but readers do not encounter graphic death scenes as part of the narratives. The presence of zombies in Whitehead's and Ma's works, however, create a narrative form where death must be encountered on a regular basis. Kyle William Bishop notes that Romero's *Night of the Living Dead* was filmed during the Vietnam War;

as a result, this film "forced its contemporary viewers to face the morbid realities of violent death: rotting corpses, dismembered bodies, and bloody bullet wounds" (10). Canavan connects the killing of zombies to Foucault's theory of bio-power to demonstrate how these narratives highlight Eurowestern racial anxiety. He first quotes Foucault's description of how biopolitics connects to issues of race:

> In the biopower system, in other words, killing or the imperative to kill is acceptable only if it results not in a victory over political adversaries, but in the elimination of the biological threat to and the improvement of the species or race. . . . In a normalizing society, race or racism is the precondition that makes killing acceptable. (qtd. in Canavan 438)

He then connects Foucault's theory of biopolitics and race to that of the zombie narrative:

> The biopolitical state . . . needs to create this sort of racial imaginary in order to retain its power to kill. Under biopower those who are imagined to threaten the population as a whole become not merely a danger but a kind of anti-life that must be sequestered from (white) life at any cost. Any contact with a zombie, after all, might lead to infection, just as the racial Other must be disciplined and quarantined to prevent "intermingling." (438)

The zombie figure was born of colonial slave violence and appropriated by white Eurowestern culture to express the anxiety of racial contamination.[21] If zombies are the biopolitical threat in a zombie narrative as Canavan argues, then zombies become a stand-in for the racial other that must be contained or killed at all costs. Contemporary zombie narratives like Whitehead and Ma's add a level of awareness of the costs of such violence for peoples of color.

Whitehead and Ma's works portray the graphic violence against zombies expected in the genre but refuse to allow readers to fantasize about racial violence against the other by including scenes with non-violent zombies. In both works, the majority of the zombie figures are passive figures engaging in repetitive mundane tasks connected to their former lives. The protagonists in both narratives express sympathy for these figures at specific points in the narrative. In *Zone One*, Mark Spitz describes how the nonvio-

---

21. For a detailed explanation of the origins of the zombie figure and its relation to colonialism, see Elizabeth McAlister's "Slaves, Cannibals, and Infected Hyper-Whites: The Race and Religion of Zombies" (2013).

lent category of zombies (or "skels,") nicknamed "stragglers" by the humans tasked with cleanup, face a more-prolonged violence at the hands of some sweepers—the ones who take sadistic pleasure in mutilating a figure that cannot fight back. He then suggests to the other sweepers in his crew that they spare one of the stragglers, a young man perpetually making copies in a dingy office environment:

> Mark Spitz had noticed on numerous occasions that while the regular skels got referred to as *it*, the stragglers were awarded male and female pronouns, and he wondered what that meant. "What's his name?" he said.
> "What do you mean, what's his name?" Gary said.
> "It has to be something."
> "Buffalo doesn't want the names."
> "Still."
> "His name is Ned the Copy Boy."
> "What if we let him stay?' Mark Spitz didn't know why he said it. "He's not hurting anyone. Look at this room. We're standing in the most depressing room in the entire city."
> His comrades looked at each other but did not comment. (102)

Mark Spitz is able to empathize with the straggler because he was working the kind of depressing, low-level corporate job Mark Spitz also worked before the zombie outbreak. He is thus willing to see the humanity in the straggler. Later, the Lieutenant whom Mark Spitz works under explains that empathy for the stragglers is dangerous, not to the stragglers, but to the mental well-being of the surviving humans. He states to the lead sweeper on Mark Spitz's team, Kaitlyn:

> "No, you're right. Mustn't humanize them. The whole thing breaks down unless you are fundamentally sure that they are not you. "I do not resemble the animal, you tell yourself, as you squat in the back of a convenience store, pissing in a bucket and cooking up mangy squirrel for dinner." (195)

The reason that Mark Spitz's crew do not address his bout of empathy for the straggler is that to do so forces them to confront the fact that they are systematically killing human beings, people who have done nothing to deserve their fate. Achille Mbembe notes in "Necropolitics" that survival is inherently bound with death; the survivor often must kill to continue surviving, and the survivor is both haunted by and relieved at the sight of death: "In the logic of survival one's horror at the sight of death turns into satisfaction that it is someone else who is dead" (36). Canavan quotes Mbembe at length to help make the point that one of the reasons survivors in a zombie narrative must kill zombies, even passive ones, is that "they infect us with their vulnerability, their killability make us 'killable' too. One's position in the state of exception is, after all, never secure; the class of dangerous anti-citizens, bound for the camps, tends only to grow" (445). Most often, the first citizens to be affected by the state of exception Canavan describes are peoples of color.[22] If one reads this scene through the lens of the zombie as person of color, the stragglers become peoples of color disadvantaged by Eurowestern cultures' privileging of whiteness and the centuries of laws designed to keep peoples of color in a lower social status. The fact that the Lieutenant mockingly refers to the stragglers as "animals" references the history of white Eurowestern colonizers and citizens dehumanizing peoples of color to justify violence.

Ma also includes multiple scenes in *Severance* where Candace shows empathy for the zombie figures, referred to as the "fevered." When the leader of the survivor group she joins refers to their situation as similar to living in a zombie film, Candace counters:

> Wait, I interjected. What are you saying? Because number one, the fevered aren't zombies. They don't attack us or try to eat us. They don't do anything to us. If anything, we do more harm to them. (29)

Candace rejects Bob's comparison of the fevered as zombie threat in this statement and also demonstrates empathy for the zombies, who, like the stragglers in *Zone One*, are likely the objectified other being used as an outlet for survivors' anger and anxiety. Later in the narrative, Candace encounters a fevered girl engaging in an endless game of hide-and-seek. She attempts to hide this fact by re-covering the girl with the curtain she was hiding behind and distracting Bob, who comes to check on her progress. Bob notices the girl, however, and forces Candace to shoot her in front of the other survivors in the group. When he asks the group why they kill the fevered, one of the members states, "It's the humane thing to do" (69). Because Candace is not adept with firearms, it takes her multiple shots to kill the girl; however, Bob refuses to let anyone else in the group help her. Candace describes the killing in detail, counting the number of shots it takes to kill the girl:

---

22. See Henry A. Giroux's "Reading Hurricane Katrina: Race, Class, and the Biopolitics of Disposability" (2016).

> She raised her blue eyes and looked at me, as the sixth shot hit her in the cheek, and then the seventh reached the forehead. The eighth shot hit her in the arm, and ninth in the stomach, the tenth in the eye, which spurted. At some point, I lost track of what I was shooting. . . . She was probably obediently dead by now, but still I was shooting, past the death barrier and into someplace else, I don't know where. (67–71)

Candace's description of the scene and her actions goes against the typical view that "the 'enemy' who is killed is always *first* the zombie—who is unthinking and unfeeling, and can be killed without regret" (Canavan 444). Nothing about the graphic killing of the fevered girl is portrayed as "humane." Bob's need to force Candace to kill is at best a desire to make her complicit in his own guilt over killing to survive, at worst a sadistic need for control over another human being. Candace's choice of the phrase "obediently dead" demonstrates her understanding that to survive, she has to display obedience to Bob, a social position that is historically common for peoples of color. Slave masters commonly quoted Bible passages that required submission of slaves to their masters in their attempts to justify slavery, a practice that Granville Sharp identifies in 1776 as "the law of passive obedience" (2). In *Severance*, the zombie figure also becomes enslaved to the desires of the survivors; it is their job to die so that the survivors can continue to view themselves as humane and just. Candace's comment that the survivors "do more harm" applies to both the fevered's and the survivors' treatment of other survivors. As Canavan notes, in most zombie narratives, each survivor's position in the group is tenuous and based solely on which members are viewed as contributing members who do not threaten the survival of the group. The actions of Mark Spitz and Candace both reject the logic of survival that Achille Mbembe describes in "Necropolitics" by refusing to be satisfied with the dominant view of nonviolent zombies as a threat that must be disposed of for survival.

Zone One and *Severance* also directly challenge the zombie narrative's dismissal of race and racism in the face of a global epidemic. Mark Spitz and Candace, both peoples of color, are forced to downplay their skills and intelligence in these narratives to appease a white majority. Canavan explains that even when diverse groups of humans band together to survive the zombie apocalypse, the violence always turns inward, which places another level of tenuousness and anxiety on the survivors:

> Anyone outside the white patriarchal community, anyone who is not already one of "us," is a potential threat to the future who must be interro-

gated intensely, if not kept out altogether. Even those inside the community have to be surveilled at all times for signs of treachery, weakness, or growing infection. (445)

While peoples of all races are in danger of being stripped of their rights and reduced to "bare life," if one assumes that racism does not simply disappear in moments of crisis but, as Giroux notes, is amplified as specific groups of peoples become even more disposable in times of crisis, then Mark Spitz and Candace are in danger of being labeled as dangerous and expelled from the group at any time.

The two protagonists each take specific measures to assimilate into the majority white, male, Eurowestern societies they find refuge in. Mark Spitz allows himself to be nicknamed by other survivors; readers never discover his real name in the narrative. Instead, Whitehead humorously gives the self-described "average" Black protagonist who cannot swim the name of an Olympic swimmer who was viewed as the embodiment of white, successful manliness in the 1970s. Rather than describing himself as lacking, however, Mark Spitz discusses his "averageness" as an asset:

> He'd never had trouble with the American checklist, having successfully executed all the hurdles of his life's stages, from preschool to junior high to college, with unwavering competence and nary a wobble into exceptionality or failure. He possessed a strange facility for the mandatory. . . . His aptitude lay in the well-executed muddle, never shining, never flunking, but gathering himself for what it took to progress past life's next random obstacle. It was his solemn expertise.
> Got him this far. (10–11)

Mark Spitz's description of a successful "American" is someone who demonstrates enough aptitude to be considered intelligent but is not so successful that he is singled out as exceptional. Ford and Whiting explain in a study titled "Beyond testing: social and psychological considerations in recruiting and retaining gifted Black students" that not all African American students and families consider gifted programs and classes to be beneficial. They note that many African American students opt out of gifted programs to avoid becoming isolated from their Black peers in the majority white gifted classes. Ford and Whiting explain, "Academically successful Black males and females complain about negative peer pressures because of their high grades, participation in gifted programs, speaking Standard English, and other conditions" (133–34). Paul Scott echoes these sentiments in his personal essay "Fear of an Intelligent Black Man," where he describes how he downplayed his intelligence because "Being an academically gifted black kid in America is a proverbial catch 22: White America fears your intelligence, and you fear yourself." Mark Spitz has been surviving the American social system his entire life; his "averageness" continues to allow him to survive after the zombie apocalypse. He integrates into several social groups throughout the novel, yet he never allows himself to become complacent. He volunteers to serve on a sweeper squad but does not try to obtain a leadership role. When his squad-mate, a white man named Gary, claims to have never heard the stereotype that Black people can't swim, Mark Spitz does not challenge him (Whitehead 287). Mark Spitz downplays his abilities and refuses to challenge Gary's color-blind claims because he knows that these choices will increase his chances for survival.

Mark Spitz also understands that the social and racial systems of preapocalypse America have not disappeared in the post-apocalyptic setting; toward the end of *Zone One*, he questions if restoring "The System" would benefit him:

> Would the old bigotries be reborn as well, when they cleared out this Zone, and the next, and so on, and they were packed together again, tight and suffocating on top of each other? Or was that particular bramble of animosities, fears, and envies impossible to recreate? If they could bring back paperwork, Mark Spitz thought, they could certainly reanimate prejudice, parking tickets, and reruns. There were plenty of things in the world that deserved to stay dead, yet they walked. (288)

Whitehead uses this scene to challenge the notion of a race-blind future that many science fiction narratives espouse.[23] Instead, he brings together the narrative of capitalism as social death and ideas of racism by comparing racism to items such as "paperwork," "parking tickets," and "reruns." While most readers might consider these items to be "inconveniences" and might think Whitehead is downplaying the experience of racism, Whitehead actually achieves the opposite: Mark Spitz's statement highlights the pervasiveness of racism in US culture. Like the zombies in *Zone One*, Whitehead understands that centuries of ingrained racism will be hard to kill.

Candace also downplays her skills as an artist throughout *Severance*. Like Mark Spitz, she describes her photography as average:

---

23. For a thorough overview of the history of science fiction's treatment of race, see Mark Bould's "The Ships Landed Long Ago: Afrofuturism and Black SF" (2007).

I didn't think much of my photographs. When I first moved to New York, I had created a photo blog called *NY Ghost*. It was mostly pictures of the city. The intent was to show new, undiscovered aspects of New York from an outsider's perspective, but in retrospect, the pictures just looked clichéd and trope-y.... For these and other reasons, I hardly updated the blog anymore. I hardly took pictures anymore. (Ma 14)

Rather than believe in her gifts as an artist and her ability to have a unique perspective, Candace downplays her photography because she feels that it is not exceptional. She tells her boyfriend, an aspiring white male writer named Jonathan, "I'm not an artist" (14). Candace's reluctance to see her art as a possible career and her decision to stay working a job with a stable salary corresponds to the pressures peoples of color feel to be financially "successful." In a personal essay titled "Failure Is Not an Option: The Pressure Black Women Feel to Succeed," Rhonesha Byng explains that because Black women are often faced with less access to educational and career opportunities, those who manage to earn a college degree or obtain a high-level position feel pressure to succeed, not just for themselves but for other Black women. She notes that these women are often trying "to excel within spaces that were not originally set up for a woman or a Black person to excel." Since the US art world is still majority white,[24] Candace does not feel she will be able to succeed unless her art is exceptional. She also does not see the idea of supporting herself on the proceeds of her art as a possibility. Jonathan, on the other hand, does not feel pressure to be exceptional; he works only to make enough money to live and decides to leave New York City because he becomes disillusioned with the city and its consumerism. Jonathan is not concerned with how he will survive because as a white male in a Eurowestern country, he has the freedom to decide to partially opt out of the capitalist system of the US.

To survive, Candace holds back personal information to better integrate into a group of survivors. She joins the group last, after the group has already bonded and chosen Bob as their leader. Though Candace refers to the group as ethnically diverse, her interactions with Bob, a religious man described as having "light grey eyes," recreate the Eurowestern privileging of white, male, Christian citizens. When Candace challenges Bob's description of the fevered as zombies, she quickly realizes her mistake: "I surprised myself when I spoke. It was rare that I did. But, having spoken, I felt short of breath, nauseated. Everyone looked at me" (29). Candace has not disclosed

---

24. See Roberto A. Ferdman's discussion of artists and racial diversity in "If you're lucky enough to earn a living from your art, you're probably white" (2014).

that she is pregnant or that she was responsible for the blog *NY Ghost*. These decisions, coupled with the statement that she does not speak much, demonstrate that she understands that her position in the group is tentative. Bob uses his position as head of the group of survivors to control Candace: He forces her to kill the fevered girl and breaks her cell phone to strip her of her only memories of the past. When Bob imprisons her, she forces herself to act out of character to placate him: "Arguing only seemed to make him angrier. Better to appear meek and fearful, better to assure him of his power" (168). Candace's experience echoes that of many women of color in Eurowestern countries that practice mass incarceration. Kimberlé Crenshaw notes that young women of color are often more subject to "discretionary decisions of gateway agents, such as police" and explains that girls are often detained when "decisionmakers perceive girls to pose threats requiring supervision when the same behavior in a boy would not" (1439). She also notes that mothers of color are particularly subject to increased surveillance and punishment because of stereotypical moral judgements that depict mothers of color as "immoral and irresponsible" and therefore in need of social control (1445). Like Mari and Orion, it is Candace's status as a future mother that opens her to Bob's complete social control: As the leader of the group, Bob views himself as justifiably imprisoning Candace to "save" her baby while also instructing her on the "right" social values she will need to be a good mother. The fact that Candace has to control her emotions and play into the gender stereotype of female meekness to escape Bob's control demonstrates the ways that Eurowestern cultures force women of color to adhere to a stereotypical white Christian portrayal of femininity and morality to survive the racist, patriarchal social order that is still in effect. Eventually, when Bob becomes fevered himself, Candace is finally able to express her anger and frustration at being controlled most of her life by white men. After she realized Bob is fevered, she hears the voice of her old boss, a white man who convinced her to stay in a job she did not enjoy, congratulating her on all her hard work for the company. At that moment, she kicks Bob repeatedly and spits in his face. When one of the other survivors, a man named Adam, tells her to stop in a tone "enunciating every word as if speaking to a child," she laughs and states, "I'm laughing because I have never had a personal conversation with Adam in all this time and he is telling me what to do. That's pretty funny" (282). In her expression of her rage, Candace finds the power to break the cycle of patriarchal, capitalist control she has been living under for years. She is no longer interested in getting along with the other survivors; she decides she is better off alone than living under constant surveillance and being punished for not adhering to Eurowestern male views of "good" behavior.

Whitehead and Ma each end their narratives with their main characters alone and facing almost insurmountable odds. At the end of *Zone One*, Mark Spitz watches as the dead stream into New York City through a crack in the barrier the new government erected as part of their revitalization campaign. In this moment, Mark Spitz accepts that the world will never go back to its pre-apocalypse systems:

> He'd always wanted to live in New York but that city didn't exist anymore. He didn't know if the world was doomed or saved, but whatever the next thing was, it would not look like what came before. (320)

The humans running the new government in Buffalo have been trying to sell the survivors on the image of a reconstructed New York City as a beacon of hope for humanity. The fact that the city cannot be "saved" demonstrates one of Whitehead's main messages: Some systems should not be saved. Mark Spitz's situation seems hopeless, yet he has survived the entire novel by refusing a nostalgic desire for a return to normalcy. If he survives, it is doubtful that he will attempt to usher in a new system. But this is Whitehead's point: Peoples of color do not have to fit into Eurowestern society's definition of "exceptional"—Mark Spitz is already exceptional because he continues to survive in a system that is not only designed to not benefit him, but that is often actively seeking to control or destroy him.

At the end of *Severance*, Candace drives away from the mall toward the city of Chicago. As she drives, she describes living in a city as being a part of a preplanned system:

> To live in a city is to live the life that it was built for, to adapt to its schedule and rhythms.
>
> To live in a city is to take part in and propagate its impossible systems. To wake up. To go to work in the morning. It is also to take pleasure in those systems because, otherwise, who could repeat the same routines, year in, year out? (289)

Candace feels comfort in the reliability of life in a city, even one that has become a ghostly reminder of the systems that sought to control her. Like Mark Spitz, she feels attached to a nostalgic view of the city as a place of promise, yet she also avoids wishing for a return to pre-apocalyptic systems. Readers never discover if she finds another group of survivors to join, but Ma seems to suggest that Candace is better off alone than being oppressed by other survivors. *Severance* seems to suggest that until the survivors decolonize their racist and sexist views, the survival of humanity will be in jeopardy.

Is There a Post-Apocalypse for Peoples of Color?

The works discussed in this chapter bring to light a disturbing truth about the treatment of peoples of color worldwide: In many countries, particularly those with a history of Eurowestern colonization, peoples of color are subject to criminalization leading to state-sanctioned violence. The irony is that most peoples of color do not have enough power to threaten the white privilege pervading Eurowestern cultures, and yet their lives and rights as citizens are in jeopardy because they are perceived as a threat. Whether it is the need to proclaim that Black Lives Matter, the incarceration of Latinx asylum seekers, or the policing of Indigenous protest, peoples of color worldwide find themselves living a zombified experience, where the sacrifice of their lives is deemed acceptable or necessary for the safety of the white majority. As the works in this chapter demonstrate, the apocalypse does not change this position for peoples of color—in fact, it generally amplifies the anxiety of the white majority and increases tactics of criminalization against peoples perceived as threats.

So can there be a post-apocalypse for peoples of color, a narrative where such peoples can escape zombification and live as full and free citizens? A Fourth World scenario where all races and cultures live with respect for one another? Perhaps. The endings of the four works discussed give a glimpse into the two avenues that science fiction authors of color envision for the future of race in post-apocalyptic settings. Vourvoulias and Rivera imagine the beginnings of state reform in their works, where laws are being passed to combat the dehumanizing of specific groups and where politicians begin to view citizens as individuals deserving of freedom. However, both texts also caution that radical change happens slowly if at all. Whitehead's and Ma's narratives at first seem to suggest a complete lack of hope for structural change. The solitary figures of Candace and Mark Spitz embrace the chaos that is the ending of the world as it was. But with their precarious endings may come the end of red tape, the end of racism, and the end of state-sanctioned criminalization. *Zone One* and *Severance* both end before readers discover if their worlds die out completely, and in this liminal space of uncertainty at the end of these two novels lies the possibilities of the Fourth World. The only question left is whether humans are ready to decolonize not only their systems of government, but also their minds and hearts.

CHAPTER 4

"Our Knowledge Is Not Primitive"
Indigenous and Eurowestern Science

In her introduction to *Walking the Clouds*, Grace L. Dillon (Anishinaabe) defines the concept of "Indigenous scientific literacies" and explains how Indigenous knowledge of science differs from the Eurowestern scientific method:

> In contrast to the accelerating effect of techno-driven western scientific method, Indigenous scientific literacies represent practices used by Indigenous peoples over thousands of years to reenergize the natural environment while improving the interconnected relationships among all persons (animal, human, spirit, and even machine). Some of its features include sustainable forms of medicine, agriculture, architecture, and art. Since Indigenous scientific literacies historically are shaped by the diverse natural environments of the groups that use them, no single set of practices summarizes the possibilities. ("Imagining" 7–8)

A large contributor to the fact that Indigenous knowledge is not viewed as being scientific is the continued belief in Eurowestern cultural superiority, which includes privileging the scientific method over non-Eurowestern cultural knowledge. The notion that Indigenous cultures have a "primitive" view of the planet because they often view "lesser" species as equal beings means that this knowledge is in danger of not being recorded and remembered. In recent years, Indigenous scientists have attempted to bridge the gap between Indigenous scientific literacies and the Eurowestern scientific method while also creating a record of Indigenous scientific and cultural knowledge. Botanist Robin Wall Kimmerer (Anishinaabe) explains in *Braiding Sweetgrass: Indigenous Wisdom, Scientific Knowledge, and the Teachings of Plants* (2013) that Eurowestern scientific methods, which express themselves as the only rational form of scientific belief, are not impervious to issues of bias. She cites scientific views of plants as one example:

> Science pretends to be purely rational, completely neutral, a system of knowledge-making in which the observation is independent of the observer. And yet the conclusion was drawn that plants cannot communicate because they lack the mechanisms that animals use to speak. The potentials for plants were seen purely through the lens of animal capacity (18).

Indigenous cultures, explains Kimmerer, already understand that plants and animals have their own languages and that humans often lack the capacity to understand why or how they act in specific ways. She goes on to argue that Indigenous culture's decentering of humanity, with its biases and politics, creates a more reciprocal, symbiotic relationship between humans and the planet (112), a view that has the potential to combat planetwide issues such as climate change.

Ultimately, Kimmerer argues, scientists should make room for both Indigenous scientific literacies and Eurowestern science through ethical, decolonizing practices of study and research. She uses the metaphor of the relationship between the "Three Sisters" (corn, beans, and squash), three plants that share a reciprocal relationship, to explain:

> The Three Sisters offer us a new metaphor for an emerging relationship between indigenous knowledge and Western science, both of which are rooted in the earth. I think of the corn as traditional ecological knowledge, the physical and spiritual framework that can guide the curious bean of science, which twines like a double helix. The squash creates an ethical habitat for coexistence and mutual flourishing. I envision a time when the intellectual monoculture of science will be replaced with a polyculture of complementary knowledges. And so all may be fed (139).

I argue that Kimmerer's vision of a world that values and utilizes both Indigenous knowledge and Eurowestern science is already being imagined by science fiction authors of color. This chapter examines four literary works—Nalo Hopkinson's *Brown Girl in the Ring* (1998), Tananarive Due's *African Immortals* series (1997–2011), Carlos Hernandez's "The Assimilated Cuban's Guide to Quantum Santeria" (2016), and Rivers Solomon's *An Unkindness of Ghosts* (2017). These texts combine elements of Indigenous[1] scientific literacies and Eurowestern sciences and technologies to argue that the incorporation of Indigenous practices such as environmental sustainability, the promotion of balance, and "conjure science"[2] expand the definitions of science and technology in science fiction. Such an expansion is a direct challenge to Eurowestern notions of Indigenous cultures as "primitive." These texts demonstrate a truth only now beginning to be understood: that Indigenous sciences, which have been passed down in Indigenous cultures for centuries, have the ability to teach Eurowestern culture how to adapt and survive.

Because each of the authors discussed in this chapter comes from a different cultural background, the Indigenous scientific and technological practices they discuss differ widely. However, they do share some commonalities, such as the use of local knowledge for healing practices and the use of ritual to communicate with deities or spirits. This is not to imply that all Indigenous cultures share these commonalities; while there are beliefs that cross several Indigenous cultures, each culture has its own unique set of cultural practices that are passed down from generation to generation. Each of the texts also makes references to Eurowestern science: sometimes to highlight connections in beliefs, at other times to demonstrate the limitations of relying solely on the Eurowestern scientific method. While some science fiction critics might argue that the presence of Eurowestern science is what makes these texts science fiction, critics of Indigenous science fiction note that many texts that appear to employ "magic" or religious practices should be studied as science fiction.[3]

Examining science fiction texts with Indigenous scientific literacies requires an expansion of what constitutes "science" and "technology." Robert Conley (United Keetoowah Band of Cherokee) connects the concept of *duyulta*, translated as "the right way" or "the path of being in balance"[4] to

---

1. I define Indigenous cultures as the first peoples to be present in a country. Many Indigenous peoples, such as Native Americans, have been removed from the lands they originally lived on, while other Indigenous groups may be nomadic. However, they typically share the experiences of colonization and forced relocation.

2. See Dillon's "Haint Stories Rooted in Conjure Science."

3. See Nisi Shawl's "Ifa: Reverence, Science, and Social Technology" (2016).

4. This translation appears in Dillon's "Haint Stories Rooted in Conjure Science," p. 106.

Indigenous practices of dreaming, the sweat lodge, prayer, and other Indigenous ceremonies (qtd. in Teuton 199). If *duyulta* is considered in the Eurowestern scientific terms of symbiogenesis or quantum entanglement, then the ceremonies that promote balance for Indigenous culture are forms of science, and the objects that aid in such ceremonies are a form of technology. Nisi Shawl expands this argument in "Ifa: Reverence, Science, and Social Technology" through her explanation of how the practice of "Ifa," the religion or practice of divination utilized by the Yoruba peoples to promote balance, connects the concepts of Eurowestern science, religion, and Indigenous knowledge:

> The idea that science may reject spirituality in general, and African religious traditions in particular[,] . . . has very little impact on its complementary acceptance by Ifa practitioners. We're used to belittlement of that sort. Christianity rejects and has always rejected African-born philosophies such as Vodun, Lucumi, and Santeria, yet these and related religions equate Christian saints with members of our pantheons. Some rituals require the use of holy water, or the recitation of Bible verses. The Afrodiasporic religious outlook is deeply pragmatic; it makes use of what is useful. A scientific approach to the world is useful. Scientific knowledge is useful—also, at times, awe-inspiring and breathtakingly beautiful. What's not to like? We ain't mad at you, pretty science; don't be mad at we. (224)

Shawl goes on to draw connections between major deities in Ifa and their scientific counterparts. When she discusses the objects used in Ifa ceremonies to connect with Egun and Orisha deities, which include Christian religious artifacts such as holy water, elements of nature such as shells, and images, she argues, "If science is a system of knowledge, technology is the systematic use of that Knowledge" (224). She concludes by explaining four elements of Ifa rituals—altars, music, offerings, and divination—as aspects of "social technology," a term she creates to explain how social elements of a culture (such as justice) can be employed to remedy "human-generated ecological problems"[5] (225). Many of the works discussed in this chapter depict Indigenous rituals that remedy issues that cannot be solved by the Eurowestern scientific method or "modern" technologies.

Dillon goes further to argue that conjuring in Indigenous cultures is a form of science and to expand the definition of conjuring itself: "As a native

---

5. Although this phrase is Shawl's, she is referencing Kim Stanley Robinson's Guest of Honor speech at WisCon 39 in May 2015.

science, conjuring may have multiple layers, including not merely its symbiogenesis and coevolution, in quantum mechanics and organic physics terms... but also forms of conjuration such as reading, writing, and literacy in general" ("Haint" 107). Dillon reminds us that for cultures that have been refused the ability to document their history through the denial of reading and writing skills, pen and paper become important elements of social technology. Many of the characters in the works of this chapter reclaim Indigenous knowledge through books and journals passed down or preserved or through recording the experiences of traumatized peoples. Toni Morrison has also noted in discussions of her neo-slave narrative *Beloved* that writing this novel was an attempt to recreate a lost history, a writing practice she labels "rememory" (Noudelmann 36). Morrison argues that employing the technology of writing is critical to creating a future for African Americans because "so much of our history has been erased, distorted and reconstructed to a level of fantasy. It's as though avoiding the truths of the past is somehow so degrading that no one can function. But I think clarity about the past plays a very important role in how we handle the present and what we might be able to do for the future" (qtd. in Noudelmann 36). Shawl, Dillon, and Morrison make it clear that the study of science fiction by authors of color requires readers to look beyond the Eurowestern scientific method as the only viable form of science while also reclaiming "old" forms of technology like pen-and-paper.

Although an understanding of Indigenous science and medicine is important to the analysis of this chapter, I would like to take this opportunity to note that my position as a non-Indigenous scholar of science fiction, means that the definitions of Indigenous science and healing I provide in this chapter are limited. Wendy Makoons-Geniusz explains in *Our Knowledge Is Not Primitive: Decolonizing Botanical Anishinaabe Teachings* (2009) that Eurowestern cultures' attempts to colonize Indigenous peoples through assimilationist practices combined with Eurowestern sciences' biased study of Indigenous practices has resulted in a colonized record of Indigenous beliefs and practices. In her introduction, Makoons-Geniusz explains the need for decolonization practices in Indigenous research:

> Individuals from alien cultures have taken our lands, brainwashed our children, stolen our dead, and tried to make every part of our bodies and minds just like theirs. The colonizers have also collected and critiqued our knowledge and cultures, resulting in volumes of written materials that attempt to explain and present us to the rest of the world. Decolonization efforts seek to reclaim all these aspects of indigenous lives. (7)

Makoons-Geniusz's description of Indigenous experiences with colonization speak to themes of science fiction: being invaded by an "alien" culture, brainwashing, and desecration of the dead. It is no wonder that many of the science fiction texts discussed in this chapter represent attempts by authors of color to recover cultural knowledge lost through slavery or assimilation. Makoons-Geniusz also highlights an important issue for academic scholars of Indigenous cultures; Indigenous academics often find themselves torn between using primary, oral Indigenous sources of knowledge that are not recognized by Eurowestern scholars or relying on colonized written reports that demonstrate a biased view of Indigenous culture as primitive. For the purposes of this chapter, I will only use sources from non-Indigenous scholars when such sources provide useful basic definitions or historical background information about Indigenous cultures. However, I will abstain from using the portions of these texts that critique Indigenous practices or that draw conclusions about Indigenous cultural practices. I believe that such writing is not the place of Eurowestern scholars. The science fiction authors discussed in this chapter do not often refer to specific Indigenous cultures when describing Indigenous healing or sustainability practices; instead, they draw on the practices of multiple Indigenous cultures to demonstrate a need for humanity to restore balance between all beings, which include spirits and inanimate objects. Hopkinson, Due, Hernandez, and Solomon all look to Indigenous healing and ritual to demonstrate the limitations of Eurowestern cultures' reliance on "rational" thought and the scientific method.

"Serving the Spirits": Indigenous Healing and Spirituality

Each of the texts addressed in this chapter has characters who employ Indigenous scientific literacies for healing purposes. Indigenous medicinal practices vary, depending particularly on the current location of the Indigenous group and what materials are available to these groups. Gayle Madeleine Randal identifies two elements of healing linked to spirituality that are found across multiple Indigenous cultures: a holistic healing approach that "emphasizes treatment of body, mind, emotion, and spirit"; and a belief in animism, or "the belief that nature has sentient life force and all physical beings have a spiritual essence that is related to but separate from their physical aspect" (S127). She also explains that Indigenous healing practices can be difficult to study because such practices are typically learned through hands-on apprenticeship and are not often recorded or written (S127). Indigenous healers, sometimes referred to as Medicine Men or Women, are typically tasked with the responsibility of teaching advanced Indigenous healing practices, including the making of medicines, healing rituals, and spiritual knowledge, to apprentices. However, as Makoons-Genuis explains, many Indigenous peoples have a *gikendaasowin* ("public" or "unguarded") knowledge of cultural practices, which includes a basic knowledge of herbal remedies. In an interview Makoons-Genuis conducts with Dora Dorothy Whipple, an elder from the Leech Lake Reservation in Minnesota, Dora explains that Medicine men typically possess more advanced, specialized healing abilities that go beyond *gikendaasowin*, which include the ability to "see inside a person" and to heal sicknesses that do not respond to basic herbal remedies (65–66). Makoons-Geniusz also notes that Anishinaabe Indigenous healing practices come from many sources, including dreams, spirits, and observation of nature (68–69). Indigenous healing practices are thus simultaneously generalized and highly specified; some healing practices are passed down from family to family while others are known only to healers who have undergone apprenticeship.

Because the art of healing is one of the fundamental sources of Indigenous scientific literacy, combining a knowledge of botany, oral history, and social and spiritual practices, the suppression of Indigenous healing practices in the Americas by Eurowestern cultures has had a devastating effect on efforts to recover Indigenous knowledge. Laws such as the US Indian Health Care Improvement Act (IHCIA), enacted in 1976 to "improve" the healthcare status of Native Americans, only served to impose Eurowestern medicine on Indigenous communities by a culture that believed its medicinal practices to be superior. Holly T. Kuschell-Haworth notes that the act did not attempt to understand the practices and beliefs of Indigenous healing and did not provide Indigenous healers as part of its healthcare system (844). Although Kuschell-Haworth notes that beginning in the 1990s, some US government healthcare initiatives did start approving the use of Indigenous healers, the centuries of suppression of Indigenous practices and forced assimilation of Indigenous peoples by colonizing Eurowestern cultures means that Indigenous healers are often in short supply. Makoons-Geniusz notes that Anishinaabe cultural revitalization programs of the US and Canada often have trouble finding written texts that do not present a biased or inaccurate view of Indigenous languages, practices, and cultural beliefs (5). Without a written record or a knowledgeable elder, Indigenous communities may struggle to preserve Indigenous knowledge and cultural practices. This struggle to preserve or restore knowledge is a common theme in the works discussed in this chapter.

Although spirits are often regulated to the fantasy genre of writing, the science fiction authors discussed in this chapter frequently depict characters engaged in Indigenous healing practices linked to some form of spirituality.[6] *Brown Girl in the Ring* has the most complete depiction of Indigenous healing and spiritual practices; Hopkinson highlights Indigenous healing practices through the actions of "Mami" Gros-Jeanne, a first-generation Caribbean Canadian who possesses knowledge of both herbal medicines and Eurowestern medicine. As a part of her healing practice, Mami also "serves the spirits" of an unidentified, African-based religion (59).[7] Hopkinson's text demonstrates a generational divide in the acceptance and practice of Indigenous healing and religious practices: She highlights the destructive results of Eurowestern colonization by creating a tension in the novel between Mami and her granddaughter, Ti-Jeanne, who has been taught to believe that Mami's rituals are "obeah,"[8] or black magic, and thus resists being taught Indigenous knowledge. Hopkinson makes it clear that the source of Caribbean cultures' fear of African religious ritual stems from Eurowestern influences when Mami explains to Ti-Jeanne why she has never tried to teach her the African-based spiritual rituals: "I used to hide it from you. . . . I don't really know why, doux-doux. From since slavery days, we

---

6. I am aware that the spiritual aspect of Indigenous healing is linked to its other aspects, like the use of herbal medicines or diet, through a holistic healing approach found in many Indigenous cultures. For the purposes of my analysis, however, I am going to discuss the spiritual aspect in the novels first and then move to a discussion of how Indigenous medicinal practices are portrayed alongside Eurowestern medical practices.

7. I should mention here that Hopkinson is an author with many cultural influences. She was born in Jamaica and has also lived in Trinidad, Guyana, Canada, and the US. She therefore considers herself to be both a Caribbean and a Canadian author. The titles of her main female characters also stem from Derek Walcott's "Ti-Jean and His Brothers," a play that includes Voudon ritual and that seems to be set in Haiti rather than Walcott's home, Trinidad. Monica A. Coleman describes Hopkinson's depiction of multiple Caribbean dialects in the novel as a "pan-Caribbean identity" and explains that Hopkinson's use of the term "obeah" "denotes a Pan-Caribbean understanding of African-derived spiritual practices" (3). Wherever Mami was born, she has been brought up with Indigenous knowledge stemming from African cultures brought to these islands, knowledge that was actively suppressed throughout the Caribbean by Eurowestern missionaries.

8. Although Ti-Jeanne and Tony both refer to Mami's practice as obeah, they are referring to the term's negative connotation, not the religion. "Obeah" is a term used specifically in the Caribbean to refer to African belief systems and rituals, but it often has a negative connotation. Mami tells Ti-Jeanne several times that her practice is not obeah, and Coleman notes that Hopkinson uses aspects of several "African-derived religious traditions" in Mami's practice, so I will refer to Mami's religion as an African-based religious practice rather than calling it obeah or Voudon.

people get in the habit of hiding we business from we own children even, in case a child open he mouth and tell somebody story and get them in trouble. Secrecy was survival, oui" (50). The practice of obeah, a creolized African-Caribbean term that came to refer to rituals viewed by Eurowestern colonizers of the Caribbean as black magic, was outlawed because of its ability to create communities among African slaves, and thus to incite rebellion. Indigenous knowledge of poisonous plants, in particular, was a great fear for Eurowestern slave owners (Olmos and Paravisini-Gebert 132). For African slaves in the Caribbean, obeah was a source of knowledge and power, but it also had to be hidden because of the risks involved in its practice.[9] Although Ti-Jeanne initially resists learning Mami's Indigenous knowledge beyond herbal remedies, she eventually has to come to terms with her Indigenous spiritual heritage in the story to save her life and the life of her mother.

Mami passes down to Ti-Jeanne one example of Indigenous spiritual ritual before she dies when she calls on Papa Osain, the healing spirit, to help Ti-Jeanne's boyfriend, Tony, escape the influence of Rudy, the leader of a local gang who uses obeah for evil. The ritual Mami engages in involves drawing complex designs, bestowing ritual gifts, drumming, and spiritual possession. She gives ritual gifts of rum, candy, and the blood of a chicken to Eshun, the messenger between heaven and Earth, and asks him to allow her to speak to the spirits. She also references the Ogun, the Orisha (spirit) of iron and warriors when she kills a chicken to gift Eshun with lifeblood (Hopkinson 89–93). This ritual results in Ti-Jeanne being possessed by The Prince of Cemetery/Eshu, the dual Orisha of life and death, who is revealed to be her spirit-father. He tells Mami how to conceal Ti-Jeanne and Tony from the gang. Mami is then possessed by her father-spirit, Osain, who tells Ti-Jeanne to tell Mami that she must destroy Rudy's duppy bowl, a tool used by Rudy to capture and hold the duppies (spirits) of his victims, to restore the balance of life and death (98). Hopkinson uses this scene to demonstrate the connection between humans and spirits in Indigenous culture, the importance of balance between all life, and the role of ritual in spiritual practice. She makes it clear that if the balance between worlds is not restored, the result will be the destruction of Ti-Jeanne's entire community.

Hopkinson draws attention to the ways that Indigenous healing is connected to the powers of both life and death in her narrative. Like the Haitian slaves that frightened European colonizers with their knowledge of poisons,

---

9. Margarite Fernández Olmos and Lizabeth Paravisini-Gebert note that many Caribbean islands still have active laws forbidding obeah practices, but they also state that enforcement of these laws has become lax as peoples become more tolerant of Indigenous religious practices (133).

healers in *Brown Girl* have knowledge of which ceremonies and plants can be used to harm or kill others. When Tony comes to try to win back Ti-Jeanne, Mami threatens to put "mal 'jo," or the *evil eye,* on him (26). Mami's practice of serving the spirits is also contrasted with the character Rudy, who uses obeah and a combination of drugs and Haitian herbs to create "zombies," by stripping people of their will, or "duppies," which are people whose souls have been disconnected from their physical bodies. These people, including Ti-Jeanne's mother, must serve Rudy unless their souls are freed. Mami and Rudy both demonstrate that knowledge of Indigenous healing practices is linked with knowledge of how to use spirits and plants to do harm; however, Rudy's choice to abuse obeah for personal gain is causing friction between the human and spiritual world because he is doing more harm than good. By taking more than he needs to prolong his own life, he is placing the mortal world in jeopardy. When Ti-Jeanne breaks his duppy bowl and calls on the eight oldest spirits to stop him, she gains the power to overcome his obeah (221). Ti-Jeanne demonstrates a respect and understanding of the spirits during this scene; her eventual willingness to "serve the spirits" restores balance and frees the souls Rudy has trapped.

Hopkinson connects Ti-Jeanne's acceptance of her new Indigenous knowledge to the salvation of her family and community. Once Ti-Jeanne realizes that she is tasked with finishing the job Osain gave Mami to confront Rudy, she uses the ritual knowledge Mami taught her to call the spirits to conceal her presence from Rudy. Mami is dead at this point, and the responsibility of restoring balance has fallen on Ti-Jeanne. As she calls on her father spirit, Papa Legbara (Eshu), she acknowledges the bond between herself and the spirits: "She knew that by calling the spirit 'Papa,' she was acknowledging a bond between them. Strangely, that felt safe and right, not the imposition on her that she thought it would be" (195). Ti-Jeanne is able to reenact a rough copy of the ceremony Mami taught her; she has limited resources, so the gifts she gives are peppermints and a cigarette (195). Once Ti-Jeanne acknowledges her connection to the spirit world, which she now realizes is "right," she is able to defeat Rudy, and by the end of the novel, she takes over Mami's role of healer in her community. Without Ti-Jeanne's healing knowledge, there is a chance that her community would not be sustainable. Hopkinson uses Ti-Jeanne's recovery of Indigenous healing and spirituality to demonstrate in *Brown Girl* that decolonization practices are crucial to the survival of humanity.

Carlos Hernandez's "The Assimilated Cuban's Guide to Quantum Santeria," the title story of his short story collection that shares the same name, tells the story of a young Cuban American boy named Salvador, or Sal, who turns to the Indigenous practice of Santería to enact a love spell and heal his father's heart. Salvador's mother dies from complications during an operation, but Hernandez uses flashbacks to let his readers understand that she has a very Catholic mistrust of "magic," which includes magic tricks and the practice of Santería. Sal's father, on the other hand, practiced Santería as a young man and eventually gave up the practice for his wife. Sal's father explains later in the story why he gave up being a Santero, or practitioner of Santería: "Before I met your mother, back when we were in Cuba, I was a Santero. A cabeza of Elegua. But I gave it up for her. It really scared her. She equated it with witchcraft, and the bible says witchcraft will get you a one-way ticket to hell" (248). Like Hopkinson, Hernandez creates a tension in the story between Indigenous practice and Catholicism, a belief system imposed upon Cubans by European colonizers. Sal's father explains to him that Cubans who did not give up their Santería/Yoruba practices had to hide them by using Catholic Saints as stand-in images for African gods (247). Hernandez utilizes the tension between the differing beliefs systems of Sal's parents as a commentary on the effects of colonization on Cuban and Latinx cultures.

When Sal creates a magic trick involving a stuffed black cat and performs the trick at school, his mother's spirit returns to their home and tells him and his father that "No quiero la magia negra en esta casa" (244). Sal's father, a science teacher, has his entire belief system challenged by her reappearance, and he attempts to understand what happened by returning to the practice of Santería. He creates a shrine to Elegua, "the pathfinder god, the guide to travelers" (247), and attempts to ask the spirits for guidance. Like Mami in *Brown Girl*, he gives the god gifts—rum, candies, and fruit; however, he does not know if he truly believes in the spirits and keeps drinking the rum. It is clear in this scene that Sal's father has forgotten how to be a Santero, and now, after years of training in the sciences, he has doubts about whether spirits exist. He explains to Sal that he has forgotten most of the rituals and states, "Connecticut isn't exactly a Santeria Mecca, you know. Where the hell do you get aguardiente in Handcock? But Santeria was born of adaptation. I will do the best I can with the materials at hand. If Elegua wants to hear me, he will hear me" (249). Like Ti-Jeanne, Sal's father is forced to make do with an adaptation of the original Indigenous ritual, which has been lost. His statement that Santería is "born of adaptation" demonstrates how formerly colonized cultures are working to revive Indigenous rituals and beliefs, often by adapting them to new materials and locations, as a decolonizing practice.

When Sal tries to research Santería, he finds no books in his school library on the subject. Ms. Anbow, the Assistant Principal, finds a master's thesis from the University of Connecticut's library that helps him understand the basics of the practice. Sal discovers that his father's altar is incorrect (perhaps the reason that the spirits are not communicating with him). He also discovers that the book has instructions for different "ebos," or spells, to help the Santo achieve specific goals. Sal finds that he cannot complete any of the love ebos from start to finish, mainly because they involve collecting samples of excrements from the desired lovers, so he decides to adapt his practice to his needs:

> There wasn't a single love ebo in the thesis I could—or would—follow all the way through. But there were ingredients of different love ebos I didn't mind, like cinnamon sticks and wine and hard candies and incense and Borax. So why couldn't I combine those to make my own ebo? Papí said that Santeria was born of adaptation; if the orishas wanted to help me, they would. I just had to prove I was serious. Willing to sacrifice for the sake of my desire." (253)

For Sal, who is not brought up in Cuba with the practice of Santería, the ritual matters less than his belief. He is following the instructions of a text written by a master's student named Ines Guanagao. Although the author would have been schooled in a Eurowestern university environment, her name indicates that she may be Latinx. Hernandez does not make it clear whether the author of the thesis had previous knowledge of Santería before starting her research, and she does not reveal anything about her research process in the narrative, so the audience cannot determine the accuracy of the instructions in the thesis. Like many other contemporary Indigenous peoples, Sal is left to adapt this text, written by a Eurowestern student, to his own healing needs. Hernandez uses humor and the "magic" of conjure science to discuss the difficulties of decolonizing not just Indigenous cultural practice, but also internalized cultural hatred of Indigenous beliefs and rituals imposed by Eurowestern colonization.

One theme that runs across many Indigenous oral tales is that healing is not meant to be a quick-and-easy process; rather, it is a relationship with all living things, including spirits, that requires several steps and sometimes the participation of an entire community. Hopkinson creates a communal gathering system in *Brown Girl* where those who have access to specific plants—by using greenhouses or by gathering in the wild—barter medicinal herbs with Mami for medicine. The ritual to protect Tony also involved taking the life of an animal, a chicken. Sal finds himself in a similar position when he is required to take the life of a pigeon to complete his ebo. He seems to instinctively understand enough about Indigenous ritual at this point to honor the bird's sacrifice by thanking it. This gesture or Sal's belief may be the reason the makeshift ebo works; his mother comes walking into the house a minute later with bags of groceries. However, Hernandez also forces the reader to question if it is the ebo that brings the spirit of Sal's mother to the home or the fact that he has once again, in her eyes, practiced "black magic." When Sal's mother sees the dead bird, she is furious and beats him with a sneaker, an experience he humorously describes as "the happiest moment of my childhood" (264). Once again, Hernandez asks his reader to acknowledge the effects of colonization on Cuban culture: Although Cuban Catholics like Sal's mother fear Indigenous ritual, the rituals and the belief in sprits remain. The fact that Sal's mother keeps returning demonstrates that the Latinx belief in the fantastic has never truly been erased. Sal and his father continue to practice Santería at the end of the story when they want to communicate with Mami's spirit, an act that demonstrates a successful decolonization of belief for a Cuban immigrant and his Latinx son.

Solomon's *An Unkindness of Ghosts* and Due's *African Immortals* series do not follow a specific Indigenous belief system; instead, they each include spirit-like, ghostly characters that represent the past as well as a transcendence of the physical body. *An Unkindness of Ghosts* is set in a distant future where a specific race of peoples, named "Tarlanders," are subjugated and treated as slaves. The reference to "tar," a black substance, may be one clue as to why these peoples are treated differently. However, Solomon also adds an additional element of sexual identity when the main character, a healer named Aster,[10] explains that Tarlanders often do not present as male or female, which makes them "not of the Heavens" (19). This justification, based on a Eurowestern-like religious belief in two distinct sexes, means that Tarlanders can be treated as slaves; that is, they are forced to work as manual laborers and are not allowed to move up to a higher "deck" on the

---

10. Although Solomon uses the pronoun "she" to describe Aster and "he" for Theo in *Unkindness*, it is clear in their "cross-dressing" scene and in the descriptions of Tarlanders as non-gender-conforming that they are not following the Eurowestern, heteronormative notion of femininity and gender roles. Solomon explains their decision to avoid contemporary LGBTQIA labels, stating, "To me, all of these labels are context dependent and therefore it does not feel authentic or organic to use words that have developed out of our contemporary discourse to describe my characters. For example, largely everyone in Q-deck, where the protagonist Aster lives, uses she/her pronouns and are generally interpreted as women, and most people are intersex. 'Lesbian' doesn't make sense as a meaningful word in a world where almost everyone someone would be attracted to is a woman. Certainly neither does 'straight' when everything about their bodies and sexual expression is otherised" (qtd. in Falck). I will, therefore, try to use the characters' proper names as much as possible. I will also use Solomon's preferred pronoun of "they."

ship, a metaphor for social class. Aster escapes the class system of the ship for a brief period of time when her interest in and inherent gift for creating medicines catch the notice of the ship's surgeon, Theo, who is also able to overcome the view of his slightly darker skin through his position as the ship's Surgeon. Aster and Theo both subvert the class system of the ship through a knowledge of healing.

Solomon includes references to Indigenous cultural belief in *Unkindness* by making references to oral histories of "the Ancestors,'" or spirits of the dead who have remained on the ship. When the ship begins experiencing random blackouts, the grandmother of one of Aster's patients, whom she calls by the title "Eldwa," tells Aster that "the Ancestors are real and their spirits are at work" (22). The use of the term "Eldwa" seems to reference the term "elder," which is significant because Indigenous cultures demonstrate a great respect for the beliefs and teachings of elders. However, like Ti-Jeanne and Sal's father, Aster does not believe in spirits. While trying to decipher notes that her mother left behind, notes about her family history and inheritance, Aster states, "The Sprit World was as much a myth as a planet or a real star. Signs, however, didn't rely on the existence of the supernatural. History wanted to be remembered. . . . *That's what ghosts really are*, Aint Melusine had said, *the past refusing to be forgot*" (59, original italics). Aster takes a pragmatic view of the existence of spirits. However, Solomon, like Hernandez, uses humor to ask readers to believe that the spirit world does exist, the same way they know that the planets and stars are real. Unlike the Orisha spirits of Hopkinson's and Hernandez's novels, Solomon creates an intentionally vague notion of spirits and juxtaposes them with ghosts to comment on the loss slavery has created for the African diaspora. Aster asks herself at one point while thinking about the loss of her mother: "A part of each person lay in their past, in their parentage and grandparentage, and if that history was missing, were said people incomplete?" (23). Aster also comments on the "impressiveness" of oral histories (23). Solomon is less optimistic about colonized cultures' ability to recover lost histories than Hopkinson or Hernandez; however, the fact that Aster and her friend Giselle are able to discover that Aster's mother's notes are written in code and that therefore they can decipher them demonstrates that some of Aster's history, while incomplete and difficult to understand, has survived.

Eventually, Aster learns that the entire ship was designed by the Ancestors to pay homage to "The Celestial Sphere," or a theoretical model of Earth, also named "The Great Lifehouse," and its surrounding stars:

> In the model, the Great Lifehouse rests at the center of an imaginary sphere, stars revolving around it along various axes. . . . the Celestial Sphere was

distinct from the worldview pretelescope scientists held that the universe revolved around a single, insignificantly sized planet. Rather, the Celestial Sphere provided a way of understanding relationships in the horizon, the poles, and the night sky to determine the location of stars relative to one's location on the Great Lifehouse at a given time. (104)

Solomon references the "pretelescope" belief in Eurowestern cultures that Earth was the center of the universe, which highlights early Eurowestern peoples as a "primitive" culture. Naming Earth "The Great Lifehouse" references Indigenous belief in the value of all life. Solomon's choice to highlight "relationships" between Earth and the stars also demonstrates the Ancestors' valuing of mutual relations between inanimate objects, another belief that is expressed in multiple Indigenous cultures. Although Solomon does not reference a specific Indigenous culture, her references to slavery and lost oral history mean that belief in the Ancestors may have come from an African belief system. The theme that emerges from Solomon's references to the spirit world is that colonized cultures will have to find a way to heal the trauma of losing their history and connection to their Ancestors before they can find a way forward to a decolonized mindset.

Due also uses a nonspecific description of spirits in her *African Immortal* series to demonstrate the need to address the spiritual as part of healing both individuals and communities. Unlike the other authors discussed, who represent cultures where people have forgotten their history and cultural practices as a result of slavery and colonization, Due's immortal characters can remember the entirety of their personal histories going back centuries. One of her main characters is an African man named Dawit, or David, who has lived through centuries of war and who has experienced slavery firsthand. Due positions Dawit as a living testimonial that directly challenges Eurowestern bias in historical narratives. His firsthand experience of slavery, told to his mortal (later made immortal) wife, Jessica, creates a powerful narrative that demonstrates in first person the traumatic loss experienced by Black enslaved peoples. Because Dawit can remember all the abuse he has experienced over centuries, he embodies the trauma of past and contemporary Black peoples. To prove this point, Due explains that Dawit chose to remain in the US after gaining his freedom because his experiences with slavery connect him to African American communities; few other peoples would be able to understand his experiences. Although Dawit is not a spirit, he is haunted by his past experiences with slavery, a haunting that he must engage with by recounting his experiences to Jessica. Dawit is a professor and an author of a book on jazz culture, while Jessica is a newspaper reporter who is also considering writing a book about inequality in the nursing care system. Both recognize the need to chronicle the experiences of peoples who have been abused, and Due uses the power of the written word as a metaphor for the restoration of these peoples' history. Looking at this restorative aspect of Due's writing through Dillon's concept of literacy and writing as "conjure sciences," Dawit and Jessica become healers who are using writing to restore spiritual balance to enslaved and traumatized peoples.

Due also uses the concept of evil spirits in her series to further demonstrate the consequences of spiritual imbalance on enslaved and colonized peoples. One of her characters, Lucas Sheppard, is a Eurowestern-trained doctor who becomes interested in Indigenous healing practices because of a childhood experience he has with an evil spirit. After Lucas spends the night at his friend's house—a household riddled with alcoholism and abuse—his grandmother explains that the bed-shaking spirit he encounters is a manifestation of the misery found in the home. She speculates that this sickness could be "left in that old house from slavery" and explains that the spirit "wanted to be reckoned with" (*The Living* 138). Indigenous cultural practices would explain Lucas's "supernatural" experience as a spiritual imbalance caused by both the past traumas of slavery and the current traumas of alcoholism and abuse that may stem from the socioeconomic imbalances created by racist institutions in Eurowestern cultures. Dillon advocates for *biskaabiiyang*, or a return to self through decolonization practices, as the solution to the dangers of imbalance ("Imagining" 9–10). However, at this time Lucas is a young boy who is powerless to heal the trauma of his friend's home, and his experience with the spirit also marks his family as a target for "the shadows," a phrase that Due creates to explain the source of the evil spirits in her series. Due creates the shadows to represent the lasting traumas of colonization on black and brown bodies.

When Lucas's wife, Rachel, falls ill with a sickness modern medicine cannot treat, Lucas turns to Indigenous medicine to heal her. The shaman Lucas consults tells him that his wife is "swimming in shadows" that refuse to release her (30). Lucas's son is also marked by the shadows and, seemingly as a result, is unable to be cured of his leukemia without the intervention of "The Living Blood," the source of the immortal characters' immortality that their leader, Khaldun, claims is the blood of Christ. Due uses this reference to Christ to juxtapose the spiritual beliefs of Indigenous practice with the Christianity that many African American communities have turned to in the face of devastating cultural loss. Due uses references to "spirits" and "shadows" in conjunction with spiritual and physical illness to demonstrate how both Indigenous cultures and colonized Christian communities incorporate the spiritual into their healing and sustainability practices.

Each author discussed in this chapter includes scenes in their books that highlight the connection between spiritual belief and healing practices for Indigenous and colonized communities. Whether this belief is highlighted in a return to a specific Indigenous cultural practice or through the use of spirits in a more metaphorical sense, each author demonstrates the power that comes from retaining, recovering, and recording the histories of enslaved and colonized peoples. Eurowestern cultures have at times dismissed Indigenous healing practices as "magic" while at the same time fearing the power that this communal knowledge and practice gives communities of color. This juxtaposition is one of many reasons why the incorporation of Indigenous spiritual healing into science fiction texts is so significant. The texts in this chapter provide blueprints for how humans, if they decolonize their thinking, can employ Indigenous scientific literacies as "powerful acts[s] of reciprocity with the more-than-human world" (Kimmerer 252).

Blending Eurowestern and Indigenous Science and Technology

Each of the authors discussed in this chapter addresses the role of both Eurowestern and Indigenous science and technologies in their texts. Sometimes this discussion is comparative, while at other times one science or technology complements or supplements the other. The authors also ensure that Indigenous scientific literacies are depicted as equal or superior to Eurowestern sciences. Several of the novels create a dichotomy between a Eurowestern-trained doctor and a doctor or healer who employs Indigenous healing practices. Despite the differences in their depictions of the relationship between Eurowestern and Indigenous sciences, all the authors discussed ask readers to think about the possibilities of blending both knowledge-sets to create a view of science that is more inclusive and adaptable.

Hopkinson explains multiple times in *Brown Girl* how Mami adapts her Caribbean Indigenous knowledge of herbal medicines to her new home in a near-future dystopic Canada. Ti-Jeanne notes that Mami "freely mixed her nursing training with her knowledge of herbal cures" (12). At the beginning of the novel, the town librarian, Mr. Reed, gives Ti-Jeanne four books he thinks might interest Mami: "an encyclopedia of medical symptoms, two gardening books, and the real find: *Caribbean Wild Plants and Their Uses*" (12).

The librarian knows that Mami should be able to use these books to enhance her healing knowledge, which will allow her to better treat the people who come to her for care. The book also represents a return of lost Indigenous knowledge about Caribbean herbal medicines. Ti-Jeanne, a third-generation Caribbean-Canadian, demonstrates her distrust of Mami's reliance on herbal remedies in the same scene: "Ti-Jeanne just hoped that the ointment would work. Sometimes the plants Mami used had lost their potency, or perhaps were just a weak strain. Too sometimes-ish for Ti-Jeanne's taste. She'd slipped some vitamin B tablets and a tube of anti-inflammatory cream into Mr. Reed's package" (13). Ti-Jeanne, who was born in Canada, has adopted the belief that Eurowestern medicine is more "advanced" than herbal medicines. Hopkinson uses Ti-Jeanne's suspicion of Indigenous knowledge and the symbolism of the books to comment on the effects of colonization and immigration on Caribbean peoples. Ti-Jeanne will eventually have to overcome her suspicion and restore her lost cultural knowledge to survive.

Hopkinson reinforces the tension between Indigenous and Eurowestern medicinal practices through Ti-Jeanne's relationship with Tony, a Caribbean immigrant who has been trained as a nurse in Canada. At the beginning of the novel Tony states that he does not believe in spirits; the narrator explains, "Tony had once teased Ti-Jeanne to tears about her grandmother: 'What's that crazy old woman doing over there . . . obeah? Nobody believes in that duppy business any more!'" (36). Tony does, however, have the traditional colonized Caribbean fear of obeah. Hopkinson explains, "Tony was terrified of the small-boned seer woman [Mami]. Ti-Jeanne knew that for all his medical training and his Canadian upbringing, he'd learned the fear of Caribbean obeah at his mother's knee" (26). Tony and Ti-Jeanne both fear obeah because they have witnessed the rituals and effects without a true understanding of the Indigenous knowledge behind them. Although Tony claims he does not believe in obeah, he turns to Ti-Jeanne, and through her Mami, for help escaping Rudy because he recognizes that her healing ability is the only thing that may be able to save him. Tony and Ti-Jeanne represent the tension and contradiction in beliefs held by many younger generations of Caribbean immigrants.

Hopkinson further critiques Eurowestern medicinal practices by characterizing Tony as a drug addict, which highlights the effects of Eurowestern medicine's reliance on drugs such as opioids.[11] She also describes the Canadian state doctors, who are too expensive to call on unless a person has

---

11. For information on the scale of the opioid crisis in the US, see the US Department of Health and Human Services page titled "What Is the U. S. Opioid Epidemic?": https://www.hhs.gov/opioids/about-the-epidemic/index.html.

died, as "vultures." Tony becomes addicted to "Buff," a chemical substance injected into the veins, while treating patients; he loses his job as a result and becomes indebted to Rudy's gang. When Papa Osain possesses Mami's body during the spiritual ceremony she enacts to save Tony from Rudy, the Orisha notices the buff slashes on his arms and states that he is angry with him: "Don't touch me. So long you ain't use your hands to heal. Don't touch me. You not my son anymore. . . . Healer turn to dealer. What I business with you?" (96–99). Amanda D. Concha-Holmes explains that in Yoruba culture, Papa Osain is considered both a deity and a force of nature:

> Osain (spelled Osanyin in Yorùbàland) is an orisha who may be understood as the embodiment of nature and medicine including herbs, plants, trees, and the forest. Osain embodies many different aspects of the religion, particularly the embodiment of ashé, orisha and nature. He is not only a deity, but it is also a ceremony that allows the powers to be extracted from the plants. Osain is also considered to be an omiero, sacred water that holds the powers of the plants. Thus, I found out, I had to distinguish between asking *What* is Osain? and *Who* is Osain? (207)

Papa Osain comes because Mami, a true healer, has called him. Osain is considered the Orisha connected to healing, and it is his being and ceremony that allow healers to succeed in their practices. Osain's statement that Tony is no longer his "son" demonstrates how working in the Eurowestern medical community, with access to addictive drugs and no spiritual connection to his practice, has caused Tony to become disconnected from his role as a healer. Hopkinson utilizes Mami's practice to critique the idea that Eurowestern medicine is superior to Indigenous healing.

Hopkinson also demonstrates the negative side of Eurowestern healing practices in her description of Canadian Premier Uttley's heart transplant. Due to a lack of human donors, most peoples in Hopkinson's near-future Canada receive pig hearts for a transplant. However, Premier Uttley decides to use a recent disease to scare the public into supporting her bill for the reinstation of voluntary human organ donation. In order to get reelected to her position, she claims that she will not have a transplant unless the medical system finds her a compatible human heart. To increase her chances, one of her aides hires Rudy's gang to kill a donor and secure the Premier a heart. To save his own life, Tony kills Mami and sends for the "vultures," or medical personnel, to deliver her heart to Uttley. In an ironic twist, Mami's heart affects Uttley, and she wakes to find that the heart has influenced her worldview by giving her a "social consciousness," which causes her to support a plan to fund small businesses and rejuvenate Toronto. The Premier's transplant represents the ways in which Eurowestern countries favor wealthy patients who are more likely to have their names listed on multiple donor waiting lists and less likely to die while waiting due to better access to healthcare (Marchione). Hopkinson understands that countries like the US and Canada often fail to provide adequate healthcare to poor and middle-class citizens. In 1986, the US Congress had to enact the Emergency Medical Treatment and Labor Act (EMTALA) to make it illegal for hospitals to engage in "patient dumping," or the early release of patients who did not have health insurance and who, therefore, could not afford medical treatment (Dalen). In 2010, the US Congress and then-President Barack Obama enacted the Patient Protection and Affordable Care Act to attempt to provide all Americans with affordable healthcare ("Patient"). After the change in administration, Trump and other Republican lawmakers attempted to repeal the law, which would have left millions of Americans without healthcare ("Obamacare"). Although Canada has publicly funded healthcare, the government admits that healthcare disparities still exist due to social, political, and economic disadvantages. Indigenous Canadians, in particular, have been affected by colonialism and the imposition of Eurowestern medical practices, which the First Nations Information Governance Centre and Métis National Council states has "been largely responsible for destabilizing the determinants of Indigenous health" ("Key Health"). Hopkinson demonstrates that a major flaw in the medical systems of Eurowestern countries is that they are still seeking capitalist gain rather than helping citizens most in need. The fact that Mami, an Indigenous healer, dies to further a Canadian government official's political agenda shows the consequences of Eurowestern colonization for immigrant and Indigenous groups, who are often the most affected by the flaws and biases of the Eurowestern medical system.

But Hopkinson refuses to leave readers with no hope. The fact that Mami's heart takes over Uttley's consciousness and influences her worldview demonstrates the influence of Indigenous and grassroots social movements. Mami forces Uttley to serves the spirits, which the Jab Jab (another form of Papa Legbara) explains to Ti-Jeanne is something that anyone with social awareness can do: "Gros-Jeanne [Mami] woulda tell you that all she doing is serving the spirits. And that anybody who try to live good, who try to have respect for life, and age, and those who go before, them all doing the same thing: serving the spirits" (219). Indigenous peoples[12] have been instrumental in the protests of the Dakota Access Pipeline in the US and

---

12. Specifically, the Standing Rock Sioux and Cheyenne River Sioux tribes.

Keystone XL Pipeline, which runs from Canada to Nebraska (Medina). The Dakota Access Pipeline protest, in particular, has received media attention as Indigenous tribes and environmental activist groups worldwide joined the Standing Rock Sioux in their protest (Wehelie); media coverage of the protest also allowed Indigenous peoples to discuss the contrast between Indigenous environmental beliefs and the profit-driven capitalist view of Eurowestern corporations. As younger generations consider the impact of climate change on the future of the planet, young climate change activists like Xiye Bastida, Mari Copeny, Jamie Margolin, Isra Hirsi, and Greta Thurnberg, who at age sixteen is nominated for a Nobel Peace Prize, are influencing public opinion about the issue. Educational Organizations such as the United Nations Educational, Scientific and Cultural Organization (UNESCO) are currently recognizing Indigenous knowledge through its Local and Indigenous Knowledge Systems program (LINKS), which "promotes local and indigenous knowledge and its inclusion in global climate science and policy processes" ("Indigenous Knowledge"). As Eurowestern citizens begin to see the consequences of lax environmental laws in their cities and towns, Indigenous activism is influencing social movements and drawing attention to the effects of climate change.

Due describes both Indigenous and Eurowestern medical practices in her *African Immortal* series, but does not blend the two practices; instead, she makes two key characters in the series African American doctors who demonstrate respect for Indigenous healing. She also employs scenes of Indigenous healing to highlight how Indigenous practices account for influences that Eurowestern medicine dismisses as non-rational. Dr. Sheppard studies under South American, Lakota, Haitian, and Zimbabwean healers to broaden his knowledge of medicinal plants and healing ceremonies (*The Living* 26–30). When his wife's cancer refuses to respond to Eurowestern medicines, he employs Indigenous healer Three Ravens Perez to conduct a sweat lodge ceremony to heal her and asks his friends and family to participate. The narrator notes that everyone at the ceremony feels the ground shake as the healer attempts to drive the shadows away from Rachel (30–31). Although Perez is unsuccessful because the shadows refuse to release her, the fact that he knows about the shadows makes his medicine superior to Eurowestern attempts according to the most powerful Life Brother, Khaldun, who says:

> Many mortal cultures understand this already and have always passed knowledge through generations to combat them. They avoid grounds that are accursed; they know incarnations and rituals to keep them safe. The

cultures that have forgotten the Shadows' existence consider these beliefs primitive . . . but, if anything, those who know and respect the Shadows are the more enlightened. (*African Immortals* 276)

Due uses the sweat lodge scene and Khaldun's explanation to argue that Indigenous knowledge should not be dismissed by Eurowestern doctors as primitive; it is important knowledge that has been passed down and preserved for the benefit of all. She understands that Indigenous knowledge accounts for the entire being, physical and spiritual, and therefore has the potential to heal ailments still not entirely understood by Eurowestern medicine.

Another key scene that links Indigenous and Eurowestern medicine in Due's series is when Alex, a US-trained doctor and Jessica's sister, opens a clinic in Botswana to heal people with Jessica's blood. Alex and the local medicine man demonstrate a mutual respect for each other's practices by referring patients back and forth between one another. Alex refers patients who are able to be healed using local medicines, while the medicine man sends her patients who cannot be healed without the blood. Each healer understands the need for the other in their community, and both respect the knowledge of the other practitioner. Lisa Lopez Levers argues that more Eurowestern doctors and counselors need to incorporate Indigenous scientific knowledge to treat illness in African communities successfully:

Euro-American understandings of indigenous knowledge, in general, and indigenous healing practices, in particular, have been limited. However, as the philosophy and history of science literatures have indicated a shifting scientific paradigm, our understandings have been moving gradually away from the hegemony of scientific method and Cartesian logic as the only valid dictum of knowledge. If this is the case . . . it behooves academics and practitioners interested in multiple epistemological paradigms to investigate systems of indigenous knowledge and practices that historically have been considered as outside the parameters of the Euro-American scientific paradigm. (87)

The assumption of Eurowestern technological superiority means that doctors in these countries typically dismiss valuable resources of local knowledge. However, the "shifting scientific paradigm" Levers refers to demonstrates that some Eurowestern scientists and doctors are beginning to shift to acknowledge other ways of thinking about science. Due's fiction provides one example of how Eurowestern doctors could respect local knowledge by creating a scenario where a US-trained doctor and an Indigenous healer work together for the good of the community. Alex creates a relationship with the Botswanan community that allows for trust and respect; this is one reason that the local peoples accept her help.

While Hopkinson and Due employ Indigenous knowledge to critique Eurowestern medicine, Solomon describes the character Aster in *An Unkindness of Ghosts* as a healer who uses a combination of Indigenous and Eurowestern medical knowledge in her healing efforts. The fact that Aster blends both types of healing highlights her intelligence and adaptability, both traits that help her survive the brutal colonial system of the ship. Aster learns Eurowestern medical practices from Theo, but she also supplements these practices with her knowledge of herbal medicines. The first time Aster meets Theo, she claims to have synthesized benzodiazepine to give to her friend Giselle, who suffers from anxiety. Theo is impressed by her knowledge of medicines, but Aster thinks to herself:

> In truth, she'd not synthesized anything at all, only dissolved pills she'd stolen from an upperdeck woman into an herbal solution that heightened the calming effects of the drug. She's tried to make it herself . . . but the books she found confused and then upset her. (Solomon 191)

Though Aster does not discuss the specifics of her "herbal solution" or where she learned this knowledge, it is clear that she has a basic knowledge of herbal medicines and their uses. Like Sal in "Quantum Santeria," Aster is left to figure out how to heal using incomplete or confusing written records and observation. The fact that Aster steals the medicine demonstrates its rarity, especially among the Tarlanders, who are probably not considered worth medicating. Aster is able to refine her knowledge of herbal medicines because she has created a hidden greenhouse on the ship where she grows the plants she needs to create herbal remedies. Aster's knowledge of plants and herbal medicines and her willingness to nurture the plants necessary to create the medicines give her a form of currency on the ship: Aster can barter her healing abilities for necessities. Working as Theo's assistant also gives Aster a layer of protection from the abusive overseers on the ship and the freedom to move about the ship. Aster's survival is therefore intimately connected to her knowledge of both Eurowestern and Indigenous medicines.

Solomon further references the power of Aster's knowledge of poisons when Theo asks Aster whether she poisoned the Sovereign Nicholas, the leader of the entire ship. Theo cannot figure out what substance killed the

Sovereign, and he believes that only Aster, with her greenhouse and knowledge of herbal medicine, could have created an unknown poison. Theo acknowledges in this scene that Aster has knowledge he does not, knowledge linked to Indigenous healing. Theo is trained in Eurowestern medicines and has more knowledge of surgery, but Aster's knowledge of herbal medicines makes her a healer on equal footing. As Aster performs an autopsy on Nicholas with Theo, she comments to him, "Believe me, if I could make a poison that did this, you better believe I'd give it to every upperdecker on this ship. Excluding you, of course. You were right to suspect me" (139). Aster has no moral issue with killing the upperdeckers, whom she views as either responsible for or complacent in the social order that results in her enslavement and mistreatment. Solomon uses this scene to remind readers of the power of Indigenous knowledge and the fear that this knowledge rightly instilled in Eurowestern colonizers. They remind us that Indigenous knowledge should not be dismissed or undervalued, and they also point out the consequences of doing so for Eurowestern societies.

As Theo acknowledges Aster's superior knowledge of herbal medicine, Aster acknowledges that plants have healing abilities she will never understand or possess. She describes a dandelion root as "smaller and less complicated than she was, genetically, but possessing the ability to locate and destroy cancerous cells where Aster herself could not" (255). Ovadje et al. note that Eurowestern medical treatments have not been able to successfully eradicate cancer or slow its progress among humans:

> There are over 12 million new cancer cases arising annually and over 7 million cancer-related deaths worldwide, and even with the introduction of many chemotherapy and chemopreventive approaches, cancer is still one of the leading causes of deaths in the world today, with a statistic of one in four deaths being attributed to cancer alone (73080).

They then note that based on their research, dandelion root extract has the potential to become "a non-toxic and effective anti-cancer alternative, instrumental for reducing the occurrence of cancer cells drug-resistance" (73080). This study points to acceptance of plant-based medicines as effective and demonstrates how Eurowestern scientists are beginning to combine chemical and herbal treatments to achieve a more successful treatment of patients worldwide. Aster, like most other Indigenous healers, demonstrates a relationship with and respect for the plants that she cultivates. While Eurowestern doctors and scientists may not achieve a symbiotic relationship with plants, they can still benefit from a knowledge of herbal medicines.

Although Sal plays the role of an Indigenous healer in "Quantum Santeria," Hernandez's concern is less with actual healing practices than with the healing of family or generational trauma. Sal doesn't want to heal peoples in his community; he only wants to utilize his cultural inheritance of Santería to heal his father's grief. While "Quantum Santeria" addresses healing on a more personal level, Hernandez also employs the concept of nonlinear time, a belief of many Indigenous cultures, to demonstrate how Latinx culture makes room for the fantastic. When Sal researches Santería and grief, he finds no books on Santería (not unexpected in a Eurowestern cultural knowledge model), but he does discover several psychology texts. One of the texts notes that children do not see time as linear:

> But not children. They think time can go forward, backwards, sideways, and loop like a Hot Wheels racecar track. You need to understand how children see time to help them understand that the dead stay dead forever.
>
> Unless the dead show up one day to tell you to get rid of your stuffed black cat. (250)

Hernandez uses humor to make space for multiple theories of time. A Eurowestern psychologist views time as only linear because this form of time is considered "rational" and observable. However, the fact that Sal's mother comes back from death to scold him twice in the story suggests that an alternate theory of time is working in this story, one that blurs the distinction between life and death. Hernandez's story fits the definition of "Native Slipstream," which Dillon defines as texts that reference a nonlinear view of space time through use of "time travel, alternate realities and multiverses, and alternative histories" ("Imagining" 3). Dillon also notes that Indigenous views of time anticipate current scientific theories in physics:

> Native slipstream thinking, which has been around for millennia, anticipated recent cutting-edge physics, ironically suggesting that Natives have had things right all along. The closest approximation in quantum mechanics is the concept of the "multiverse," which posits that reality consists of a number of simultaneously existing alternate worlds and/or parallel worlds. (4)

Hernandez uses references to Eurowestern sciences and research methods as a foil for his alternate or parallel theories of time. Eventually, Sal becomes a scientist like his father, with a specialization in quantum physics, yet both men still employ Sal's Santería ritual whenever they want to see Sal's mother. Sal states at the end of the story, "Nobody knows the first thing about quantum physics. Except maybe Elegua" (266). His choice to reference an Orisha in a discussion of physics shows that Sal has not forgotten his Indigenous heritage after being trained in Eurowestern science. Instead, Hernandez depicts Eurowestern and Indigenous science coexisting in harmony through his portrayal of a father and son who value both science and Santería. "Quantum Santeria" gives readers a glimpse into what Eurowestern science could achieve if it acknowledged Indigenous scientific literacies.

Balance and Survivance

Indigenous cultures' history of resistance to Eurowestern colonization and forced assimilation leads some scholars to discuss Indigenous culture in terms of already surviving the apocalypse. Deborah L. Madsen quotes Anishinaabe scholar Lawrence W. Gross's description of Anishinaabe culture as recovering from "Post-Apocalypse Stress Syndrome" and goes on to note, "Along with many other Native American peoples, the Anishinaabe have seen the end of the world, which has created tremendous social stresses" (65). But Indigenous culture is not only significant because it is still present; Gerald Vizenor (Anishinaabe) notes in his theory of survivance that without an "active sense of presence over absence, deracination, and oblivion" and a resistance against a "legacy of victimry" (Vizenor 1), Indigenous cultures and their knowledge will continue to be ignored by colonizing cultures.

Dillon notes that Native Apocalypse is defined by a state of imbalance and defines Native apocalyptic storytelling as an effort to restore cultural balance:

> Imbalance further implies a state of extremes, but within those extremes lies a middle ground and the seeds of *bimaadiziwin,* the state of balance, one of difference and provisionally, a condition of resistance and survival. Native apocalyptic storytelling, then, shows the ruptures, the scars, and the trauma in its effort ultimately to provide healing and a return to bimaadiziwin. This is a path to a sovereignty embedded in self-determination. ("Imagining" 9)

As scholars and activists recover and reference Indigenous knowledge to combat the damage of internalized colonization, this knowledge also has the potential to educate Eurowestern cultures about alternate ways of viewing humanity's relationship both to other living beings and to the planet. Each of the authors in this chapter is engaging in such work by highlighting relationships between different types of beings. Whether it is humans and spirits or immortals, or humans and plants, each story showcases symbiotic relations and argues for a rebuilding of lost connections and, ultimately, a restoration of balance for survival.

Hopkinson and Hernandez address the need for balance in human/spirit relations in their works. Hopkinson employs Ti-Jeanne's relationship with the spirit world as a metaphor for all humanity. Ti-Jeanne makes it clear at the end of *Brown Girl* that her decision to take over Mami's healer role will not last forever when she tells Papa Legbara, another iteration of her father Orisha, "I go do this [healing] for a little while, but I ain't Mami. I ain't know what I want to do with myself yet, but I can't be she" (244). Ti-Jeanne's statement creates a tentative balance between humans and spirits in her generation, one that will hopefully be carried on by Ti-Jeanne's baby, who Hopkinson hints may have inherited his mother's seer abilities. But Hopkinson leaves readers questioning what will happen to humanity if Ti-Jeanne and other contemporary Indigenous peoples refuse to acknowledge their inheritance of Indigenous knowledge, which includes crucial knowledge about retaining and restoring balance both within the body and planetwide.

Hernandez creates a sense of balance at the end of "Quantum Santeria" between Latinx peoples, represented by Sal and his father and their Indigenous heritage. When Sal's father states, "Now all we need is a pigeon" and Sal answers, "No worries Pápi. . . . I've got one right here" (267), they are both acknowledging the power of Santería. Moreover, by choosing to enact the ritual that they know Sal's mother disapproves of, they are both shedding the internalized beliefs of colonized Latinx peoples who view Santería as evil and not worthy of Christian belief. Sal and his father represent balance on both a personal and a cultural level; like Ti-Jeanne, they have both accepted their inheritance of Indigenous knowledge and its power. However, while Ti-Jeanne remains uncertain as to what she and her child will do with this knowledge, Sal and his father are happy to set aside a Eurowestern dependence on rationality and utilize Santería to enhance their knowledge. Hernandez's humorous style leaves the men employing the Orishas for wish fulfillment, but Sal's mother also represents a recovery of lost family and cultural connections that many Latinx immigrants yearn for.

Due takes the personal relationship between Fana and Michael, two super-immortals who received the living blood in utero, and she employs this relationship as a metaphor for all of humanity. Fana and Michael have an extraordinary amount of power to shape humanity, but they each have differing views of what the future of humanity should look like. Fana wants to use the living blood to cure disease, which would increase the overall quality of life for all humans. However, she acknowledges that humanity is having a negative environmental impact on the planet. Michael believes that the only solution to the problem of human environmental impact is to kill off a large portion of humanity in an event he calls the Cleansing. As each immortal struggles to assert his or her desires, Due creates a bond between Fana and Michael that makes it unlikely that one can survive if they kill the other, forcing them to learn to compromise. As Fana and Michael explore each other's strengths and weaknesses, the leader of the life brothers, Khaldun, sends them three messages: "teach," "learn," and "grow" (*My Soul to Take* 335, 337, 339). Each of these words connects to the themes of balance and adaptability Due weaves into her series. Fana and Michael agree that if humanity continues to ignore its environmental impact on the planet, the entire planet will die. This view of humanity as part of a planet-wide symbiotic relationship is a central tenet of many Indigenous cultures. Dillon notes that symbiotic relations between humans, animals, spirits, and machines are an integral part of Indigenous scientific belief and a major difference between Indigenous belief and the "techno-driven western scientific method" ("Imagining" 7). Fana and Michael's solution for the imbalance currently endangering all species must consider the needs of all life on the planet. They eventually decide to limit new human births rather than cleansing the population. Due's solution decenters multiple assumptions of Eurowestern culture. As Michael's equal (acknowledged only through the threat of planetary extinction), Fana disrupts narratives of white superiority, while Fana and Michael's choice to limit human births decenters assumptions about humans as a superior species. Their solution for restoring balance to the planet privileges Indigenous scientific literacies over Eurowestern assumptions of technological superiority, which also connects the acceptance of peoples of color and non-Eurowestern beliefs to the adaptation and survival of the entire planet.

In *An Unkindness of Ghosts*, Solomon further expands the notion of balance between all life through Aster's musings on the multiple semantic meanings of the words "blood" and "medicine": "*Blood* meant/could mean cell-dense plasma, life, kinship, disease. *Medicine* meant/could mean: healing serums, both literal and metaphorical, soup, pills, cure" (214, original italics). The fact that blood can exist as life, family, and disease simultaneously (depending on the cultural views surrounding the use of the word) demonstrates a respect for multiple cultural viewpoints that mark Aster's interpretation of the world while also referencing the history of "one-drop" contamination that affected black peoples in the US for centuries. The fact that Aster states that healing serums can be both "literal" and "metaphorical" shows Aster's view of the different ways a culture can be "cured." To heal a colonized peoples involves more than access to healthcare or the ability to practice Indigenous healing. The Eurowestern viewpoint that has impacted the colonized culture's view of themselves as a people must also be healed. Solomon's novel ends with Aster burying the bodies of her mother and best friend on a planet believed to be Earth, thus completing the circle of obligation for humans to the planet.

Each of the authors discussed creates a unique vision of the Indigenous ideal of balance between all life through depictions of characters immersed in imbalance who ultimately find balance through the recovery of lost cultural knowledge or artifacts. For Hopkinson and Solomon, the dystopic conditions of their novels echo the writings of Native Apocalypse by portraying the consequences of imbalance. Hopkinson, Solomon, and Due also force readers to consider how humanity's refusal to acknowledge its contribution to climate change and other environmental issues will lead to the destruction of the planet. Hernandez discusses balance on a personal level in terms of family connections and Latinx/Indigenous relations. While each author takes a different approach to their narratives, all these works are prime examples of how authors of color are engaging in the science fiction trope of advanced or cutting-edge technologies by balancing this Eurowestern view of technology with depictions of Indigenous sciences. The incorporation of Indigenous scientific literacies allows these authors to demonstrate how Eurowestern privileging of the scientific method has devalued Indigenous knowledge. Each of these authors also employs Eurowestern and Indigenous technologies and sciences as a metaphor for the damage of colonization and, ultimately, a call for science fiction authors and readers to examine why Eurowestern sciences and technologies are privileged in science fiction writing. According to the authors in this chapter, and many other authors, our very survival as a species depends on finding balance. I argue that the first step in this process is to decolonize our thinking about science and technology, a goal that science fiction authors can help achieve.

CONCLUSION

"How Long 'Til Black Future Month?"

I borrow the title of my conclusion from author N. K. Jemisin's 2018 collection of short stories. This title identifies two important issues in representations of race and science fiction: the use of token acknowledgments of diversity to avoid systemic change in Eurowestern race relations and the tendency of science fiction critics to isolate and marginalize science fiction authors of color into subcategories of ethnic literatures, rather than embracing their work as science fiction. So far, my analysis of science fiction by authors of color has focused on authors of color writing as a response to science fiction's reputation as a "white" genre and its tendency to privilege white, Eurowestern narratives. However, I would be remiss if I did not also take time to acknowledge the authors, scholars, and fans working to create spaces where science fiction authors of color and their fans can connect to and support one another. This conclusion is not meant to be a comprehensive history of science fiction creators of color and their use of internet mediums (that would be another book project altogether), but I do want to acknowledge how the internet is shifting the ways that science fiction fans and creators of color connect with one another. This new level of engagement, where fans and creators of color literally create cyberspaces that build the futures they want to see, has the potential to influence decisions about which science fiction projects are supported and funded.

My research on science fiction and authors of color would have been impossible without the internet. To find the works that I ultimately decided to discuss in *Diverse Futures*, I read recommended reading lists by science fiction authors of color, joined the Facebook communities *Imagining Indigenous Futurisms* and *The State of Black Science Fiction*, searched the internet for science fiction fan community websites created by peoples of color, and searched science fiction and fantasy internet discussion forums on *Reddit*. What I found in my internet searches was a small, yet persistent, group of peoples of color who were science fiction lovers like myself. Moya Bailey argues that although the internet has not become the race blind, equalizing space critics theorized at its inception, it is still useful for communities of color:

> By refashioning existing social media platforms like *YouTube, Twitter*, and *Tumblr*, gender marginalized folks of color are creating the changes that they want to see in the world. Innovative webseries, projects and initiatives proliferate on the web as those of us whose genders and sexualities are labeled deviant within white supremacist capitalist heteropatriarchy, find more autonomous room online. But even within the "democratized space" of "teh interwebs" the same systems of oppression operate, pushing new digital media makers to grow new strategies that fit a rapidly shifting digital ecosystem.

As Bailey notes, the internet provides a variety of benefits for communities of color who wish to organize and raise awareness online. Women of color, in particular, have the potential to bypass the intersectional barriers to publishing and access that have been discussed by critics like Kinitra Brooks and authors like Tananarive Due.[1] However, peoples of color also need to be aware of how the internet can be used to recreate systems of oppression due to issues like access, the abolishment of net neutrality, and lack of opportunity for peoples of color in tech employment. Despite these barriers, science fiction communities of color are managing to employ the internet to create supportive online spaces that celebrate science fiction fandom in communities of color. Internet communities are also driving much of the conversations and platforms that are supporting science fiction creators of color.

---

1. See my discussion of publishing barriers for women of color in popular genres in "Alternative Futurisms: Tananarive Due's African Immortal Series" (2020), Kinitra Brooks's *Searching for Sycorax: Black Women's Hauntings of Contemporary Horror* (2017), and Farai Chideya's "A Conversation with Tananarive Due, Part 1." (2006): https://www.npr.org/templates/story/story.php?storyId=5160333.

Early on in the Afrofuturism movement, science fiction authors, critics, and fans organized online to share ideas and recommendations for books, music, and films. Rob Cameron explains that Alondra Nelson's Afrofuturism listserv was critical to building the momentum of this movement:

> Alondra Nelson founded the Afrofuturism listserv in 1998, possibly the first digital network of creatives to collectively self-identify as Afrofuturist. There they discussed works that told stories about culture, technology, science fiction imagery, futurism, and innovation as it related to Black communities. It was a sounding board and crossroads where artists, writers, and musicians collectively built the aesthetic that they called Afrofuturism.

While critic Mark Dery's 1994 interview of Samuel R. Delany, Greg Tate, and Tricia Rose, titled "Black to the Future," was crucial for bringing the term "Afrofuturism" into critical consciousness and for drawing attention to the connections between the Black experience in the US and themes of science fiction, it is ultimately an online community that gave Afrofuturist thinkers and artists the space they needed to come together in a discussion that would define this movement. Many Afrofuturist authors writing at this time did not have the visibility of an author like Samuel R. Delany; an online community where peoples interested in Afrofuturism could share literature recommendations created a word-of-mouth distribution opportunity where fans of Afrofuturist writing could learn where to purchase Afrofuturist works.

Discussions of science fiction are often split between academic study, which takes place in universities, archives, and scholarly conferences, and popular science fiction fandom, which includes science fiction "cons," or conventions, and cosplay. While this split does occur for science fiction communities of color, there is also a lot of overlap as critics of science fiction and race connect with popular science fiction events to advocate for social justice. Events like the Schomburg Center for Research in Black Culture's annual comic book festival bring together Black and Latinx authors, activists, artists, comic book creators, and academics for a two-day celebration of public panels and booths selling comic book and science fiction books, artwork, and memorabilia. Science fiction author and founder of Rosarium Publishing, Bill Campbell, notes that attending science fiction conventions has allowed this press to access science fiction readers directly, bypassing the major publishing trade houses that often create barriers for science fiction authors of color by assuming there is no market for science fiction written by authors of color (Anderson). People of color are also participating more in cosplay, despite racist backlash, as science fiction fans of color begin to express their fandom in public.[2] Cons like East Coast Black Age of Comics Convention (ECBACC), Chicago's Wakandacon, Afro Comicon, ONYXCON, Latino Comic Con, Nerdtino Expo, Latino Comics Expo, and Indigenous Comic Con/Indigipop X are also providing venues for the celebration of science fiction authors of color and science fiction fans of color.

In addition to online forums where fans share reading suggestions, the internet also provides a platform for more specialized science fiction reading lists. A physical bookstore has limited space; the science fiction and fantasy sections of bookstores typically include one or two authors of color at most but are mainly dominated by white popular and canonical science fiction and fantasy works. Online, there can be as many reading lists as can be imagined. Science fiction authors of color such as Sabrina Vourvoulias, Nalo Hopkinson, and Rebecca Roanhorse have also helped draw attention to science fiction by authors of color by writing reading guides for fans who want more diverse science fiction reading options. Additionally, science fiction websites such as *Tor.com* and *Black Girl Nerds,* and many public libraries, are highlighting science fiction writings by authors of color either as featured books or through reading lists. *Wikipedia* even has a page titled "Speculative Fiction by Authors of Color"; while this page has not always been comprehensive,[3] over time, fans, authors, and science fiction critics have added to the page to make it one of the largest listings of science fiction authors of color currently available.

There are a few online communities, like the Afrofuturism listserv, the Octavia E. Butler Legacy Network, and the Octavia E. Butler Literary Society, that have been created and maintained by academic scholars. However, because such endeavors are typically not counted as academic work by universities, many online communities for science fiction fans of color are founded by community activists and authors who are not science fiction scholars. One example is the *Afro Futurist Affair* (2011) founded by Rasheedah Phillips, Esq., Managing Attorney of the Landlord-Tenant Housing Unit at Community Legal Services of Philadelphia (CLS) who is also a speculative fiction author. This website clearly states its goals as being a combination of intellectual discussion coupled with practical action: "The

---

2. See Darcel Rockett's "Racial slurs and 'black' Superman: How cosplayers of color navigate a world of mostly white characters" (2019).

3. See Vourvoulias's discussion of the absence of Latinx science fiction authors on this page in "Putting the I in Speculative: Looking at U.S. Latino/a Writers and Stories" (2015): https://www.tor.com/2015/02/02/looking-at-us-latino-latina-speculative-writers-and-stories/.

organization aims to provide a space not only for further dialogue around Afrofuturistic ideas, but a space for actual, practical implementation of these ideas as they serve social progress and freedom" ("About"). The *Black Girl Nerds* website was founded in 2012 by Jamie Broadnax, who states on the site's information page that she founded a blog with the same name after her Google search for the term "black girl nerds" was unsuccessful. She states that the idea for the website's name comes from stereotypes she sees as limiting opportunities for women of color to express themselves: "The concept of Black women as geeky-dorky beings is somewhat of an anomaly. It's against the order of things in the 'Black Girl' world. We represent a wide array of diverse women who embrace all cultures and refuse to conform to the status quo" (Broadnax). Both of these website examples were created by women of color who noticed a lack of space for peoples of color to be able to express science fiction or geek fandom. Each site also combines information about science fiction by authors of color with information about other opportunities to express fandom, such as events and podcasts. Both sites sell merchandise as a way to both highlight artwork by artists of color and to raise money for these societies. The *Afrofuturist Affair* site even has a "Resources" page that lists many other science fiction websites created by communities of color. The internet makes it possible for these sites and others to maintain their independent missions while also supporting each other in raising awareness about science fiction fandom and peoples of color.

Science fiction scholars of color and fans of color often utilize online social platforms such as Facebook and Twitter to celebrate and support science fiction creators of color. Facebook sites such as *The State of Black Science Fiction* (18.7K members), *Black Science Fiction Society* (2 pages, each with 10K to 12K members), *Afrofuturism* (6.6K members), *Imagining Indigenous Futurisms* (3.2K members), and *Asian Science Fiction and Fantasy* (840 members) are each using these groups as spaces to share articles, book reviews, news, and artwork pertaining to science fiction creation by peoples of color. These online groups are also a great avenue for science fiction creators of color to learn about funding opportunities and to gain visibility for artwork, writing, and other projects. One great example is the *Imagining Indigenous Futurisms* Facebook page created by Anishinaabe science fiction scholar Grace L. Dillon and her daughter, Anishinaabe artist and scholar of Indigenous media Beth LaPensée. This site explains, "'Imagining Indigenous Futurisms' (iIf) is a space for artists, writers, filmmakers, designers, media makers, activists, and scholarly activists to share insights, exchange information, and highlight work on Indigenous Futurisms" (Dillon). The site also serves as a space to share information about the annual Imagining Indigenous Futurisms Science Fiction Writing Contest, now in its tenth year. This site is a great example of how Dillon and LaPensée are putting their scholarly work in Indigenous Futurisms into practice by creating an online space for shared learning and Indigenous activism and opportunities to highlight the work of Indigenous science fiction authors.

Like many other social justice movements highlighting racial disparity, science fiction fans of color have rallied under a number of Twitter hashtags to challenge stereotypes of peoples of color as non-tech-savvy or as disinterested in the science fiction genre. However, when hashtags go viral, they are often linked to heated debates where the anonymity of the internet can allow perpetrators of vicious online attacks to hide their identities while exposing individuals who have not chosen anonymity to real danger. Nathan Rambukanna notes that just as the internet is not the egalitarian space early creators imagined, digital communication is also not a perfect system:

> Digital convergence increases the sphere of global connection, but that does not, in and of itself, heal a world community broken by misunderstanding. . . . The political role of communication media cannot, therefore, be to "fix" a broken system of public sphere communication, but rather to "un-fix" staid communication patterns, to re-figure the public conversation about important issues and topics (such as inequality, racism, sexism and abuses of power) with a view to cracking open stable systems of meaning-making. (164)

Rambukanna uses an important science fiction and fantasy conversation that happened online in 2009 under the Twitter hashtag "Racefail" as an example of a conversation that both educated readers about racial inequity in the science fiction and fantasy genres, yet also exposed some of the participants to public censure. The conversation began when science fiction and fantasy author Elizabeth Bear commented on the idea of "writing the Other" in the science fiction and fantasy genres. Some critics argue that Bear downplayed issues of cultural representation and appropriation and reduced these concerns to a list of items to avoid in an attempt to provide guidelines to authors aspiring to write characters of other races or ethnicities. The conversation quickly expanded as participants began to censure Bear and comment on the overall racism and cultural insensitivity in the science fiction and fantasy genres and the white-dominated publishing industry that produces them. The conversation eventually devolved as other participants, believed to be white science fiction and fantasy fans, authors, and publishing executives, verbally attacked the participants critiquing Bear (166). The entire conversation spanned months of 2019 and involved thousands of total participants. Award-winning science fiction and fantasy author N. K. Jemisin notes that although the conversation exposed much of the racist attitudes still prevalent in science fiction and fantasy writing and publishing, #Racefail does seem to have made science fiction and fantasy authors and readers think more about the issue of diverse representation in these genres. She describes her participation in a thread where science fiction and fantasy fans of color introduced themselves as a liberating experience: "One of the most powerful moments for me in Racefail was when the participating fans of color decided to do a very informal roll call, and illustrated just how non-rare we were" ("Why I Think"). Though the Twitter conversation may have become vicious and angry, leaving many white authors and fans to argue that it had no impact beyond stirring up controversy, Jemisin's comment illustrates how the use of Twitter hashtags and online threads can be a unifying experience for fans of color, who often believe themselves to be anomalies in white-fan-dominated genres.

Another important medium for internet visibility is online science fiction magazines. The ability to publish fully online bypasses some of the costs of traditional publishing. Although the cost to produce an ebook is only slightly cheaper than that of a print book, most of what print consumers are paying for are the advances paid to popular authors and the costs of editing and marketing the book (Skildelsky). Digital magazines are much cheaper than publishing eBooks; since the pieces featured are usually shorter, authors can be paid much less than book advances, typically a flat fee or a few cents per word. There are also online platforms where non-tech-savvy users can create an online magazine for a startup cost of a few hundred dollars (Kawatu). Online magazines can be sold through a website or through platforms like apps or Amazon, for a variable fee of about 30 percent (Goldstein). Science fiction fans of color are able to take advantage of these low startup costs and create online magazines for specific science fiction fan markets. Kenesha Williams, founder of the *Black Girl Magic* website, states that she created a companion literary magazine titled the *Black Girl Magic Lit Mag* for herself and other fans who want to read more diverse science fiction and fantasy stories: "She took to heart the advice, 'If you don't see a clear path for what you want, sometimes you have to make it yourself' and created a Speculative Fiction Literary Magazine featuring characters she wanted to see" ("Our Mission"). Another recent online magazine, *FIYAH*, was named in tribute to the 1920s print publication "Fire!" edited by Wallace Thurman and supported by Langston Hughes, Zora Neale Hurston, and other prominent Black authors in this time period ("The Mission"). Science fiction authors, fans, and critics are able to continue the Harlem Renaissance's legacy of social justice and cultural celebration, but without the need to solicit mostly white patrons. The low costs of internet-magazine creation are allowing many science fiction organizations and websites to begin publishing online magazines where both new and established science fiction authors of color can showcase their work and build their fan base. Other non-mainstream online venues that highlight science fiction by authors of color include *Axxón, Genesis SF, Mithila Review,* and *La Bloga's Latino Speculative Literature Directory.*

Some authors of color have also shifted to creating anthologies, translation, and running small presses in an effort to create more diversity within the science fiction, fantasy, comic, and graphic novel genres. Bill Campbell, author and owner of Rosarium Press, has discussed in numerous interviews the fact that he had to self-publish his first few books; even after hiring a literary agent and having his work assigned in college courses, publishers would not consider his work because it did not fit the stereotypical "ghetto" literature that Campbell notes was dominating the market in the 1990s and early 2000s (David). Self-publishing typically costs thousands of dollars, and this market includes many predatory companies that upcharge even more. Additionally, self-promoting these works and finding venues to sell your work can take hours of unpaid labor and unforeseen additional costs (Pretty). Eventually, Campbell decided to create his own press to give other authors of color the support and visibility he could not obtain through mainstream publishing. Rosarium's first publication found Campbell soliciting authors for the anthology *Mothership: Tales from Afrofuturism and Beyond* (2013). The startup funds for this project were obtained through an internet crowdsourcing campaign on Indiegogo, a decision that Campbell describes as a good opportunity with a few drawbacks:

> Mothership was just supposed to be the jumpoff for Rosarium Publishing. . . . I was initially against crowdfunding because I thought it would be a lot more work . . . and I was right. The idea was great, and I'm glad it was successful, but many people with money use crowdfunding, and use it as a marketing tool. I didn't want to get into that. (qtd. in David)

Campbell's comments demonstrate the positives and negatives of crowdsourcing. As he notes, crowdsourcing is time-intensive and depends on a creator's ability to self-promote their product and find enough backers to reach a preset goal. Most crowdfunding sites work on an all-or-nothing model, which *Kickstarter* notes on their website is a deliberate choice to protect artists and backers from the costs of not being able to deliver or obtain an underfunded project ("Why Is Funding"). Of course, this strategy can mean that critics, authors, and artists of color could end up investing a lot of time into promoting a project and still end up not meeting their goals. For these reasons, science fiction creators are likely going to attempt crowdfunding for a project only if the funding amount is small or if the project already has a fan base. Campbell's point raises an important issue about publishing and science fiction authors of color: These authors cannot rely solely on crowdfunding as a source of income or even for startup funds. It is also important to have small presses, like Rosarium, Arte Público Press, and Ellipsis Press, that are willing to distribute and promote the works of science fiction authors of color.

One important project that was partially funded by crowdsourcing efforts is *Latin@ Rising* (recently renamed *Latinx Rising* for the new The Ohio State University Press printing), the first Latinx science fiction and fantasy anthology. The editor of this collection, science fiction scholar Matthew David Goodwin, wrote a description of the project for his online crowdfunding campaign that expressed the critical need for an anthology of Latinx science fiction and fantasy:

> With the exception of Edward James Olmos' *Bladerunner* and *Battlestar Galactica*, positive US Latino/a characters have been largely absent from mainstream speculative fiction novels and films. Films such as *Men in Black* and *Alien Nation*, and shows such as *X-Files*, express the anxiety that the mainstream has concerning Latinos/as and recent immigrants. *Latino/a Rising* will contest this trend, showing how Latino/a writers and artists are transforming the genres. ("Latino/a")

Goodwin also included a video discussing the history of Latinx science fiction and fantasy and explained the ways that these genres helped Latinx peoples express the alienating feelings associated with migration while also creating space to confront the racist stereotype of Latinx people as an "invading" force. He notes that the $10,000 goal of the Kickstarter campaign would not fully fund this project, so he was also working with "grants and donations from Latino/a community organizations, universities, and foundations" ("Latino/a"). Sixty percent of the funds raised were slated for author and artist compensation, which is not surprising because the anthology contains works by several well-known Latinx authors such as Daína Chaviano, Ana Castillo, Junot Díaz, and Daniel José Older.

Goodwin's Kickstarter campaign was successful but involved a lot of time and online effort. In addition to the Kickstarter page, which included a description, video, chart of donation use, and artwork examples, Goodwin had to work with other Latinx artists to create t-shirts and prints for campaign incentives. Goodwin also created a Facebook group and website for the anthology. Like Campbell, he explains that crowdsourcing is a time-consuming way to raise funds, but one that also has community-building benefits:

> Kickstarters are amazingly difficult to pull off. You really have to develop a lot of excitement around the project and to convince people that the book is not only a great book but that it will in fact happen. At the same time, the process created an online community of people interested in Latinx speculative fiction which continues in various forms until today.

Ultimately, 321 backers funded the campaign, which raised $10,476 for the project. *Latinx Rising* is a great example of how science fiction communities of color can come together to raise funds and support science fiction authors of color. The fact that 321 people contributed to the campaign, in addition to Latinx community group support, shows that there is a growing interest in science fiction written by authors of color. There are now many more anthologies celebrating science fiction and authors of color than when I began researching this project, but the number is still small compared to the overall number of anthologies celebrating white science fiction authors. A few examples include *Dark Matter: A Century of Speculative Fiction from the African Diaspora* (2000), *Dark Matter: Reading the Bones* (2005), *So Long Been Dreaming: Postcolonial Science Fiction and Fantasy* (2004), *Walking the Clouds: An Anthology of Indigenous Science Fiction* (2012), *Afrofuturism 2.0: The Rise of Astro-Blackness* (2015), *Stories for Chip: A Tribute to Samuel R. Delany* (2015), *Octavia's Brood: Science Fiction Stories from Social Justice Movements* (2015), *Black and Brown Planets: The Politics of Race in Science Fiction* (2014), *Dis-Orienting Planets: Racial Representations of Asia in Science Fiction* (2017), and *New Suns: Original Speculative Fiction by People of Color* (2019).

Comic book creators of color have found a great deal of support for projects through crowdfunding efforts. One significant example is the comic series *Black*, created by Kwanza Osajyefo, Khary Randolph, Tim Smith 3, and Jamal Igle. The comic, about a world where only Black people have superpowers, raised $91,973 through *Kickstarter* and had 2,775 backers by the end of the campaign ("Black"). Osajyefo notes that his comic series builds on the history of confronting issues of race and discrimination in comics started by creators like Stan Lee, but he also presents a new perspective of discrimination through Black creation of a comic depicting Black discrimination:

> *Black* looks at the "outsider" trope, the characters that are outside of society and not accepted even in their secret identity. Like the X-Men characters who are palatable examples of what discrimination looks like. I wanted to kind of scrape away at that trope like icing on a cake and cut into the real issues using science fiction as vehicle.

Like *Latinx Rising*, the creators of *Black* included a brief description of the premise of the comic along with a video, sketches of panels, a description of characters, and artwork for the cover and incentive posters. Osajyefo notes that his experience working in digital mediums gave him experience in online promotion of projects, which helped contribute to the success of this project:

> The thing that I noticed . . . is that editorial, print and publishing led[,] and digital and online were sort of an afterthought. But the way I saw it at the time, digital is low-cost, no-cost marketing where you can reach your audience, serve them content and really engage with them. And I think a lot of my experience from working online gave me a much broader perspective on what was possible. (Horne)

This project's massive funding success caught the attention of several film studios, which approached Osajyefo about the rights to the comic series before it had even been published. This project demonstrates how building an online fanbase not only provides funds and an immediate readership for science fiction creators of color, but also demonstrates how going viral can help science fiction creators of color bypass barriers of mainstream publishing and film production by proving that projects have a fan base ready to support and purchase their product.

Another highly visible way that science fiction authors of color are gaining lager fan bases is by collaborating with mainstream science fiction efforts or by having their works adapted for TV and film. Ted Chiang's short story "Story of Your Life" was the basis for the film *Arrival* (2016). Gabby Rivera wrote a comic series based on the Marvel character America Chavez (2017–18), which marked the first queer Latina writer hired by Marvel as well as the first queer Latina character in a comic series.[4] Nnedi Okorafor wrote for

---

4. See David Betancourt's "Marvel hired Gabby Rivera, a queer Latina writer, for its queer Latina superhero. That matters" (2017).

the new *Shuri* comic series (2018–19), and her novel *Who Fears Death* has been optioned by HBO for a television series with fantasy author George R. R. Martin as executive producer. Okorafor's novel series *Binti* is also under development by Hulu for a television series. Science fiction icon Octavia E. Butler's novel *Wild Seed* is being developed by Amazon as a TV series being written by Nnedi Okorafor and Kenyan filmmaker Wanuri Kahiu. Author Carlos Hernandez also adapted characters from his short story collection *The Assimilated Cuban's Guide to Quantum Santeria* into a book series for fantasy author Rick Riordan's children's book series (2019, 2020). These authors' willingness to diversify the types of writing they engage in creates more opportunities for them to build a fan base and, ultimately, make a living from writing science fiction.

Other internet-friendly media outlets include independent films and webseries. One good example of the power of science fiction communities of color supporting science fiction creators of color is Alex Rivera's independent film "Sleep Dealer" (2008). After winning an award at the Sundance Film Festival in 2008, the film's distributor went out of business, which left the film in danger (Montgomery). Rivera explains that science fiction scholars and fans were the only groups distributing the film until he could get the rights to the film back in 2014. He states, "It's been the pirates and the professors who have kept this film alive for the last half-decade" (qtd. in Montgomery). Once Rivera obtained the rights to the film, he turned to the internet for help by asking his Facebook friends if they knew of any distribution companies that might be interested in the film (Bogado). He was then contacted by the Sundance Institute, the nonprofit that hosts the Sundance Film Festival and supports independent artists. Today, the film is available on Amazon and iTunes. Rivera's determination, coupled with a word-of-mouth distribution of his film by science fiction communities, helped ensure the film's return. Rivera's experience also draws attention to the challenges that independent science fiction filmmakers of color face in trying to create, distribute, and make a profit from their projects.

In 2010, DeWayne Copland and Scoff F. Evans created a Black science fiction and fantasy superhero webseries named *CV Nation*. When asked about their reasons for creating the series, Evans states, "Very often Black characters are either completely marginalized or they're like chocolate kiss versions of white characters. . . . I wanted to create something where we get to save the world, we get the girl, or we make the decisions. All of that. You know everything the white dudes get to do" (Northern). While the civil rights era did see the creation of comic books featuring Black characters, such as *Blade* or the *X-Men Series*, Evans's comment is significant. *CV Nation* is a series about Black superheroes written by two African American men. The ability to post their work on the internet gives Copland and Evans access to a fan base and creative control over how to depict a community of predominately Black science fiction characters. Another notable webseries created by a woman of color is Reagan Gomez's *Surviving* (2015), a postapocalyptic zombie story that challenges stereotypes of people of color as minor or disposable characters. By making two women of color the protagonists in this series, Gomez is employing online production to tell a familiar science fiction story from the perspective of overlooked or marginalized characters.

Another significant way that creators of color are addressing inequity in science fiction communities is through online game design. Daymond Packwood explains in "The era of white male games for white male gamers is ending" that, like science fiction, gaming has a history of being stereotyped as a hobby for young white males. However, Packwood notes that today, more young peoples of color are gaming than white youth, and they are also more likely to invest more time into gaming than white youth. He also notes that women gamers are quickly joining the ranks, which is creating an economic spike in gaming revenue through the mobile-game market, which in turn is just beginning to be recognized as a legitimate investment for video game companies (Packwood). Although the cost to create a mobile game is not cheap, it is significantly less than video game development and is described as "the fastest growing segment by revenue with the lowest barrier to entry" (Dmasper). And as streaming video services like *Netflix* become involved, these companies' interest in more diverse representation in TV and film options may bleed into the mobile gaming market.

Science fiction and fantasy game creators of color are currently proving that game design and creation, a contemporary technology, can be used to celebrate Indigenous cultural knowledge and teach it to others. One example is *Thunderbird Strike,* an online and mobile game created by Anishinaabe designer Elizabeth LaPensée and available on Windows PC, Android phones, and iOS. In this 2D scrolling game, players take on the character of the thunderbird and fly from the Tar Sands to the Great Lakes to Turtle Island "with searing lightning against the snake that threatens to swallow the lands and waters whole" (LaPensée). The snake combines Indigenous stories of the Water Snake with a metaphor for the Line 5 oil pipeline currently threatening the Great Lakes. On the companion website, *Thunderbird Strikes,* LaPensée includes information about the legend of the thunderbird, information on the dangers of oil pipelines, and concrete ways that people can protect waterways through education and activism. After *Thunderbird Strikes* won an award for Best Digital Media at imagineNATIVE Film +

Media Arts Festival in 2017, Minnesota Senator David Osmek claimed that the video game was "an eco-terrorist version of Angry Birds" and objected to the support of the project by the Minnesota Legacy Fund grant program ("Sen. David"). LaPensée's work demonstrates how contemporary technologies can be repurposed to educate people about Indigenous knowledge and environmental activism. The fact that anyone can play this game on their phones for free means that the game can reach large audiences. The negative comments the game received from a US senator also demonstrates the risks that science fiction and fantasy creators of color face when attempting to enact systemic changes that challenge Eurowestern capitalistic views and stereotypes of Indigenous peoples as against "progress." As more science fiction creators of color become involved in gaming, graphic design, and digital humanities projects, it is possible that more science fiction creators and activists of color will move to online platforms and mobile games to reach a broader audience.

The internet may well be one of the most important technological advances for science fiction critics, fans, and authors of color. The different, inexpensive internet platforms available to science fiction creators of color allow them to quickly reach a large number of people, which is crucial for creators who wish to create fan bases or fund potential projects. Science fiction conventions and organizations have become another medium for new science fiction authors and directors of color to showcase their work and speak directly to science fiction fans and for fans of color to build cosplay and fandom communities. Both levels of community building give science fiction fans a voice in the science fiction marketplace; in countries where "money talks," the success of large-scale films like *Black Panther* have a significant impact on the types of science fiction books, films, comic books, and TV shows that are viewed as profitable. If science fiction fans, both online and at in-person conventions, advocate for more diverse science fiction offerings created by people of color, then the science fiction genre may shift to accommodate this new demand.

Creating the Transhistorical Feedback Loop

In his examination of the literary prehistory of Afrofuturism, *Afrofuturism Rising,* Isiah Lavender III argues that different movements examining race and its connection to science fiction have the opportunity to work together to combat the whitewashing of Eurowestern historical narratives:

To connect to the black networked consciousness, to experience the hope impulse, we readers create and maintain a transhistorical feedback loop, where we go outside the bounds of today's systematic narrative of past events related to early white America. We overload the control system with new input, original thinking, and innovative ideas, causing a systemwide adjustment and, perhaps, inspiring a response to advance the human condition. Afrofuturism functions as such an idea, generating the necessary intellectual dynamism to jolt the discovery of other truths—a revolutionary power. Enough interconnected feedback loops working together—techno-orientalism, Latinx futurism, indigenous futurism, afrofuturism—can change history's whitewashed narrative. (7)

Diverse Futures is one of many efforts to highlight connections between the various movements fighting for a more diverse representation and interpretation within science fiction. Through my discussion of science fiction written by authors of color, I add to the interconnected transhistorical feedback loop Lavender III describes by drawing attention to the ways that science fiction authors of color are working to decolonize this genre's thinking about the relationships between race, science, and technology. I understand that each of the movements named deserves recognition in its own right, and that each movement has attributes unique to specific races, ethnicities, and cultures. But there is also a need for science fiction authors and critics of color to recognize the similarities of their science-fictional experiences, specifically those of colonization, diaspora, alienation, xenophobia, and gaslighting, that create the feedback loops which limit the experiences of many peoples of color living in Eurowestern countries. The science fiction works discussed in this project speak to peoples of many races and ethnicities trying to survive in an alien environment, and these works provide hope for a different, more diverse vision of the future. This conclusion speaks to the ways in which science fiction creators and fans of color can begin to disrupt the feedback loop and create new narratives of past, present, and future.

This project also highlights the potential for science fiction authors of color to learn from races and cultures outside their experience. Indigenous science fiction, in particular, resonates with many colonized Latinx cultures that have had their Indigenous and African histories erased, whether by white colonizers or through internalized narratives of colonization and white supremacy. Afrofuturists are currently in discussion with African futurists; both groups are attempting to define their own use of future visions while also recognizing the interconnectedness of African culture and the Black diaspora. Asian American science fiction authors are making decisions about how their ethnicity and cultural history will influence the ways they write science fiction and are also forging connections with Asian science fiction authors through translation efforts and anthologies. A few science fiction authors of color are already beginning to respectfully utilize elements of other cultures to enrich their work. A prime example is Tananarive Due's *African Immortals* series. This series is set in the US, Africa, and Mexico. Due, a former reporter, has done extensive research for her series and incorporated many scenes that demonstrate the interconnectedness of Black, Indigenous, and Latinx cultures.[5] Texts like Due's continue a tradition—one that started with Samuel R. Delany and Octavia E. Butler—of writing science fiction that defies rigid boundaries and classifications. Lavender III also notes that the positive reception of texts such as Colson Whitehead's *Underground Railroad* creates even more opportunities for "literary" or experimental science fiction writing by authors of color (Lavender 193).[6] As science fiction authors of color begin to challenge the colonial history of race portrayal in science fiction, they are also refusing to adhere to the Eurowestern-dominated "rules" of this genre.

All peoples of color have an investment in decolonizing thinking about race, science, and technology because these themes connect to issues of access and opportunity across racial and ethnic divides. By supporting non-Eurowestern depictions of science and technology, science fiction creators and fans of color have the ability to begin changing the conversations about "primitive" and "advanced" cultures that have created issues of colonization, racism and xenophobia in Eurowesten cultures today. Jessica Kolopenuk (Ininiw/Cree) notes that a growing movement of Indigenous scholars and scientists are "producing methodological frameworks capable of analyzing from their own standpoints science and technology projects that affect them" (21). Kolopenuk explains that by taking control of scientific discourse, often depicted as antithetical to Indigenous knowledge, Indigenous peoples can disrupt the feedback loop of Eurowestern oppression by challenging depictions of Indigenous cultures as primitive peoples incapable of knowledge production: "The creation of Indigenous approaches to analyses of the sciences and technologies that affect Indigenous *and* non-Indigenous peoples and territories is disruptive to colonial ontologies of knowledge and sover-

---

5. See my detailed explanation of Due's cultural influences and how they combine elements of Afrofuturism, Latinx futurism, and Indigenous futurism in "Alternative Futurisms: Tananarive Due's African Immortal Series" (2020).

6. Whitehead's *Zone One* is discussed in this project as a work of science fiction; however, this text did not receive as much critical attention as *The Underground Railroad*, perhaps because the science-fictional elements are more prominent. Literary critics still have a way to go before science fiction is considered on par with "high-brow" literature.

eignty" (21, emphasis in original). Because many Indigenous cultures stress relationality between humans and space, time, location, spirits, animals, and inanimate objects, Indigenous sciences are often more willing to acknowledge the need for holistic approaches to science and technology. In terms of science fiction, Indigenous science opens possibilities for imagining futures where Indigenous scientific literacies are employed to create societies that finally learn to acknowledge the consequences of sciences driven by capitalistic gain and technological "progress." Science fiction authors can help decolonize science by showcasing the limits of Eurowestern "rational" scientific methods.

There are still many challenges ahead for science fiction creators and fans of color. From Delany's moving essay "Racism and Science Fiction," which described decades of personal abuse from science fiction authors and publishers, to the scandal of #Racefail in 2009, conversations about Eurowestern privilege in science fiction texts are still being ignored or attacked. As I noted earlier, the internet is helping to raise visibility and support for science fiction creators of color, but not every work can rely solely on these means. The science fiction publishing, TV, film, and gaming industries need to become more attuned to the demand for science fiction created by and for peoples of color. White science fiction creators can also improve equity within the genre by mentoring and supporting science fiction creators of color. There are many more visible science fiction creators of color today than there were when Delany wrote his essay in 1998, and certainly more than when he began writing in the 1960s, but these creators need a path to mainstream science fiction markets and access to funding to showcase their works on a larger scale.

And there could not be a more crucial time for science fiction authors of color to emerge into the mainstream imagination. As I write this Conclusion, the COVID-19 pandemic is moving across the globe and disproportionality affecting peoples of color, once again drawing attention to the biopolitics of disposability Giroux exposed in the wake of 2005's Hurricane Katrina. Simultaneously, thousands of Americans are protesting the murder of George Floyd, a Black man killed by a white police officer, and calling once again for reform in US legal systems. Over and over, peoples of color find themselves fighting to survive yet another post-apocalyptic landscape where a person's health and well-being are contrasted against the need to not be perceived as a threat, where masking while Black is poised to become the new driving while Black.[7] Surveillance technologies are being used to

---

7. See Derrick Bryson Taylor's "For Black Men, Fear That Masks Will Invite Racial Profiling" (2020).

track the pandemic, ushering in a new era of privacy issues worldwide.[8] Now more than ever, peoples of color need to see themselves depicted in the future, to counter the narratives of disposability thinly veiled by the Trump administration's depictions of poor peoples of color as violent mobs incapable of implementing social distancing and healthcare standards.[9] The future for peoples of color in many Eurowestern countries is under direct attack, and science fiction authors of color are crucial to the effort to warn people about the consequences of a willingness to sacrifice some lives for a perceived safety and prosperity.

Science fiction's most basic driving premise—the question, "What if?"—is also a useful tool for creators of color resisting the call for Eurowestern countries to return to "normal" post-pandemic. For peoples of color, "normal" is the continuation of the whitewashing of Eurowestern history and the cycles of violence and systemic racism that will continue to oppress these peoples in the future without systemic change. "Normal" is the refusal of predominantly white cultures to see non-Eurowestern knowledge as equal or even superior to Eurowestern scientific methods. "Normal" means peoples of color being subjected to certain technologies, such as surveillance, while being denied access to STEM opportunities to participate in the creation and implementation of such technologies. As news outlets report on the need for a "new normal" post-pandemic,[10] science fiction authors of color are already imagining new worlds that can warn readers about the consequences of returning to the norm of white supremacy while also creating hope that, this time, the world might listen.

---

8. See Natasha Singer and Choe Sang-Hun's "As Coronavirus Surveillance Escalates, Personal Privacy Plummets" (2020).

9. See "Rep. Waters Slams Surgeon General Jerome Adams for Offensive Comments During WH Coronavirus Briefing" (2020).

10. See Andrew Winston's "Is the COVID-19 Outbreak a Black Swan or the New Normal?" (2020).

BIBLIOGRAPHY

"About—AfroFuturist Affair." *AfroFuturist Affair*, 2014, https://www.afrofuturistaffair.com/about-afrofuturist-affair.

Abramson, Gunnar. "Comparative Colonialisms: Variations in Japanese Colonial Policy in Taiwan and Korea, 1895–1945." *PSU McNair Scholars Online Journal*, vol. 1, issue 1, 2004, 11 Aug. 2017, pp. 9–37. Portland State University Library.

Addison-Smith, Helen. "The Future of Race: Colonialism, Adaptation and Hybridity in Mid Century American Science Fiction." *Foundation*, vol. 35 issue 96 (2006), pp. 17–30. Accessed 1 July 2013.

Aldama, Frederick Luis, and Christopher González. *Reel Latinxs: Representation in U.S. Film and TV*. The University of Arizona Press, 2019.

Amberstone, Celu. "Refugees." *So Long Been Dreaming: Postcolonial Science Fiction and Fantasy*, edited by Nalo Hopkinson and Uppinder Mehan, Arsenal Pulp Press, 2004, pp. 161–82.

Anderson, Porter. "Rosarium's Faces of Diverse Publishing: 'Get Out of Our Way.'" *Publishing Perspectives*, 24 Jan. 2017, https://publishingperspectives.com/2017/01/rosarium-publishing-diversity-multiculturalism/.

Anzaldúa, Gloria. *Borderlands/La Frontera: The New Mestiza*. 2nd ed. Aunt Lute Books, 1999.

Bailey, Moya. "Digital Alchemy: The Transformative Magic of Women of Color Online." 2 Jan. 2013. *Moya Bailey*, https://www.moyabailey.com/2013/01/02/digital-alchemy-the-transformative-magic-of-women-of-color-online/. Accessed 24 May 2020.

Barber, Kirsten. "What Does a State of Emergency Actually Mean?" *NCDPS: North Carolina Department of Public Safety*. North Carolina Department of Public Safety. 14 Dec. 2018, https://www.ncdps.gov/blog/2018/12/14/what-does-state-emergency-actually-mean.

Becquemont, Daniel. "Social Darwinism: From Reality to Myth and from Myth to Reality." *Studies in History and Philosophy of Biol & Biomed Sci*, vol. 42, no. 1, 2011, pp. 12–19. Accessed 28 May 2020.

Belluck, Pam. "In Breakthrough, Scientists Edit a Dangerous Mutation from Genes in Human Embryos." *New York Times*. 2 Aug. 2017, https://www.nytimes.com/2017/08/02/science/gene-editing-human-embryos.html.

Bérard, Sylvie. "Alien or Alienated?" *SFS Symposium: Sexuality in Science Fiction. Science Fiction Studies*, vol. 36, no. 3, 2009, p. 386.

Betancourt, David. "Marvel Hired Gabby Rivera, a Queer Latina Writer, for Its Queer Latina Superhero. That Matters." *Washington Post*, 8 March 2017, https://www.washingtonpost.com/news/comic-riffs/wp/2017/03/08/marvel-hired-gabby-rivera-a-queer-latina-writer-for-its-queer-latina-superhero-that-matters/.

Bhabha, Homi K. *The Location of Culture*. London: Routledge, 1994.

Bishop, Kyle William. *How Zombie Conquered Popular Culture: The Multifarious Walking Dead in the 21st Century*. McFarland, 2010.

Blade. Directed by Stephen Norrington, performances by Wesley Snipes, Stephen Dorff, and Kris Kristofferson, New Line Cinema, 1998.

Bogado, Aura. "'Sleep Dealer' Has Been Re-released Digitally." *Color Lines*, 7 July 2014, https://www.colorlines.com/articles/sleep-dealer-has-been-re-released-digitally.

Bollinger, Laurel. "Symbiogenesis, Selfhood, and Science Fiction." *Science Fiction Studies*, vol. 37, no. 1, March 2010, pp. 34–53.

Britt, Ryan. "Why Aliens in Sci-Fi Look the Way They Do, Tentacles and All." *Inverse*, 4 Nov. 2016, https://www.inverse.com/article/23112-arrival-aliens-tentacles-science-fiction-ted-chiang-paul-park. Accessed 20 May 2020.

Broadnax, Jaime. "Creator." *Black Girl Nerds*, https://blackgirlnerds.com/creator/jamie-broadnax/.

Broderick, Damien. *The Spike: How Our Lives Are Being Transformed by Rapidly Advancing Technologies*. Tor Books, 2002.

Brooks, Kinitra D. *Searching for Sycorax: Black Women's Hauntings of Contemporary Horror*. Rutgers UP, 2017.

Brox, Ali. "'Every Age Has the Vampire It Needs': Octavia Butler's Vampiric Vision in Fledgling." *Utopian Studies*, vol. 19, issue 3, 2008, pp. 391–409. Accessed 19 August 2012.

Butler, Octavia E. *Dawn*. 1987. Open Road, 2012.

———. *Fledgling*. 2005. Grand Central Publishing, 2007.

Byng, Rhonesha. "Failure Is Not an Option: The Pressure Black Women Feel to Succeed." *Forbes*, Forbes Media LLC, 31 Aug. 2017, https://www.forbes.com/sites/rhoneshabyng/2017/08/31/failure-is-not-an-option-the-pressure-black-women-feel-to-succeed/#21e238253fad.

Cameron, Rob. "In Search of Afro-Solarpunk, Part 1: Elements of Afrofuturism." *Tor.com*, 29 Oct. 2019, https://www.tor.com/2019/10/29/in-search-of-afro-solarpunk-part-1-elements-of-afrofuturism/.

Carpenter, Roger M. "Womanish Men and Manlike Women: The Native American Two-Spirit as Warrior." *Gender and Sexuality in Indigenous North America, 1400–1850.* U of South Carolina P, 2012, pp. 146–64.

Césaire, Aimé. "Culture and Colonization." *Social Text 103,* vol. 28, no. 2, Summer 2010, pp. 130–41. Accessed 5 Aug. 2013.

Chabram-Dernersesian, Angie. "Bucking Tradition: Sci Fi with a Chicana/o Latina/o Twist." *Confluencia,* vol. 26, no. 1, Fall 2010, pp. 192–94. Accessed 16 July 2017.

Chiang, Ted. "Story of Your Life." *Stories of Your Life and Others.* 2002. New York: Vintage Books, 2016.

Chideya, Farai. "A Conversation with Tananarive Due, Part 1." *NPR,* 17 Jan. 2006, https://www.npr.org/templates/story/story.php?storyId=5160333.

Clarke, Arthur C. *Profiles of the Future: An Inquiry into the Limits of the Possible.* Harper & Row, 1973.

Coleman, Monica A. "Serving the Spirits: The Pan-Caribbean African-Derived Religion in Nalo Hopkinson's *Brown Girl in the Ring.*" *Journal of Caribbean Literatures,* vol. 6, no. 1, Summer 2009, pp. 1–13.

Concha-Holmes, Amanda D. Who *is Nature?: Yorùbá Religion and Ecology in Cuba.* 2010. University of Florida, PhD dissertation.

Crenshaw, Kimberlé W. "From Private Violence to Mass Incarceration: Thinking Intersectionally about Women, Race, and Social Control." *UCLA Law Review,* vol. 59, no. 6, 2012, pp. 1418–72.

Cyrenoski, David. "The CRISPR-Baby Scandal: What's Next for Human Gene-editing." *Nature,* 26 Feb. 2019, https://www.nature.com/articles/d41586-019-00673-1. Accessed 31 May 2020.

Dalen, J. E., K. Waterbrook,, and J. S. Alpert. "Why Do So Many Americans Oppose the Affordable Care Act?" *American Journal of Medicine,* vol. 128, no. 8, August 2015, pp. 807–10. 27 Feb. 2015. Accessed 26 Aug. 2019, doi: 10.1016/j.amjmed.2015.01.032.

Dar-Nimrod, Ilan, and Steven J. Heine. "Genetic Essentialism: On the Deceptive Determinism of DNA." *Psychological Bulletin,* vol. 137, no. 5, 2011, pp. 800–818. *PsycARTICLES.* Accessed 10 Jan. 2018.

David, Tiffany M. "Bill Campbell Profile." *QBR: The Black Book Review,* 2020, https://www.qbrbookreview.com/bill-campbell-profile.aspx.

"Deferred Action for Childhood Arrivals: Response to January 2018 Preliminary Injunction." *U.S. Citizenship and Immigration Services.* Department of Homeland Security, 17 July 2019, https://www.uscis.gov/humanitarian/deferred-action-childhood-arrivals-response-january-2018-preliminary-injunction.

Delany, Samuel R. "Racism and Science Fiction." *The New York Review of Science Fiction,* issue 120, Aug. 1998.

———. *Starboard Wine: More Notes on the Language of Science Fiction.* 1978. Wesleyan UP, 2012.

Dennis, Rutledge M. "Social Darwinism, Scientific Racism, and the Metaphysics of Race." *Journal of Negro Education,* vol. 64, no. 3, 1995, pp. 243–52.

Dery, Mark. "Black to the Future: Interviews with Samuel R. Delany, Greg Tate, and Tricia Rose." *Flame Wars: The Discourse of Cyberculture,* special issue of *South Atlantic Quarterly,* vol. 92, no. 4, 1993, pp. 735–78.

Desmond, Matthew, and Mustafa Emirbayer. "What Is Racial Domination?" *Du Bois Review,* vol. 6, no. 2, 2009, pp. 335–55, doi:10.1017/S1742058X09990166.

Díaz, Junot. *The Brief Wondrous Life of Oscar Wao*. Riverhead Books, 2007.

Dillon, Grace L. "Haint Stories Rooted in Conjure Science: Indigenous Scientific Literacies in Andrea Hairston's *Redwood and Wildfire*." *Black and Brown Planets: The Politics of Race in Science Fiction*, edited by Isiah Lavender III. UP of Mississippi, 2014.

———. "Imagining Indigenous Futures." *Walking the Clouds: An Anthology of Indigenous Science Fiction*, edited by Grace L. Dillon. U of Arizona P, 2012.

———. "*Miindiwag* and Indigenous Diaspora: Eden Robinson's and Celu Amberstone's Forays into 'Postcolonial' Science Fiction and Fantasy." *Extrapolation* vol. 48, no. 2, 2007 pp. 219–43. Accessed 20 June 2012.

Dillon, Grace L., and Beth LaPensée. "Imagining Indigenous Futurisms." *Facebook*, 10 Feb. 2012, https://www.facebook.com/groups/349927541693986/about/. Accessed 14 April 2020.

Dmasper. "Mobile Gaming is a $50b Industry. But Only 5% of Players are Spending Money (Part 1)." *Medium*, 5 Dec. 2017, https://medium.com/shopify-gaming/mobile-gaming-is-a-50b-industry-but-only-5-of-players-are-spending-money-f7f3375dd959.

Due, Tananarive. *Blood Colony*. Kindle Ed. Washington Square, 2008.

———. *The Living Blood*. Kindle Ed. Washington Square, 2001.

———. *My Soul to Keep*. Kindle Ed. Harper Voyager, 1997.

———. *My Soul to Take*. Kindle Ed. Washington Square, 2011.

Elia, Adriano. "The Languages of Afrofuturism." *Lingue Linguaggi*, vol. 12, 2014, pp. 83–96, doi: 10.1285/i22390359v12p83.

"Emergency Medical Treatment & Labor Act (EMTALA)." *CMS.gov: Centers for Medicare & Medicare Services*. U.S. Centers for Medicare & Medicaid Services, 26 March 2012. Accessed 24 Aug. 2019.

Eshun, Kodwo. "Further Considerations of Afrofuturism." *CR: The New Centennial Review*, vol. 3, no. 2, Summer 2003, pp. 287–302, *Project Muse*, https://doi.org/10.1353/ncr.2003.0021.

Evans, Arthur B. "The Beginnings: Early Forms of Science Fiction." *Science Fiction: A Literary History*, edited by Roger Luckhurst. The British library, 2017.

Falck, Alex. "An Interview with Author Rivers Solomon." *Intellectual Freedom Blog*. The Office for Intellectual Freedom of the American Library Association, 20 Oct. 2018, https://www.oif.ala.org/oif/?p=15918. Accessed 5 June 2020.

Faucheux, Amandine, and Isiah Lavender III. "Tricknology: Theorizing the Trickster in Afrofuturism." *Journal of Science Fiction*, vol. 2, issue 2, Jan. 2018, pp. 31–46.

Ferraro, Vincent, editor. "President Andrew Jackson's Case for the Removal Act: First Annual Message to Congress, 8 December 1829." *Documents Relating to American Foreign Policy: Pre-1898*. Mount Holyoke College, https://www.mtholyoke.edu/acad/intrel/pre1898.htm.

Ford, Donna Y., and Gilman W Whiting. "Beyond Testing: Social and Psychological Considerations in Recruiting and Retaining Gifted Black Students." *Journal for the Education of the Gifted*, vol. 34, no. 1, 2011, pp. 131–55.

Foucault, Michel. "Right of Death and Power of Life." *The Foucault Reader*, edited by Paul Rabinow, Pantheon Books, 1984.

---. *Society Must Be Defended: Lectures at the Collège de France, 1975–1976.* 1st ed. Picador, 2003.

Frederiksen, Tomas. "Authorizing the 'Natives': Governmentality, Dispossession, and the Contradictions of Rule in Colonial Zambia." *Annals of the Association of American Geographers*, vol. 104, no. 6, 2014, pp. 1273–90. Accessed 4 Oct. 2017.

Freedman, Carl. *Critical Theory and Science Fiction.* UP of New England, 2000.

---. "The Fugitive Slave Acts of 1793 and 1850." *African American History of Western New York*, State U of New York P, 1996, http://www.math.buffalo.edu/~sww/ohistory/hwny.html. Accessed 29 April 2020.

"Genetic Engineering." *National Human Genome Research Institute*, National Human Genome Research Institute, 2014, https://www.genome.gov/genetics-glossary/Genetic-Engineering. Accessed 5 May 2019.

George-Warren, Delesslin. "Native Technology: Colonialism and the Indigenous Technological Ecosystem." *Six by Eight Press*, 4 May 2017. https://www.sixbyeightpress.com/native-technology/. Accessed 13 May 2020.

Giroux, Henry A. "Reading Hurricane Katrina: Race, Class, and the Biopolitics of Disposability." *College Literature*, vol. 33, no. 3, Summer 2006, pp. 171–96.

Golash-Boza, Tanya Maria. *Immigration Nation: Raids, Detentions, and Deportations in Post-9/11 America.* Paradigm Publishers, 2012.

Goldstein, Jacob. "How to Start A Magazine (And Make A Profit)." *NPR*, 21 Feb. 2013, https://www.npr.org/sections/money/2013/02/21/172588471/how-to-start-a-magazine-and-make-a-profit.

Goodwin, Matthew David. Interview. Conducted by Joy Sanchez-Taylor, 14 April 2020.

---. "Latino/a Rising." *Kickstarter*, 3 Jan 2018, https://www.kickstarter.com/projects/2019038492/latino-a-rising/description.

---. *Latinx Rising.* The Ohio State University Press, 2020. Originally published as *Latin@ Rising*, Wings Press, 2017.

Hampton, Gregory Jerome. *Changing Bodies in the Fiction of Octavia Butler: Slaves, Aliens, and Vampires.* Rowman & Littlefield, 2010.

Haraway, Donna J. "A Cyborg Manifesto: Science, Technology, and Socialist-Feminism in the Late Twentieth Century." *Simians, Cyborgs, and Women: The Reinvention of Nature.* Routledge, 1991.

Hastings, Christobel. "The Timeless Myth of Medusa, a Rape Victim Turned into a Monster." *Vice*, 9 April 2018, https://www.vice.com/en_us/article/qvxwax/medusa-greek-myth-rape-victim-turned-into-a-monster. Accessed 27 May 2020.

Hernandez, Carlos. *The Assimilated Cuban's Guide to Quantum Santeria.* eBook, Rosarium Publishing, 2016.

Hernandez, Jillian. "'Miss, You Look Like a Bratz Doll': On Chonga Girls and Sexual Aesthetic Excess." *NWSA Journal*, vol. 21, no. 3, Fall 2009, pp. 63–90. Accessed 15 Jan. 2018.

"Hi, r/Fantasy. (Again.) I'm N. K. Jemisin. Ask Me Anything!" *Welcome to /r/Fantasy.* Reddit, https://www.reddit.com/r/Fantasy/comments/413h8g/hi_rfantasy_again_im_n_k_jemisin_ask_me_anything/#bottom-comments. Accessed 29 Oct. 2017.

Hopkinson, Nalo, and Uppinder Mehan "Introduction." *So Long Been Dreaming: Postcolonial Science Fiction and Fantasy.* Arsenal Pulp Press, 2004.

Horne, Karama. "Indie Comics Spotlight: Kwanza Osajyefo Is Black AF." *SY FY Wire*, 8 Feb. 2018, https://www.syfy.com/syfywire/indie-comics-spotlight-kwanza-osajyefo-is-black-af.

Hyman, Louis, and Natasha Iskander. "What the Mass Deportation of Immigrants Might Look Like." 16 Nov. 2016, *Slate*, https://slate.com/news-and-politics/2016/11/donald-trump-mass-deportation-and-the-tragic-history-of-operation-wetback.html.

Jager, Rebecca K. *Malinche, Pocahontas, and Sacagawea: Indian Women as Cultural Intermediaries and National Symbols*. 2015. U of Oklahoma P, 2016.

James, C. L. R. *The Black Jacobins: Toussaint L'Ouverture and the San Domingo Revolution*. 2nd ed., rev. ed. Vintage Books, 1989.

Jemisin, N. K. *The Fifth Season*. Orbit, 2015.

———. *The Obelisk Gate*. Orbit, 2016.

———. *The Stone Sky*. Orbit, 2017.

———. *How Long 'Til Black Future Month?* Orbit, 2018.

———. "Why I Think RaceFail Was the Bestest Thing Evar for SFF." *N. K. Jemisin*, 18 Jan. 2010, http://nkjemisin.com/2010/01/why-i-think-racefail-was-the-bestest-thing-evar-for-sff/.

Jones, D. Marvin. *Dangerous Spaces: Beyond the Racial Profile*. Praeger, 2016.

Jones, Jeremy L. C. "Peculiar Notes of Contradiction: A Conversation with N. K. Jemisin." *Clarkesworld*, issue 43, April 2020.

Kawatu, Rafael. "How to Create a Digital Magazine: Steps, Cost, and Platforms." *Mag Loft*, 11 Jan. 2019, https://www.magloft.com/blog/how-to-create-a-digital-magazine/.

Kevles, Daniel J. "The History of Eugenics." *Issues in Science and Technology*, vol. 32, issue 3 Spring 2016, pp. 45–50. Proquest. Accessed 10 Jan. 2018.

"Key Health Inequalities in Canada: A National Portrait—Executive Summary." *Government of Canada*. 31 July 2019. Accessed 26 Aug. 2019, https://www.canada.ca/en/public-health/services/publications/science-research-data/key-health-inequalities-canada-national-portrait-executive-summary.html.

Kilgore, De Witt Douglass. "Afrofuturism." *The Oxford Handbook of Science Fiction*, edited by Rob Latham, Oxford UP, 2014, pp. 561–72.

Kimmerer, Robin Wall. *Braiding Sweetgrass: Indigenous Wisdom, Scientific Knowledge, and the Teachings of Plants*. Milkweed Editions, 2015.

Kirby, David A. "The New Eugenics in Cinema: Genetic Determinism and Gene Therapy in Gattaca." *Science Fiction Studies*, vol. 27, no. 2, 2000, pp. 193–215.

Klein, Christine A. "Treaties of Conquest: Property Rights, Indian Treaties, and the Treaty of Guadalupe Hildago." *New Mexico Law Review*, vol. 26 (Spring 1996): pp. 201–55, http://lawlibrary.unm.edu/nmlr/volumes/26/2/05_klein_treaties.pdf. Accessed 15 Aug. 2013.

Kolata, Gina. "With a Simple DNA Test, Family Histories Are Rewritten." *New York Times*. 28 Aug. 2017. https://www.nytimes.com/2017/08/28/science/dna-tests-ancestry.html. Accessed 15 Aug. 2017.

Kolopenuk, Jessica. "Miskâsowin: Indigenous Science, Technology, and Society." *Genealogy*, vol. 4, no. 1, 2020, p. 21.

Kurtz, Malisa. "'Race as Technology' and the Asian Body in *The Bohr Maker* and *Salt Fish Girl*." *Disorienting Planets: Racial Representations of Asia in Science Fiction*, edited by Isiah Lavender III, UP of Mississippi, 2017, pp. 117–30.

Kuschell-Haworth, Holly T. "Jumping through Hoops: Traditional Healers and the Indian Health Care Improvement Act." *DePaul Journal of Health Care Law*, vol. 2, issue 4, Summer 1999, pp. 843–60.

"Kyle Traded His Lederhosen for a Kilt/Testimonial/Ancestry." *YouTube*, 9 Dec. 2015, https://www.youtube.com/watch?v=Yfz2KJQvH-0. Accessed 28 May 2020.

"Labor Force Statistics from the Current Population Survey." *U.S. Bureau of Labor Statistics*, 22 Jan. 2020, https://www.bls.gov/cps/cpsaat11.htm.

Lai, Larissa. *Salt Fish Girl*. Thomas Allen, 2002.

Lai, Paul. "Stinky Bodies: Mythological Futures and the Olfactory Sense in Larissa Lai's *Salt Fish Girl*." *MELUS*, vol. 33, no. 4, 2008, pp. 167–87.

Landon, Brooks. "Dime Novels and the Cultural Work of Early SF." *Science Fiction Studies*, vol. 36, no. 2, 2009, p. 198. *JSTOR*. Accessed 19 May 2020.

LaPensée, Elizabeth. "Indigenous Futurisms in Games." *Indigenous Game Devs*, 25 Jan. 2020, https://www.indigenousgamedevs.com/blog/indigenous-futurisms-as-game-design?fbclid=IwAR10CusizPbDj29E0f62IjIx124Tl3s5SwVhsrhaW6yBud205A7iy5Tgeno. Accessed 6 June 2020.

———. *Thunderbird Strike: A Lightning Searing Sidescroller*, https://www.thunderbirdstrike.com/about. Accessed 14 April 2020.

Lavender, Isiah III. *Afrofuturism Rising: The Literary Prehistory of a Movement*. The Ohio State UP, 2019.

———. "Ethnoscapes: Environment and Language in Ishmael Reed's 'Mumbo Jumbo,' Colson Whitehead's 'The Intuitionist,' and Samuel R. Delany's 'Babel-17.'" *Science Fiction Studies*, vol. 34, no. 2, 2007, pp. 187–200.

———, editor. "Introduction." *Black and Brown Planets: The Politics of Race in Science Fiction*. UP of Mississippi, 2014.

———. *Race in American Science Fiction*. Indiana UPress, 2011.

Legesse, A. *Gada: Three Approaches to the Study of African Society*. 1973.

Leonard, Elisabeth Anne. "Race and Ethnicity in Science Fiction." *The Cambridge Companion to Science Fiction*, Cambridge UP, 2003, pp. 253–63.

Le Roux-Kemp, Andra. "A Legal Perspective on African Traditional Medicine in South Africa." *The Comparative and International Law Journal of Southern Africa*, vol. 43, no. 3, 2010, pp. 273–91, *JSTOR*, www.jstor.org/stable/23253084.

Lopez Levers, Lisa. "Traditional Healing as Indigenous Knowledge: Its Relevance to HIV/AIDS in Southern Africa and the Implications for Counselors." *Journal of Psychology in Africa*, 2006, vol. 1, pp. 87–100.

Ma, Ling. *Severance*. Picador, 2019.

Madsen, Deborah L. "On Subjectivity and Survivance: Reading Trauma through *The Heirs of Columbus* and *The Crown of Columbus*." *Survivance: Narratives of Native Presence*, edited by Gerald Vizenor, U of Nebraska P, 2008.

Makoons Geniusz, Wendy. *Our Knowledge Is Not Primitive: Decolonizing Botanical Anishinaabe Teachings*. Syracuse UP, 2009.

Manuel, George, and Michael Posluns. *The Fourth World: An Indian Reality*. 1974. Kindle ed. U of Minnesota P, 2019.

Marchione, Marilynn. "Organ Transplant Lists in the US Favor the Rich, According to New Study." *Business Insider*, 9 Nov. 2015, https://www.businessinsider.com/organ-transplant-lists-favor-therich-2015-11. Accessed 6 June 2020.

Marks, Jonathan. "Racism: Scientific." *Encyclopedia of Race and Racism*, edited by Patrick L.

Mason. 2nd ed., vol. 3. Macmillan Reference USA, 2013, pp. 445–60. Gale Virtual Reference Library. Accessed 8 Jan. 2018.

Martin, Douglas. "The X-Men Vanquish America." *New York Times*, 21 Aug. 1994, pp. 21, 27, https://www.nytimes.com/1994/08/21/arts/the-x-men-vanquish-america.html.

Mbembe, Achille. "Necropolitics." *Public Culture*, vol. 15, no .1, 2003, pp. 11–40.

Medina, Daniel A. "Dakota Access Pipeline: Easement Expected to Allow Project to be Completed." *NBC News*, NBC Universal, 1 February 2017. Accessed 27 Aug. 2019.

Merla-Watson, Cathryn Josefina. "The Altermundos of Latin@futurism," *Alluvium*, vol. 6, no. 1, 2017, https://doi.org/10.7766/alluvium.v6.1.03.

Merla-Watson, Cathryn Josefina, and B. V. Olguín. *Altermundos: Latin@ Speculative Literature, Film, and Popular Culture*. UCLA Chicano Studies Research Center P, 2017.

Miller, P. Andrew. "Mutants, Metaphor, and Marginalism: What X-actly Do the X-Men Stand For?" *Journal of the Fantastic in the Arts*, vol. 13, no. 3 (51), 2003, pp. 282–90. https://www.jstor.org/stable/43308614. Accessed 27 April 2020.

"The Mission." *FIYAH: Magazine of Black Speculative Fiction*, 2019, https://www.fiyahlitmag.com/.

Montgomery, David. "Alex Rivera's Lost Cult Hit 'Sleep Dealer' About Immigration and Drones is Back." *Washington Post*, 7 July 2014, https://www.washingtonpost.com/news/arts-and-entertainment/wp/2014/07/07/alex-riveras-lost-cult-hit-sleep-dealer-about-immigration-and-drones-is-back/.

Moon. Directed by Duncan Jones, performances by Sam Rockwell, Kevin Spacey, and Dominique McElligott, Sony Pictures Classics, 2009.

"More Than 5,400 Children Split at Border, According to New Count." *NBC News*, 25 Oct. 2019, https://www.nbcnews.com/news/us-news/more-5-400-children-split-border-according-new-count-n1071791.

Moynihan, Donald, and Pamela Herd. "Red Tape and Democracy: How Rules Affect Citizenship Rights." *The American Review of Public Administration*, vol. 40, no. 6, 2010, pp. 654–70.

Nelson, Alondra. *The Social Life of DNA: Race, Reparations and Reconciliation after the Genome*. Kindle ed. Beacon Press, 2016.

Nelson, Alondra, and Thuy Linh N. Tu, editors, with Alicia Headlam Hines, contributor. "Introduction: Hidden Circuits." *Technicolor: Race, Technology, and Everyday Life*. New York UP, 2001.

"Non Zero Sum Game." Monash University, Monash Business School, 2020, https://www.monash.edu/business/marketing/marketing-dictionary/n/non-zero-sum-game. Accessed 21 May 2020.

Noriega Sánchez, M. Ruth. *Challenging Realities: Magic Realism in Contemporary American Women's Fiction*. Universitat de València, 2011, eBook, https://play.google.com/store/books/details?id=vYhfrpPjXfUC&rdid=book-vYhfrpPjXfUC&rdot=

1&source=gbs_vpt_read&pcampaignid=books_booksearch_viewport. Accessed 18 May 2020.

Northern, Trodayne. "CV Nation: A Black Superhero Webseries: An Exclusive Interview With the Creators of CV Nation." *BlackSci-Fi.com*, 28 Feb 2014.

Noudelmann, François. "Interview with Toni Morrison." *Black Renaissance,* vol. 12, no. 1, 2012, pp. 36–43, 151. ProQuest, https://rpa.laguardia.edu/login?url=https://search-proquest-com.rpa.laguardia.edu/docview/1349919200?accountid=11946.

"Obamacare: Has Trump Managed to Kill the Affordable Care Act?" *BBCNews.* BBC News Services, 29 March 2019. Accessed 26 Aug. 2019.

Octavia E. Butler Papers (OEB) 598. The Huntington Library. San Marino, CA.

Okorafor, Nnedi. *The Book of Phoenix.* Kindle ed. Daw Books, 2015.

———. *Who Fears Death.* Kindle ed. Daw Books, 2011.

Oliviero, Katie. "The Immigration State of Emergency: Racializing and Gendering National Vulnerability in Twenty-First-Century Citizenship and Deportation Regimes." *Feminist Formations,* vol. 25, no. 2, 2013, pp. 1–29.

Olmos, Margarite Fernández, and Lizbeth Paravisini-Gebert. *Creole Religions of the Caribbean: An Introduction from Vodou and Santería to Obeah and Espiritismo.* New York UP, 2003.

"Our Mission." *Black Girl Magic Lit Mag,* 2016, https://www.blackgirlmagicmag.com/.

Ovadje, Pamela, et al. "Dandelion Root Extract Affects Colorectal Cancer Proliferation and Survival Through the Activation of Multiple Death Signaling Pathways." *Oncotarget,* vol. 7, no. 45, 8 Nov. 2016, pp. 73080–3100. doi: 10.18632/oncotarget.11485. Accessed 5 Sept. 2019.

Packwood, Damon. "The Era of White Male Games for White Male Gamers is Ending." *Quartz,* 31 Oct. 2018, https://qz.com/1433085/the-era-of-white-male-games-for-white-male-gamers-is-ending/.

"Patient Protection and Affordable Care Act." *HealthCare.org.* US Centers for Medicare & Medicaid Services, Accessed 26 Dec. 2020.

Podruczna, Agnieszka. "The Diaspora in Space. The Question of Home, Ancestry, and Heritage in Celu Amberstone's 'Refugees.'" *TransCanadiana,* issue 6, 2013, pp. 263–72. Accessed 4 Oct. 2017.

Pretty, Jacqui. "It Costs HOW MUCH?! The Price of Self-Publishing a Book." *Medium,* 22 May 2016, https://medium.com/@JacquiPretty/it-costs-how-much-the-price-of-self-publishing-a-book-6c4809dbde2.

Rambukanna, Nathan. "FCJ-194 from #RaceFail to #Ferguson: The Digital Intimacies of Race—Activist Hashtag Publics." *Fibreculture Journal,* 1 June 2015, issue 26, pp.159–88, doi: 10.15307/fcj.26.194.2015.

Ramírez, Catherine. "Afrofuturism/Chicanafuturism: Fictive Kin." *Aztlan: A Journal of Chicano Studies,* vol. 33, no. 1, Spring 2008, pp.185–94.

———. "Deus ex Machina: Tradition, Technology, and the Chicanafuturist Art of Marion C. Martinez." *Aztlán: A Journal of Chicano Studies,* vol. 29, no. 2, pp. 55–92.

Randal, Gayle Madeleine. "Native American Medicine: An Introduction." *Gynecologic Oncology,* vol. 99, 2005, pp. S127–28.

"Rep. Waters Slams Surgeon General Jerome Adams for Offensive Comments during WH Coronavirus Briefing." *Congresswoman Maxine Waters: Serving California's 43rd District,* US House of Representatives, 10 April 2020. Accessed 16 April 2020, https://waters.house.gov/media-center/press-releases/rep-waters-slams-surgeon-general-jerome-adams-offensive-comments-during.

Rich, Danielle Leigh. *Global Fandom: The Circulation of Japanese Popular Culture in the U.S.*, 2011. University of Iowa, PhD dissertation, https://ir.uiowa.edu/etd/4905/.

Richards, Leah. "This Land Was Made for You and Me: The Rise of the Oppressed in George A. Romero's Land of the Dead." *Journal of Popular Culture*, vol. 51, no. 3, Wiley Subscription Services, Inc, June 2018, pp. 657–73. doi:10.1111/jpcu.12682.

Rieder, John. *Colonialism and the Emergence of Science Fiction*. Wesleyan UP, 2008.

Rivera, Gabby. "1.0." *A People's Future of the United States: Speculative Fiction from 25 Extraordinary Writers*, edited by Victor LaValle and John Joseph Adams, One World, 2019.

Rivera, Lysa. "Future Histories and Cyborg Labor: Reading Borderlands Sf after NAFTA." *Science Fiction Studies*, vol. 39, no. 3, Nov. 2012, pp. 415–36. Accessed 1 June 2013.

Rockett, Darcel. "Racial Slurs and 'Black' Superman: How Cosplayers of Color Navigate a World of Mostly White Characters." *Chicago Tribune*, 23 Aug. 2019, https://www.chicagotribune.com/entertainment/ct-ent-black-cosplayers-ttd-20190822-20190822-seybrucxfzgd3ls4efrzhvuit4-story.html.

Roh, David S., et al. *Techno-Orientalism: Imagining Asia in Speculative Fiction, History, and Media*. Rutgers UP, 2015.

Ruíz, Gina. "Chanclas and Aliens." *Ban This! the Bsp Anthology of Xican@ Literature*. Broken Sword Publications, 2012.

Said, Edward W. *Orientalism*. Vintage Books, 1979.

Saldívar, Karina. "A Muted Voice? Red Tape and Latino Political Participation." *Public Administration Quarterly*, vol. 39, no. 1, 2015, pp. 51–84.

Samson, Jane. *Race and Empire*. Routledge, 2004. ProQuest Ebook Central, http://ebookcentral.proquest.com/lib/cunymain/detail.action?docID=4045426.

Sánchez, Rosaura, and Beatrice Pita. *Lunar Braceros 2125–2148*. Calaca Press, 2009.

Sanchez-Taylor, Joy. "Alternative Futurisms: Tananarive Due's African Immortal Series." *Extrapolation*, vol. 61, issue 1–2, 2020, pp. 91–108.

Sandoval, Chela, and Angela Y. Davis. *Methodology of the Oppressed*. U of Minnesota P, 2000.

Schalk, Sami. "Experience, Research, and Writing: Octavia E. Butler as an Author of Disability Literature." *Palimpsest: A Journal on Women, Gender, and the Black International*, vol. 6, no. 1, 2017, pp. 153–77. Project MUSE, doi:10.1353/pal.2017.0018.

Scott, Paul. "Fear of an Intelligent Black Man." *Durham Herald Sun*, 30 Aug. 2018, https://www.heraldsun.com/opinion/article217585490.html.

See, Lisa. "PW Interviews: Octavia E. Butler." *Conversations with Octavia Butler*, edited by Conseula Francis. UP of Mississippi, 2010.

"Sen. David Osmek: MN Taxpayers Should Not Be Funding Angry Birds for Eco-Terrorists." *MSNRC: Minnesota Senate Republican Caucus*. Minnesota Senate Republican Caucus, 26 Oct. 2017, https://www.mnsenaterepublicans.com/sen-david-osmek-mn-taxpayers-not-funding-angry-birds-eco-terrorists/.

Sharp, Granville. *The Law of Passive Obedience, or, Christian Submission to Personal Injuries Wherein is Shewn, That the Several Texts of Scripture, Which Command the*

Entire Submission of Servants or Slaves to their Masters, Cannot Authorize the Latter to Exact an Involuntary Servitude, nor, in the Least Degree, Justify the Claims of Modern Slaveholders. Printed for B. White and E. and C. Dilly, 1776.

Shawl, Nisi. "Ifa: Reverence, Science, and Social Technology." *Extrapolation*, vol. 57, no. 1–2, 2016, pp. 221–VII.

Singer, Natasha, and Choe Sang-Hun. "As Coronavirus Surveillance Escalates, Personal Privacy Plummets." *New York Times*, 23 March 2020. https://www.nytimes.com/2020/03/23/technology/coronavirus-surveillance-tracking-privacy.html. Accessed 16 April 2020.

Solis, Gabriel A. "The Revolutionary History of Lowriders." *Vice*, 11 May 2017, https://www.vice.com/en_us/article/9aeamy/the-revolutionary-history-of-lowriders. Accessed 7 May 2020.

Solomon, Rivers. *An Unkindness of Ghosts*. Akashic Books, 2017.

Sorensen, Leif. "Against the Post-Apocalyptic: Narrative Closure in Colson Whitehead's *Zone One*." *Contemporary Literature*, vol. 55, no. 3, 2014, pp. 559–92.

Suvin, Darko. *Metamorphoses of Science Fiction*. Yale UP, 1980.

Taylor, Derrick Bryson. "For Black Men, Fear That Masks Will Invite Racial Profiling." *New York Times*, 14 April 2020, https://www.nytimes.com/2020/04/14/us/coronavirus-masks-racism-african-americans.html. Accessed 16 April 2020.

Teuton, Christopher B. *Deep Waters: The Textual Continuum in American Indian Literature*. U of Nebraska P, 2010.

"'There Are Black People in the Future'—Tale of a Billboard." *Pittsburgh Post Gazette*, 6 April 2018, https://www.post-gazette.com/local/city/2018/04/06/There-Are-Black-People-in-the-Future-billboard-Eve-Picker-Jon-Rubin-Alisha-Wormsley/stories/201804060115.

Thomas, P. L. *Science Fiction and Speculative Fiction: Challenging Genres*. Sense Publishers, 2013.

Tiki, Waktole, et al. "An Indigenous Time-Related Framework for Reconstructing the Impact of Disasters on Ancient Water Systems in Southern Ethiopia, 1560–1950. (Report)." *Journal of Historical Geography*, vol. 41, 2013, pp. 33–43.

"Top questions about AncestryDNA." *AncestryDNA*, 1997–2020, Ancestry, https://www.ancestry.com/dna. Accessed 28 May 2020.

Travis, Mitchell. "We're All Infected: Legal Personhood, Bare Life, and The Walking Dead." *International Journal for the Semiotics of Law*, vol. 28, no. 4, 2015, p. 787.

Turner, Sasha. *Contested Bodies: Pregnancy, Childrearing, and Slavery in Jamaica*. 1st ed., 2017.

Vigil, James Diego. "Cholo!: The Migratory Origins of Chicano Gangs in Los Angeles." *Global Gangs: Street Violence across the World*, edited by Jennifer M. Hazen, and Dennis Rodgers, University of Minnesota Press, 2014. *ProQuest Ebook Central*, https://ebookcentral.proquest.com/lib/lagcc-ebooks/detail.action?docID=1719860.

Vint, Sherryl. *Bodies of Tomorrow: Technology, Subjectivity, Science Fiction*. U of Toronto P, 2007.

———. "Don't Let the Future Be Written for You: Sabrina Vourvoulias's 'Ink.'" *Los Angeles Review of Books*, 27 Dec. 2012, https://lareviewofbooks.org/article/dont-let-the-future-be-written-for-you-sabrina-vourvouliass-ink/.

———. "Only by Experience": Embodiment and the Limitations of Realism in Neo-Slave Narratives." *Science Fiction Studies*, vol. 34, no. 2, July 2007, pp. 241–61.

Vizenor, Gerald. *Survivance: Narratives of Native Presence*. U of Nebraska P, 2008.

Vourvoulias, Sabrina. "Putting the I in Speculative: Looking at U.S. Latino/a Writers and Stories." *Tor.com*, 2 Feb. 2015, https://www.tor.com/2015/02/02/looking-at-us-latino-latina-speculative-writers-and-stories/.

Wade, Nicholas. *A Troublesome Inheritance: Genes, Race, and Human History*. Penguin Books, 2014.

Wali, Nidhi, and Andre M N Renzaho. "'Our Riches Are Our Family': The Changing Family Dynamics & Social Capital for New Migrant Families in Australia." *PloS One*, vol. 13, no. 12, 2018, p. e0209421.

Wang, Xin. "Asian Futurism and the Non-Other." *E-flux Journal*, no. 81, April 2017, https://www.e-flux.com/journal/81/126662/asian-futurism-and-the-non-other/.

Washington, Harriet A. *Medical Apartheid: The Dark History of Medical Experimentation on Black Americans from Colonial Times to the Present*. 1st paperback ed., Harlem Moon, 2006.

"What Is Mutation?" *Genetic Science Learning Center*, U of Utah P, 1 Aug. 2017, https://learn.genetics.utah.edu/content/evolution/mutation/. Accessed 29 April 2020.

Whitehead, Colson. *Zone One: A Novel*. Anchor, 2011.

"Why Is Funding All or Nothing?" *Kickstarter*, 10 April 2020, https://help.kickstarter.com/hc/en-us/articles/115005047893-Why-is-funding-all-or-nothing-.

Winston, Andrew. "Is the COVID-19 Outbreak a Black Swan or the New Normal?" *MIT Sloan Management Review*, 16 March 2020. Accessed 16 April 2020. https://sloanreview.mit.edu/article/is-the-covid-19-outbreak-a-black-swan-or-the-new-normal/.

Wolinsky, Richard. "Growing the Hell Up: From Middle Earth to NJ." *Guernica*, 1 Nov. 2012, https://www.guernicamag.com/growing-the-hell-up-from-middle-earth-to-nj/. Accessed 1 May 2019.

Womack, Ytasha. *Afrofuturism: The World of Black Sci-Fi and Fantasy Culture*. Chicago Review Press, 2013.

Wong, Rita. "Troubling Domestic Limits: Reading Border Fictions Alongside Larissa Lai's *Salt Fish Girl*." *BC Studies*, no. 104, Winter 2003/04, pp. 109–24. Accessed 10 Aug. 2017.

"World Shaker." *Wired*, Aug. 2016, p. 29. *General OneFile*, go.galegroup.com/ps/i.do?p=ITOF&sw=w&u=cuny_laguardia&v=2.1&id=GALE%7CA459234809&it=r&asid=8caa3f49a03f7722b7372581d3f43d9c. Accessed 15 Aug. 2017.

Yaszek, Lisa. "Afrofuturism, Science Fiction, and the History of the Future." *Socialism and Democracy*, vol. 20, no. 3, November 2006, pp. 41–60.

INDEX

"0.1" (Rivera), 10, 85, 87–92, 88n6, 95–101, 106, 116, 157, 157n4
2010 Haitian earthquake, 102

abortion, 92, 92n9
academically gifted Black children, 111–13
adaptation as survival strategy, 10, 22–26, 33, 38–46, 38n13, 53–54, 72, 99, 101, 115, 120, 128–29, 134, 140, 145
Addison-Smith, Helen, 39
Affordable Care Act. *See* Patient Protection and Affordable Care Act
Africa: Eurowestern depictions of, 15; modernity and technological advancement of, 15–16
African chattel slavery/slaves, 11, 15, 20, 23, 32–33, 33n8, 55–56, 60–72, 74–75, 79–81, 91–93, 103, 107, 107n21, 122–23, 125–27, 131–34, 141; as cultural interpreters, 33, 33n8; justification of, 55, 55n6, 60, 65, 68, 71, 81, 110; punishment of, 63, 63n17; separation of children from slave mothers, 62–63, 62n16
Africanfuturism, 14, 14n15, 161

African Immortal series (Due), 11, 24n24, 120, 130–32, 138–39, 148n1, 162, 162n5
Afro Comicon, 150
Afrodiasporic religions, 121, 127–29, 142–44
Afrofuturism, 3–4, 9–16, 12n12, 13n13, 13n14, 14–15, 14n15, 15n17, 16, 16n18, 20–26, 24n24, 30–38, 46–49, 47n23, 54, 56–57, 61–65, 67–72, 67n24, 68, 74, 76–78, 78n33, 80–82, 85–86, 101–7, 104n19, 111–16, 120, 123, 125–27, 129–41, 130n10, 144–51, 153, 148n1, 156, 157–58, 160–64, 162n5; definitions of, 13–16, 14n15, 15n17
Agamben, Giorgio, 102, 102n15
Alien (1979), 47
alienation, 15, 17, 20, 27, 30, 46–54, 56, 67, 76–77, 161; cultural, 7–8; racial, 7–8, 8n8
alien invasion trope, 1, 26–54
Alien Nation (1988), 155
alien trope, 6–7, 10, 17, 20, 25–54, 46n22, 80n36, 102: human-based, 46–54; patterned after cultures of color, 46n22; tentacled trope, 47, 47n24

177

Amberstone, Celu, 9–10, 22–23, 26, 30–54
Anderson, Porter, 149
Anderson, Reynaldo, 156
anger, women's, 114–15
animism, 123, 136
Anishinaabe culture, 23n22, 53, 64n19, 94, 98–99, 118–19, 124, 143
Anzaldúa, Gloria, 7–8, 17
Arrival (2016), 47, 157
Arte Público Press, 155
art world, whiteness of, 113, 113n24
Asian cultures, 19, 75n30, 78–79
Asian futurism, 9–10, 16, 18–24, 26, 46–57, 62n14, 74–79, 75n30, 85, 101–10, 112–16, 157, 161
Asian Science Fiction and Fantasy (Facebook site), 151
"Assimilated Cuban's Guide to Quantum Santeria, The" (Hernandez), 11, 120, 123, 127–31, 142–46
Assimilated Cuban's Guide to Quantum Santeria, The (Hernandez), 158
assimilation, 38–46, 38n12, 75n30: forced, 32, 38n13, 40–41, 54, 69, 85, 85–86n2, 122–24, 143
asylum-seekers. *See* refugees
authoritarian governments, 85–101
Avatar (2009), 74
averageness as a survival strategy, 111–14
Axxón, 154

Bad Indians (Miranda), 54
Bailey, Moya, 21, 148
balance, promotion of, 11, 22, 37, 37n11, 52, 97–98, 98n13, 118–46, 120n4, 162–63
Barber, Kirsten, 87
bare life. *See homo sacer*
Bastida, Xiye, 138
Battlestar Galactica (miniseries), 155
Bear, Elizabeth, 152–53
Bear, Greg, 38n14, 74
Beggars trilogy (Kress), 74
Belluck, Pam, 57–58n6
Beloved (Morrison), 122
Bérard, Sylvie, 76–77

Berthier-Foglar, Susanne, 32–33n7
Besson, Luke, 74
Bhabha, Homi, 34
Binti series (Okorafor), 157–58
Biomapping Indigenous Peoples: Towards an Understanding of the Issues (Berthier-Foglar), 32–33n7
biopolitics of disposability, 11, 43–45, 84–88, 101, 107, 109n22, 159, 163–64
bio-power, 84, 84n1, 107
birthright citizenship, denial of to people of color, 93
Bishop, Kyle William, 106–7
Biskaabiiyang, 53, 99, 133
Black (Osajyefo, Randolph, Smith, and Igle), 156–57
Black and Brown Planets: The Politics of Race in Science Fiction (Lavender), 8, 85, 156
Black Girl Magic Lit Mag, 153
Black Girl Nerds, 150–51
#BlackInTheIvory, 85–86n2
Black No More (Schuyler), 55–56, 66
Black Panther (2018), 16, 24, 160
Black Science Fiction Society, 151
"Black to the Future" (Dery), 13, 23n23, 149
Bladerunner (1982), 18, 155
Blade series, 81, 158
Blood Music (Bear), 74
Bodies of Tomorrow (Vint), 48n25, 49n28
Bogado, Aura, 158
Bollinger, Laurel, 22
Book of Phoenix, The (Okorafor), 11, 56, 61–65, 72
Braceros program, 27, 27n3, 42, 42n19
Braiding Sweetgrass: Indigenous Wisdom, Scientific Knowledge, and the Teachings of Plants (Kimmerer), 75–76n31, 119–20, 134
Brave New World (Huxley), 57n4, 74
Brief Wondrous Life of Oscar Wao, The (Díaz), 1
Briggs, Laura, 32–33n7, 61n11
Britt, Ryan, 47
Broadnax, Jamie, 151
Broken Earth trilogy (Jemisin), 56, 67–72, 67n24, 77

Brooks, Kinitra D., 3, 5, 9, 24n24, 148, 148n1
Brother from Another Planet (Sayles), 14
Brown, Adrienne Maree, 156
Brown Girl in the Ring (Hopkinson), 11, 120, 123, 125–27, 129–31, 134–37, 140, 144, 146
Brox, Ali, 82
Bush, George H. W. administration, 87
Butler, Octavia E., 3, 9–10, 22, 26, 30–38, 46–49, 54, 56–57, 74, 80–82, 80n35, 80n36, 150, 158, 162
Byng, Rhonesha, 113

Cameron, Rob, 149
Campbell, Bill, 149, 154–56
Canavan, Gerry, 102, 102n15, 107, 109–10
capitalism, effects of, 43–44n20, 85, 88n6, 90n1, 102–6, 103n16, 103n17, 105, 112
Carpenter, Roger M., 77
Castillo, Ana, 155
Catholicism, 127–30. *See also* Christianity
cephalopods, 47, 49–53
Césaire, Aimé, 53
Challenging Realities: Magic Realism in Contemporary American Women's Fiction (Sánchez), 41–42n18
"Chanclas and Aliens" (Ruiz), 10, 26–29
Chavez, America (character), 157
Chaviano, Daína, 155
Cheyenne River Sioux tribe, 46n21, 137n11
Chiang, Ted, 9–10, 26, 46–54, 157
Chicanafuturism, 8, 16–17, 21, 28
Chicanx laborers, 43–44n20
Chicanx people and culture, 8, 16–17, 16n19, 26–29, 26n2, 43: Eurowestern view of as premodern, 28
Chideya, Farai, 24n24, 148n1
children's literature, 158
Chinese culture and mythology, 78–79, 106
cholo culture/peoples, 27–29, 27n2, 54
Christianity, 113–14, 121, 127–30, 133–34, 144. *See also* Catholicism
citizenship, challenges faced by people of color in Eurowestern countries, 86–101, 87n4–5, 104–5. *See also* birthright citizenship
civilized/modern vs. primitive binary, 3–4, 11, 15–17, 22–23, 23n22, 25–28, 35–36, 36n33, 50, 57n3, 118–46, 162
civil rights, suspension of, 85–101
climate change, 22, 119, 121, 138, 146
clones, 38n14, 74–78
coevolution, 4, 122
cognitive estrangement (Suvin), 7, 20
Coleman, Beth, 76
Coleman, Monica A., 125n7, 125–26n8
colonialism, 6, 9–13, 11n10, 20–61, 38n13, 43–44n20, 65, 68–70, 75–80, 77n32, 100–101, 107, 107n21, 120n1, 122–37, 144–46, 162. *See also* decolonization and postcolonialism
Colonialism and the Emergence of Science Fiction (Rieder), 5–6, 5n6, 11n10, 12, 25n1, 77n32
colonial treaties, 33–34
comic books, 16n18, 65–66, 149–50, 154, 156–60
Concha-Holmes, Amanda D., 136
conjure science/conjuring practices, 4, 11, 11n9, 120–22, 120n2, 129, 133
Conley, Robert, 120–21
consumer capitalism, 90, 90n7, 102–3, 105–6. *See also* capitalism, effects of
containment of people of color, 91–92, 106
contamination, racial, 48, 81, 85–87, 94, 97–98, 107
Contested Bodies: Pregnancy, Childrearing and Slavery in Jamaica (Turner), 93
Copeny, Mari, 138
Copland, DeWayne, 158–59
cosplay, 19, 149–50, 150n2
COVID-19 pandemic, 163–64, 163n8, 164n9, 164n10
Crenshaw, Kimberlé, 114
criminalization of people of color/immigrants, 27–29, 44, 54, 84–102, 87n3–5, 116–17
CRISPR (Clustered Regularly Interspaced Short Palindromic Repeats), 73, 73n28
CRISPR baby scandal, 65n20, 73
crowdsourcing of projects, 147, 154–57

Cuban culture, 127–30
cultural mediator figure, 30–31, 31n6, 34, 37, 60, 60n8
CV Nation (Copeland and Scott), 158–59
cyberspace, 17, 24, 147–60, 163
cyborgs, 43–44, 43–44n20, 64: cyborg gender roles, 79; cyborg narratives, 78–79
"Cyborg Manifesto, A" (Haraway), 43–44n20, 79
Cyrenoski, David, 73

DACA (Deferred Action for Childhood Arrivals), 96–97
Daedalus, or Science and the Future (Haldane), 73–74
Dakota Access Pipeline, protests against, 137–38, 137n12, 159
Dangerous Spaces: Beyond the Racial Profile (Jones), 87n3, 91–92
Dark Matter: A Century of Speculative Fiction from the African Diaspora (Thomas), 156
Dark Matter: Reading the Bones (Thomas), 156
Dar-Nimrod, Ilan, 58, 58n7
Darwin, Charles, 57, 57n3
David, Tiffany M., 154
Davis, Angela Y., 9
Dawn (Butler), 9, 26, 30–38, 46–49, 54
Dawn of the Dead (Romero), 85, 105
decolonization, 23n22, 53–54, 75–76, 75–76n31, 98–101, 116–17, 119, 122, 127–34, 146, 161–64
dehumanization, 43, 54, 56, 62–63, 71, 79, 81–82, 88–89, 108–10, 116
Delany, Samuel R., 2, 12, 12n12, 77, 149, 156, 162–63
Deloria, Vine Jr., 101
Dennis, Rutledge M., 5
deportation, 27–29, 89, 95, 99
Dery, Mark, 7, 13, 13n14, 23, 23n23, 49n28, 149
Descent of Man, The (Darwin), 57
Desmond, Matthew, 55–56
detention of people of color, 87, 93–96

diaspora, 8–9, 23, 161: African, 15, 131, 161; interplanetary, 38–46, 40n15. *See also* displaced peoples
"Diaspora in Space, The" (Podruczna), 13, 26, 36–37, 41, 54
Díaz, Junot, 1, 1n1, 20, 155
digital divide, 148. *See also* technology, access to
digital magazines. *See* online science fiction magazines
Dillon, Grace L., 4, 6–7, 11n9, 17–18, 22–23, 23n22, 25, 30n5, 36n9, 52–54, 98–99, 118, 120n2, 121n4, 121–22, 133, 142–43, 145, 151–52, 156
Dis-Orienting Planets: Racial Representations of Asia in Science Fiction (Lavender), 8, 156
displaced peoples, 8, 39–41, 40n15
disposable bodies, people of color viewed as. *See* biopolitics of disposability
Dmasper, 159
DNA testing, 80, 80n34
Dolezal, Rachel, 60, 60n9
double consciousness (DuBois), 7, 7n7
double estrangement, 7, 7n7
DuBois W. E. B., 7, 7n7, 14
Due, Tananarive, 11, 23–24, 24n24, 120, 123, 130, 132–34, 136, 138–40, 145–46, 148, 148n1, 162, 162n5
Duyulta, 120–21, 120n4
dystopian future trope, 11, 30–54, 60–64, 67–79, 86–116

East Coast Black Age of Comics Convention, 150
education, access to, 113, 122. *See also* literacy, denial of
Elia, Adriano, 4n3, 15
Ellipsis Press, 155
Emirbayer, Mustafa, 55–56
emotional labor, 101, 103–4
endosymbiotic theory, 22
environmental activism, 137–38, 137n11, 160
environmental destruction, 5, 37–40, 49n28, 66, 84–117, 136–38, 145–46. *See also* climate change

INDEX • 181

environmental sustainability, 11, 35–38, 118–46
Eshun (god), 22, 126
Eshun, Kwodo, 15, 20n21, 23, 23n23
ethnic cleansing, 70, 70n26. *See also* racial/ethnic purity
ethnic essentialism. *See* genetic essentialism; racial/ethnic essentialism
ethnic purity. *See* racial/ethnic purity
ethnoscape, 3, 23
eugenics, 57, 57n3, 57n4, 70, 73, 93
Eurocentric visions of the future, 3, 7–9, 11–13, 15
Eurowestern/Indigenous relations, 38–46, 46n21
Eurowestern sciences and technologies, 4–5, 22–23, 52, 118–46: medicine/healing practices, 22–23, 124–46; racial bias in, 118–46
Evans, Arthur B., 73
Evans, Scott F., 158–59
evil spirits, 132–33, 138–39
evolution, 48–49, 49n27: Darwinian theories of, 22, 57, 57n3; theories of marking people of color as inferior, 57–59
Examining Tuskegee: The Infamous Syphilis Study and Its Legacy (Reverby), 32–33n7, 61n10
experimental science fiction by authors of color, 162, 162n6
experimentation on people of color. *See* medical experimentation on people of color
exploitation of immigrants, 38–46, 38n14, 42n19, 43–44n20, 70–72, 75–76, 88–101

Facebook platforms, 21–22, 148, 151–52, 156–58
family unity, threats to, 37, 37n10, 62–63, 62n16, 89–97
Faucheux, Amandine, 18, 22
feminine gender norms, pressure to conform to, 114–15
Ferraro, Vincent, 33
Fifth Element, The (Besson). *See* Besson, Luke

Fifth Season, The (Jemisin), 10, 67–70, 67n24, 77
film adaptations of works by authors of color, 157–59
financially successful, pressures on people of color to be, 112–13
Fire!, 153–54
Firefly (television series), 18
first contact narratives, 10, 25–54
FIYAH, 153
Fledgling (Butler), 3, 9–10, 56–57, 74, 80–82
Floyd, George, 163
forced breeding/reproduction, 33, 46–48, 47n24, 85; of slaves, 70, 93
forced labor, 70–72, 85, 131. *See also* slavery
forced migration/immigration, 9, 11, 23, 27–28, 39–41, 79, 120n1
forced sterilization of people of color, 32, 32–33n7, 57, 61, 61n11, 93
Ford, Donna Y., 111–12
Foucault, Michel, 84, 84n1, 88n6, 107
Fourth World: An Indian Reality, The (Manuel and Poslun), 98–99, 101
Fourth World Theory, 40n15, 98–101, 98n12–13, 116–17
Frankenstein (Shelley), 73
Frederiksen, Tomas, 44
Freedman, Carl, 6
free/freedom as descriptors, 89–91
Fugitive Slave Acts of 1793 and 1850, 69

gamers/game creators of color, 159–60
Gattaca (1997), 74, 74n29
generational trauma, 24, 72, 122, 132–33, 142–43
Genesis SF, 154
genetic engineering/manipulation trope, 10, 19, 22, 33–34, 47–54, 56–57, 57n5, 57–58n6, 61, 73–83
genetic essentialism, 48–49, 48n25, 55–83, 58n7
genetic experimentation trope, 56, 60–65
genetic genealogy testing, 59–60, 79–80. *See also* DNA testing
genetic mutation trope, 10, 56, 65–72, 67n23

Geniusz, Wendy Makoons, 23n22, 64n19, 75–76n31, 122–24
George-Warren, Delesslin, 35
Gernsback, Hugo, 6
ghost trope, 17, 130–31
gifted programs, Black students in, 111–12
gikendaasowin, 124
Gilda Stories, The (Gomez), 81
Giroux, Henry A., 84–85, 87, 102, 109n22, 111, 163
Golash-Boza, Tanya Maria, 87n3, 94–95, 97
Goldstein, Jacob, 153
Gomez, Jewelle, 81
Gómez-Peña, Guillermo, 21, 44, 98n12
Gomez, Reagan, 159
Gross, Lawrence W., 143

Hairston, Andrea, 4, 11
Haldane, J. B. S., 73–74
Hall, Edward Austin, 154
Hampton, Gregory Jerome, 82
Haraway, Donna J., 43–44n20, 49, 79
Harlem Renaissance, 154
healthcare disparities, 137, 140
Heine, Steven J., 58, 58n7
herbal remedies, 124–26, 125n6, 134–35, 140–41: knowledge of viewed as dangerous, 140–41
Herd, Pamela, 104–5
Hernandez, Carlos, 11, 120, 123, 127–31, 142–46, 158
heteronormative relations, Eurowestern privileging of, 76, 93–95
Hines, Alicia Headlam, 4n4, 21
Hirsi, Isra, 138
historical narratives: absence of colonized voices from, 64–65, 64n19; whitewashing of, 160–61, 164
histories and knowledge of colonized peoples, 122–33: erasure of, 102, 122–33, 161; recreation of, 122, 128–29
holistic healing approach, 123, 125n6
homicide, justifiable, 107
homo sacer, 102
Hopkinson, Nalo, 4, 8, 11–12, 15, 22, 120, 123–27, 125n7, 125–26n8, 129–31, 134–37, 140, 144, 146, 150, 156

horror, 20, 24, 24n24, 66, 103
Hughes, Langston, 153
Hugo awards, 5, 12n12, 67n24, 78n33
Human Genome Project, 58, 73
humanity, definition of, 47–54, 48n25
Hurricane Katrina, 84, 102, 163
Hurston, Zora Neale, 153
Huxley, Aldous, 57n5, 74
hybrid figures/hybridity, 17, 43–44n20, 56, 74–76, 82
Hyman, Louis, 27

Ifa, practice of, 121
"Ifa: Reverence, Science and Social Technology" (Shawl), 4n5, 120–21
Igle, Jamal, 156–57
Imarisha, Walidah, 156
Independence Day (1996), 47
Indian Removal Act, 33
Indiegogo, 154
Indigenismo, 16
Indigenous children, removal of, 37, 37n10. See also family unity, threats to
Indigenous Comic Con/Indigipop X, 150
Indigenous cultures, 17–18, 35–38, 37n11, 97–98: documentation of, 101
Indigenous futurism, 4, 6–10, 16–18, 20–24, 26, 30–54, 30n5, 97–101, 98n13, 99n14, 120, 123, 148–52, 156, 161–63, 162n5
Indigenous knowledge, sciences, and technologies, 4–5, 11, 11n9, 23, 23n22, 36, 36n9, 52, 52n31, 64n19, 118–46, 125n7, 160, 162–63: blending with Eurowestern science and technology, 134–43; Indigenous healing practices/medicine, 23, 118, 122–46, 125n6
Indigenous post-apocalyptic literature, 97–98, 98n13
Indigenous spirituality, 122–46, 125n6: trickster figure, 18
individuality, 46–54
infertility, 88, 88n6
Ink (Vourvoulias), 10, 85–89, 94, 97, 99–101, 106, 116, 150
internalized colonization, 12, 36, 143–44, 161

internalized racism, 54, 65, 129
"Interview with Toni Morrison" (Noudelmann), 15, 122
in-vitro fertilization, 57, 73
"Imagining" (Dillon). *See* Dillon, Grace
Imagining Indigenous Futurisms, 18, 148, 151–52
immigration/immigrants, 27–28, 38n14, 42, 42n19, 75n30, 87–88: undocumented, 76, 94, 104–5, 105n20
Immigration Nation: Raids, Detentions, and Deportations in Post 911 America (Golash-Boza), 87n3, 94–95, 97
immortality trope, 7, 133
Iskander, Natasha, 27

Jager, Rebecca K., 31, 31n6, 60n8
Jemisin, N. K., 10, 12, 12n12, 25, 56, 67–72, 67n24, 76–78, 78n33, 147, 153
Jiankui, He, 73
Johnson, Andrew, 33
Jones, Charles E., 156
Jones, D. Marvin, 87n3, 91–92
Jones, Jeremy L. C., 25
Jupiter Ascending (Wachowski), 74
Jurassic Park (1993), 74

Kahiu, Wanuri, 158
Kawatu, Rafael, 153
Kevles, Daniel J., 57, 57n4
Kickstarter, 155–56
Kilgore, De Witt Douglass, 13n14, 15
Kimmerer, Robin Wall, 75–76n31, 119–20, 134
Kindred (Butler), 3
Kirby, David A., 73–74
Klein, Christine, 33–34
Kolopenuk, Jessica, 162
Kress, Nancy, 74
Kurtz, Malissa, 75–76
Kuschell-Haworth, Holly T., 124

La Bloga's Latino Speculative Literature Directory, 154
Lai, Larissa, 10, 19, 56–57, 62n14, 74–79, 75n30
Lakota Sioux tribe, 138
language, alternative forms, of, 48–51

LaPensée, Elizabeth, 99n14, 151–52, 159–60
La Pocha Nostra (Gómez-Peña), 21
Last Man, The (Shelley), 85
Latin@futurism, 17, 21
Latin@ Rising (Goodwin), 155
Latino Comic Con, 150
Latino Comics Expo, 150
Latinx futurism, 9–11, 16, 16n19, 20–24, 26–29, 38–46, 38n14, 85–92, 88n6, 94–101, 106, 116, 120, 123, 127–31, 142–46, 150, 155–57, 157n4, 161–62, 162n5
Latinx Rising (Goodwin), 16n19, 155–56
Lavender, Isiah III, 3, 8, 11n12, 15n17, 18, 20n21, 22, 30n5, 82–83, 85, 160–63
Lavín, Guillermo, 43–44n20
Lee, Stan, 65–66, 156
Leonard, Elizabeth Anne, 15
Levers, Lisa Lopez, 23, 139
Lincoln Park, California, 27n2, 29
literacy, denial of, 62, 92, 122. *See also* education, access to
literary science fiction by authors of color, 162, 162n6
Local and Indigenous Knowledge Systems program (UNESCO), 138
Location of Culture, The (Bhabba), 34
Love Beyond Body, Space, and Time (Nicholson), 18
Lovecraft, H. P., 47, 47n23
Lucumi, 121
Lunar Braceros 2125–2148 (Sánchez and Pita), 9, 26, 38–46, 38n14

Madsen, Deborah L., 143
Malinche, Pocahontas, and Sacagawea: Indian Women as Cultural Intermediaries and National Symbols (Jager), 31, 31n6, 60n8
Ma, Ling, 10, 85, 101–10, 112–16
Manuel, George (Shuswap), 98–99, 101
Margolin, Jamie, 138
Margulis, Lynn, 22
Martin, Douglas, 66
Martinez, Marion C., 21
Martin, George R. R., 157
Mashigo, Mohale, 14, 14n15
Mbembe, Achille, 108–10

184 • INDEX

Medical Apartheid: The Dark History of Medical Experimentation on Black Americans from Colonial Times to the Present (Washington), 32–33n7, 60, 63
medical experimentation on people of color, 32–33, 32–33n7, 56, 61, 61n10, 80n34
Medusa, 48, 48n26
Mehan, Uppinder, 8, 11–12, 156
Men in Black (1997), 155
Merla-Watson, Cathryn Josefina, 17, 20–21
Mestizaje, 16
Methodology of the Oppressed (Sandoval and Davis), 9
Mexican American culture, 26–29, 27n2, 54
Mexican immigrants/laborers, 27–28, 38n14, 42, 42n19
Mexican land treaties, 33–34
migrant laborers, 42–46, 42n19
Mindscape (Harrison), 4
Miranda, Deborah A., 54
Mithila Review, 154
Montgomery, David, 158
Morrison, Toni, 15, 23, 23n23, 122
Mothership: Tales from Afrofuturism and Beyond (Campbell and Hall), 154
Moynihan, Donald, 104–5
multiracial/mixed race characters, 8n8, 77, 80–82
mutants, 65–75: as humans with enhanced abilities, 67n22; as monstrous "othered" beings, 67n22

Narrative of the Life of Frederick Douglass, an American Slave (Douglass), 62n16
National Human Genome Research Institute, 73
national security, 89–91, 91n8, 95–96, 102, 105
Native American DNA: Tribal Belonging and the False Promise of Genetic Science (TallBear), 75–76n31
Native American land treaties, 33–34
"Native Slipstream," 52–53, 142
Native survivance, 17, 23, 98, 98n11, 143–46
natural disasters, 85–87, 102–16, 163–64

naturalization fees, high cost of, 105, 105n20
Nebula Awards, 5, 19
"Necropolitics" (Mbembe), 108–10
Nelson, Alondra, 4n4, 16, 21, 75–76n31, 79–80, 80n34, 149
Nerdtino Expo, 150
New Suns: Original Speculative Fiction by People of Color (Shawl), 156
New World Border: Prophecies, Poems & Loqueras for the End of the Century, The (Gómez-Peña), 98n12
Nicholson, Hope, 18
Night of the Living Dead series (Romero), 103, 106–7
non-binary gender identities, 77, 130, 130n10, 148
non-heteronormative sexualities/identities/families, 19, 77–78, 93–95, 130n10, 95n10
non-zero-sum game, 49–50, 50n29
Northern, Trodayne, 158
Noudelmann, François, 15, 122

Obamacare. *See* Patient Protection and Affordable Care Act
Obama, President Barak, administration of, 137
Obeah, 125–27, 125n7, 125–26n8, 126n9, 135: suppression of, 125–26, 126n9
Obelisk Gate, The (Jemisin), 56, 67–71, 67n24, 122
Octavia E. Butler Legacy Network, 21, 150
Octavia E. Butler Literary Society, 150
Octavia's Brood: Science Fiction Stories from Social Justice Movements (Brown and Imarisha), 156
Ojalehto, 52
Okorafor, Nnedi, 4, 10, 14, 14n15, 16, 16n18, 23, 47n23, 56, 61–65, 68, 157–58
Older, Daniel José, 155
Olguín, B. V., 20
Oliviero, Katie, 93–94
Olmos, Edward James, 155
Olmos, Margarite Fernández, 126, 126n9
one-drop rule, 66, 93
online fanbases, 147–60

online forums, 149–50. *See also* social media platforms
online science fiction magazines, 153–54
On the Origin of Species (Darwin), 57
ONYXCON, 150
Operation Wetback, 27
opioid crisis, 135, 135n11
oral histories, 123, 131–32
Orisha, 121, 129, 131, 136, 143–44
Osajyefo, Kwanza, 156–57
Osmek, Senator David, 159–60
Our Knowledge Is Not Primitive (Geniusz), 23n22, 64n19, 75–76n31, 122–24
Ovadje, Pamela et. al., 141
over-policing of people of color, 27–29, 91, 114
Oxford Handbook of Science Fiction, The (Latham), 15

Packwood, Daymond, 159
pan-Caribbean culture, 125–46, 125n7, 125–26n8, 126n9
pandemics, 88, 88n6
Papa Legbara, 137, 144
Papa Osain, 126–27, 136
Paravisini-Gebert, Lizabeth, 126, 126n9
passing, racial, 55, 55n1, 66–67, 69
patient dumping, 137
Patient Protection and Affordable Care Act, 137
personhood, 48–49, 49n28
Phillips, Rasheedah Esq., 150
physical body and identity formation, 48–54, 49n28
Pita, Beatrice, 9, 26, 38–46, 38n14
Podruczna, Agnieszka, 13, 26, 36–37, 41, 54
police brutality, 163, 163n7
political rights, lack of access to, 104–5
polygenism. *See* scientific racism
Poslun, Michael, 98–99
post-apocalyptic landscapes, 10–11, 22, 84–117
post-apocalyptic narratives/trope, 10–11, 20, 22, 84–117, 159, 163. *See also* Indigenous post-apocalyptic literature; post-Native Apocalypse world
post-apocalyptic science fiction, 84–117

post-apocalyptic space, 10–11
Post-Apocalypse Stress Syndrome, 143
post-colonialism, 13, 16, 34, 53
post-Native Apocalypse world, 23, 53, 98–99
pregnancy, 88–93, 92n9, 99–100, 105, 113–14: narratives, of, 20, 88–92, 94, 105, 114
pregnant women, legal personhood of, 92, 92n9, 114
Pretty, Jacqui, 154
privacy, 90–91, 91n8, 95, 163
publishing, barriers to for authors of color, 148–57, 148n1, 161: for women of color, 148, 148n1

quantum: physics, 142–43: entanglement, 121; mechanics, 4, 142
queer identities, 76–77, 89–91, 95, 95n10, 157, 157n4

race and sexuality, link between in colonial discourse, 76–77
race as a form of technology, 75–76
race-blind future, 10, 92, 112, 112n23
#Racefail, 152–53, 163
Race in American Science Fiction (Lavender), 82–83
racial diversity, loss of, 74
racial/ethnic essentialism, 10–12, 48, 56–83, 58n7
racial/ethnic purity, 11, 48, 70, 76, 81–82
racial hierarchy. *See* Eurowestern racial hierarchy
racial identity, 56–57
racialized science fiction/fantasy, 25–28, 25n1
racial profiling, 92, 163n7
racial reconciliation, 74, 79–80
"Racism and Science Fiction" (Delany), 12n12, 163
radiation, 65–67, 67n22
Rambukanna, Nathan, 152
Ramírez, Catherine, 16–17, 21, 28
Randal, Gayle Madeleine, 123
Randolph, Khary, 156–57
"Reading Hurricane Katrina: Race, Class, and the Biopolitics of Disposability"

(Giroux), 84–85, 87, 102, 109n22, 111, 163
refugees, 30–41: viewed as imminent threats, 87–89, 87n5, 94
"Refugees" (Amberstone), 9–10, 22–23, 26, 30–54
rememory, 122
reproduction, control of, 32–33, 32–33n7, 46–48, 47n24, 57, 57n3, 57n4, 61, 61n11, 70, 73, 85, 92–93. *See also* eugenics; forced breeding/reproduction; forced sterilization of people of color
Reverby, Susan, 32–33n7, 61n10
Rieder, John, 5–6, 5n6, 11n10, 12, 25n1, 77n32
Riordan, Rick, 158
ritual to communicate with deities or spirits, 120, 120n3, 125–26, 136, 143
Rivera, Alex, 44, 158
Rivera, Gabby, 10, 85, 87–92, 88n6, 95–101, 106, 116, 157, 157n4
Rivera, Lysa, 43–44, 43–44n20
Roanhorse, Rebecca, 18, 150
Romero, George A., 85, 103, 105–7
Rosarium Publishing, 149, 154–55
Rose, Tricia, 149
Ruiz, Gina, 10, 26–29

Sad Puppies/Rabid Puppies Hugo Awards controversy, 12, 12n12
Saldívar, Karina Moreno, 105
Salt Fish Girl (Lai), 10, 19, 56–57, 62n14, 74–79, 75n30
Samitar, Sofia, 14
Samson, Jane, 86
Sánchez, M. Ruth Noriega, 41–42n18
Sánchez, Rosaura, 9, 26, 38–46, 38n14
Sandoval, Chela, 9
Santeria, 121, 127–29, 142–44
Sayles, John, 14
Schalk, Sami, 80
Schomburg Center for Research in Black Culture's annual comic book festival, 149
Schuyler, George, 55–56, 66
science, definitions of, 120–21, 120n3

science fiction, definitions of, 3–6, 120, 120n3
science fiction, Eurocentricity of, 3, 15
science fiction fan community websites, 147–49
science fiction fan conventions, 149, 160
science fiction fans of color, 2, 7, 12, 14, 24, 147–54, 160–63
science fiction, racism in, 2, 12, 12n11, 12n12, 15
scientific ethics, 57, 57–58n6, 65, 65n20, 73–74, 79, 119; unethical scientist trope, 73n27
scientific racism, 55–83, 55n2, 57n3, 89
Scott, Paul, 111–12
Searching for Sycorax: Black Women's Hauntings of Contemporary Horror (Brooks), 3, 5, 24n24, 148, 148n1
self-publishing, 154–56
self-silencing, 113–14
sexual exploitation, 33, 46–48, 47n24, 70, 85, 92–93
sexual fluidity, 76–77
Severance (Ma), 10, 85, 101–10, 112–16
Sharp, Granville, 110
Shawl, Nisi, 4n5, 13, 120–22, 121n5, 156
Shelley, Mary, 6, 73, 85
Shuri comic series (Okorafor), 14n15, 157
Sims, James Marion, 61
Sioux tribes, 46n21, 137–38, 137n11. *See also* Cheyenne River Sioux tribe; Lakota Sioux tribe; Oglala Sioux tribe; Standing Rock Sioux tribe
Skildelsky, William, 153
slavery, 32–33, 38, 55–56, 62n14, 62n16, 63n17, 60–75, 79–81, 89, 91–93, 92n9, 103, 107, 107n21, 110, 130–31, 140; genetically engineered individuals used as, 62, 62n14, 74–76. *See also* African chattel slavery/slaves
Sleep Dealer (Rivera), 44, 158
small presses, 154–55
Smith, Linda Tuhiwai, 53, 99
Smith, Tim, 3, 156–57
Snipes, Wesley, 81
social Darwinism, 4, 57, 57n3. *See also* Darwinian theories of evolution
social justice activism/activists, 149–54

Social Life of DNA, The (Nelson), 75–76n31, 79–80
social media platforms, 147–60: subversive use of, 21
social mobility, lack of, 42–43
social rights, lack of access to, 104–5
social technology, 121–22
Society Must Be Defended (Foucault), 88
Solis, Gabriel A., 28
Solomon, Rivers, 11, 23, 120, 123, 130–32, 130n10, 140–41, 145–46
So Long Been Dreaming: Postcolonial Science Fiction and Fantasy (Hopkinson and Mehan), 8, 11–12, 156
Sorensen, Leif, 103
Souls of Black Folk, The (DuBois), 7, 7n7
Space Is the Place (Sun Ra), 14
space mining, 38–38n14
space travel narratives, 10, 25–54
spiritual practices, 120–46
Standing Rock Sioux tribe, 137–38, 137n11
State of Black Science Fiction, The, 148, 151
state of emergency, 85, 87, 101, 109, 109n22, 164: permanent, 87, 87n4, 91
state-sanctioned violence, 84–117
Stone Sky, The (Jemisin), 56, 67–72, 67n24
Stories for Chip: A Tribute to Samuel R. Delany (Shawl and Campbell), 156
"Story of Your Life" (Chiang), 9–10, 26, 46–54, 157
streaming video services, 158–59
Sun Ra, 14
superheroes, 157–59, 157n4
surveillance, 43–44, 61–62, 86–101, 106, 163–64
survivance. See Native survivance
Surviving (Gomez), 159
Suvin, Darko, 7, 20
symbiogenesis, 4, 121–22
symbiosis/symbionts, 22, 80–81, 80n36, 144

TallBear, Kim, 75–76n31
targeted administrative policies, 104–5, 112
Tate, Greg, 7, 149

Technicolor: Race, Technology, and Everyday Life (Nelson and Tu), 4n4, 21
technology: access to, 3–4, 20–21, 28, 37–38, 38n12, 43–44, 148, 152; as a marker of civilization, 3–4, 15–17, 22–23, 34–46, 41, 50; as restrictive rather than liberating, 34–35, 44; definitions of, 3–4, 4n5, 11, 34–35, 120–22, 134–46, 161–63; subversive reworking of, 4, 4n4, 17, 20–22, 28–29. *See also* Indigenous knowledge, sciences, and technologies; race as technology; social technology
television adaptations of works by authors of color, 157–58
Teuton, Christopher B., 120–21
Thomas, P. L., 5
Thomas, Sheree Renée, 156
Thunderbird Strike, 159–60
Thurman, Wallace, 153
Thurnberg, Greta, 138
Tiki, Waktole, 51–52, 52n30
time, alternative perceptions of, 51–53, 142
time travel trope, 7, 20, 142
transgenic organism, 56, 80–82, 81n37. *See also* hybrid
transhistorical feedback loop, 160–64
Travis, Mitchell, 92, 102n15
trickster figure, 18, 22
trickster technologies, 22
trolls, 152–53
Troublesome Inheritance: Genes, Race, and Human History (Wade), 58–59
Trump, Donald J. administration, 87, 87n4, 89, 96–97, 137, 164, 164n9
Turner, Sasha, 93
Tuskegee Syphilis Experiment, 61, 61n10, 80n34
Tu, Thuy Linh N., 4n4, 21
Twenty Thousand Leagues under the Sea (Verne), 47
Twitter, 21, 148, 151–53; Black Twitter, 21
two-spirit peoples, 77

Underground Railroad (Whitehead), 162, 162n5
United Nations Educational, Scientific and Cultural Organization, 138

Unkindness of Ghosts, An (Solomon), 11, 23, 120, 123, 130–32, 130n10, 140–41, 145–46
US Indian Health Care Improvement Act, 124

vampires, 3, 9, 74, 80–82
Verne, Jules, 6, 47
Vigil, James Diego, 27
Vint, Sherryl, 3, 48n25, 48n28
virtual fan communities, 147
Vizenor, Gerald, 17, 23, 23n23, 52, 98, 98n11, 143
Vodun, 121
Vourvoulias, Sabrina, 10, 85–89, 94, 97, 99–101, 106, 116, 150, 150n3

Wachowski, Lana, 74
Wade, Nicholas, 58–59
Wakandacon, 150
Walking the Clouds: An Anthology of Indigenous Science Fiction (Dillon). *See* Dillon, Grace
War of the Worlds, The (Wells), 12, 47
Washington, Harriet A., 32–33n7, 60, 63
webseries, 158–59
Wells, H. G., 12, 47
Whipple, Dora Dorothy, 124
Whitehead, Colson, 10, 85–86, 101–7, 104n19, 111–16, 162, 162n6
whitening of non-white characters, 66, 66n21

Whiting, Gilman W., 111–12
Who Fears Death (Okorafor), 16n18, 68, 72, 157
Wild Seed (Butler), 158
Williams, Kenesha, 153
Wilson, Daniel H., 18, 73n27
witnessing the narratives of others, 100–101
Womack, Ytasha, 13n13, 14–15
Wong, Rita, 76
World War Z (2006), 85
Womack, Ytasha 13n13, 14–15
Wormsley, Alisha B., 2, 2n2

Xenogenesis trilogy (Butler), 26, 30–38, 46–54, 48n25, 74, 80
xenophobia, 46, 66–72, 82–83, 93, 161–62
X-Files (television series), 155
X-Men (comics), 65–66, 158

Yoruba peoples and culture, 121, 128, 136

zombie apocalypse narratives, 10, 85–86, 101–16, 102n15, 103n18, 104n19, 107n21, 127, 159: restoration of order afterwards, 103, 103n18; zombies as sympathetic characters, 107–8
zombies, 101–16, 127: as people of color, 109
Zone One (Whitehead), 10, 85–86, 101–7, 104n19, 111–16, 162, 162n6

NEW SUNS: RACE, GENDER, AND SEXUALITY IN THE SPECULATIVE
Susana M. Morris and Kinitra D. Brooks, Series Editors

Scholarly examinations of speculative fiction have been a burgeoning academic field for more than twenty-five years, but there has been a distinct lack of attention to how attending to nonhegemonic positionalities transforms our understanding of the speculative. New Suns: Race, Gender, and Sexuality in the Speculative addresses this oversight and promotes scholarship at the intersections of race, gender, sexuality, and the speculative, engaging interdisciplinary fields of research across literary, film, and cultural studies that examine multiple pasts, presents, and futures. Of particular interest are studies that offer new avenues into thinking about popular genre fictions and fan communities, including but not limited to the study of Afrofuturism, comics, ethnogothicism, ethnosurrealism, fantasy, film, futurity studies, gaming, horror, literature, science fiction, and visual studies. New Suns particularly encourages submissions that are written in a clear, accessible style that will be read both by scholars in the field as well as by nonspecialists.

Diverse Futures: Science Fiction and Authors of Color
    JOY SANCHEZ-TAYLOR

Impossible Stories: On the Space and Time of Black Destructive Creation
    JOHN MURILLO III

Literary Afrofuturism in the Twenty-First Century
    EDITED BY ISIAH LAVENDER III AND LISA YASZEK

Jordan Peele's Get Out: *Political Horror*
    EDITED BY DAWN KEETLEY

Unstable Masks: Whiteness and American Superhero Comics
    EDITED BY SEAN GUYNES AND MARTIN LUND

Afrofuturism Rising: The Literary Prehistory of a Movement
    ISIAH LAVENDER III

The Paradox of Blackness in African American Vampire Fiction
    JERRY RAFIKI JENKINS

www.ingramcontent.com/pod-product-compliance
Lightning Source LLC
Chambersburg PA
CBHW020948230426
43666CB00005B/221